Kaplan Business Books

Dictionary of Business Terms

British Library Cataloguing-in-Publication Data
A catalogue record for this book is available from the British Library.
Published by Kaplan Publishing UK
Unit 2 The Business Centre
Molly Millars Lane
Wokingham
Berkshire
RG41 2QZ

ISBN 978-1-84710-707-7

Printed and bound in Great Britain

Preface

This book is the perfect aide memoire for the busy professional in any business environment. It will prove invaluable as a reference tool during the learning phase of any business or accountancy course and when revising these fundamental terms and will last well beyond the end of the course as a reference book and a quick and easy way of refreshing knowledge.

With terms explained concisely in plain English that is easy to understand and uncluttered presentation that makes it easy to look up any reference:

- know your SOX from your SOGA
- find out if the Cadbury Report says anything about chocolate
- understand what the difference is between Higgs and Turnbull
- distinguish gross domestic from gross national product
- find a quick summary of the roles of the World Trade Organisation or the Bank of England and find out what responsibilities the European Central Bank has
- relax with the floating exchange rate or joust with the balance of payments
- talk confidently about stagflation and the paradox of thrift
- impress your colleagues with a reference to cobweb theory and be sure that you know what it means.

A

Abnormal gain

The actual loss is less than the normal loss or the output is more than expected. Abnormal gain is valued at the same value as good output.

Abnormal gain account

The abnormal gain account is:
- credited with the value of abnormal gain
- debited with any scrap value of abnormal gain.

The balance is written to the income statement.

* EXAMPLE *

Abnormal gain

	kg	*$*		*kg*	*$*
Normal loss account	20	180	Process account –	20	880
Income statement		700	Abnormal gain		
	20	880		20	880

Abnormal loss account

The abnormal loss account is:
- debited with the value of abnormal loss
- credited with any scrap value of abnormal loss.

The balance is written off to the income statement.

* EXAMPLE *

Abnormal loss

	kg	*$*		*kg*	*$*
Process account-	50	2,200	Scrap account	50	450
Abnormal loss			Income statement		1,750
	50	2,200		50	2,200

Abnormal losses

The actual loss is more than the normal loss or the output is less than expected. Abnormal loss is valued at the same value as good output.

Absorption costing - procedure

Step 1	Allocate whole overhead costs to cost centres.
Step 2	Apportion all other overhead costs to cost centres.
Step 3	Reapportion service cost centre overheads to production cost centres.
Step 4	Absorb production cost centre overheads into cost units.

Accelerator principle

Explains how an initial change in aggregate demand may lead to a greater than proportionate change in investment. This is particularly linked to the business cycle. In recovery an initial increase in aggregate demand will cause entrepreneurs to forecast further increased demand and so invest in capital equipment. As capital equipment lasts for more than one year, this will be a high initial injection into aggregate demand. Conversely, in recession entrepreneurs may expect a fall in demand and therefore stop capital investment which accelerates the decline in demand.

Accounting equation

Assets = Capital + Liabilities
The business' assets must have been funded from some source, either the owners (capital) or third parties (liabilities). The double entry bookkeeping system ensures that the total value recorded for assets is, in fact, equal to the combined totals for capital and liabilities.

Accounting estimates

Estimates that arise from the uncertainties inherent in business activities. The use of reasonable estimates is an essential part of the preparation of financial statements, but estimates may need to be changed in the light of experience or new information.

Accounting for payroll

The bookkeeping system has to keep track of the gross cost of wages and salaries. Employers are responsible for deducting taxes and other amounts from the gross cost and paying these to the government, pension fund or whichever other recipient is entitled to a deduction from the employees' gross pay.

Accounting packages

There are numerous computerised accounting packages on the market. These vary in complexity and sophistication to meet the needs of a range of businesses of differing sizes and with different information needs.

Accounting policies

The specific principles, bases, conventions, rules and practices applied by an entity in preparing and presenting financial statements. Management should select and apply appropriate accounting policies so that the financial statements comply with all applicable accounting standards.

Accounting records

Used to keep track of all transactions and adjustments so that it is possible to aggregate their effect and prepare up to date and accurate accounting statements.

Accounting standards

The authoritative statements of how particular types of transactions and other events should be reflected in financial statements. The most influential standards are those set by the International Accounting Standards Board (IASB).

Accounting statements – analysis

By definition, accounting is intended to inform economic decisions. Decision-makers analyse financial statements in a variety of ways, most notably by calculating ratios in order to identify relationships within the figures.

Accruals/matching concept

One of the fundamental accounting concepts. Income and expenses should be matched together and dealt with in the income statement for the period to which they relate regardless of the period in which the cash was actually received or paid. Therefore all of the expenses involved in making the sales for a period should be matched with the sales income and dealt with in the period in which the sales themselves are accounted for.

Accrued expenses

Charges which are brought into the financial statements at the end of a period because, although goods and services have been provided, they have not yet been charged for by the suppliers.

Accumulated fund/General fund

A club's capital account.

Addition law for mutually exclusive events

Two or more events are said to be mutually exclusive if the occurrence of any one of them precludes the occurrences of all the others, i.e. only one can happen. Mutually exclusive events may be written in symbols as:
P(A and B) = 0

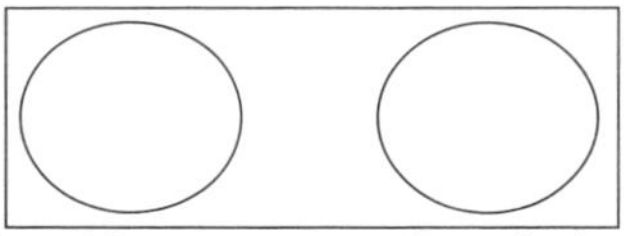

If A and B are two mutually exclusive events, then the probability that either A or B occurs in a given experiment is equal to the sum of the separate probabilities of A and B occurring:
P(A or B) = P(A) + P(B)

* EXAMPLE *

The probability of drawing an ace or king, when one card is drawn from a pack of 52 playing cards is calculated as follows:
∴ P(ace) = 4/52   P(king) = 4/52
∴ P(ace or king) = P(ace) + P(king)
= 4/52 + 4/52
= 8/52 (or 0.15)

Addition law for non-mutually exclusive events

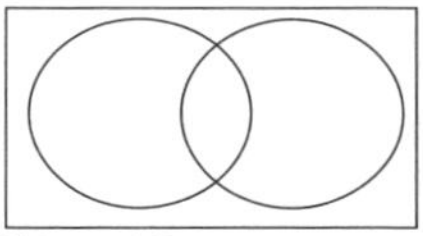

If A and B are two non-mutually exclusive events, then the probability that either A or B occurs in a given experiment is equal to the sum of the separate probabilities minus the probability that they both occur:
P(A or B) = P(A) + P(B) – P(A and B)

* EXAMPLE *

What is the probability of selecting a heart or a queen, when one card is drawn at random from a pack of playing cards? The probability of selecting a heart or a queen is an overlap situation, as the queen of hearts would be included in both events. To avoid including this probability twice, it must be subtracted once.
P(any heart) = 13/52 P(any queen) = 4/52 P(queen of hearts) = 1/52
∴ P(heart or queen) = P(heart) + P(queen) – P(queen of hearts)
= 13/52 + 4/52 – 1/52
= 16/52 (or 0.31)

Administrative controls

A domestic government can subject imports to excessive levels of administration, paperwork and red tape to slow down and increase the cost of importing goods into the home economy.

Aggregate demand

Represents the sum of demand for the output from an economy and is calculated as:

$$AD = C + I + G + X - M$$

where
C = private sector consumption expenditure
I = private sector investment expenditure
G = government expenditure
X = exports
M = imports

By manipulating aggregate demand government is able to promote/suppress growth in the economy.

Algebra

Algebra is the branch of mathematics that uses letters and other general symbols to represent numbers and quantities in formulae and equations. Formulae can be devised using algebra to describe general problems and then those formulae can be used with whatever actual values apply in specific situations.

- The individual parts of an expression are called terms, e.g. the expression 100x + y contains two terms, 100x and y.
- 100 is called the coefficient of x. The coefficient of y is 1.

Like terms

If an expression contains terms that involve the same letter and differ only in the coefficients, then they are called like terms. The important point is that 'like terms' can be added or subtracted by adding or subtracting the coefficients.

* EXAMPLE *

$5a + 6b + 2a - 3b$
$= (5 + 2)a + (6 - 3)b$
$= 7a + 3b$

Evaluation of algebraic expressions

Numerical values of algebraic expressions can be calculated simply by substituting definite numbers for the letters.

Manipulation of algebraic expressions

The rules are exactly the same as the rules for the manipulation of non-algebraic expressions.

Allowance for receivables

An amount deducted from receivables to allow for the estimated non-recovery of a proportion of the debts. The balance is adjusted at the end of each year to reflect the estimated non-recovery. The movement from one year end to the next is charged to the income statement as part of the cost of receivables written off.

Annual general meeting (AGM)

Every company must hold a first AGM within 18 months of incorporation and thereafter no more than 15 months apart and once in every calendar year. The following business is usually transacted at an AGM:

- consideration of the accounts and the reports of the directors and the auditor
- declaration of a dividend
- election of directors in place of those retiring
- appointment of auditors and fixing their remuneration.

Annual percentage rate (APR)

Two rates are usually quoted by financial institutions, the first is the nominal rate, and the other, the rate actually earned, is known as the annual percentage rate (APR).

* EXAMPLE *

A credit card company charges 3.5% interest per month. Assume a customer has purchased £100 worth of goods on their card and does not pay anything against this sum for a full year. Calculate the amount they will owe after one year, and also the annual percentage rate (APR).

At the end of a 12-month period the amount which will be owed is:

$$V = X(1 + r)^n$$

where:

X = original sum
r = interest rate
n = time period
V = amount at end of period

So $V = 100 \times (1 + 0.035)^{12} = £151.11$

The APR (which we shall call r_1 to avoid confusion with the r above) is therefore:

$$100 \times (1 + r_1) = 151.11$$

Hence:

$$100\, r_1 = 51.11$$

$$r_1 = 0.5111 = 51.11\%.$$

The APR is 51.11%.

Annuities

A fixed periodic payment that continues either for a specified time, or until the occurrence of a specified event.

* EXAMPLE *

Find the present value of an annuity of £300 for 5 years, using compound interest at 4% pa, the first receipt being in one year's time.

Time	Cash flow £	Discount factor	PV £
1	300	$1/(1.04)^1 = 0.962$	289
2	300	$1/(1.04)^2 = 0.925$	277
3	300	$1/(1.04)^3 = 0.889$	267
4	300	$1/(1.04)^4 = 0.855$	256
5	300	$1/(1.04)^5 = 0.822$	247
Total present value			1,336

Cash flows of the same amount received or spent at regular intervals. Annuity factors (given in tables) can be applied to the cash flow to discount to the present value.

* EXAMPLE *

A cash flow of £1,000 for three years at an interest rate of 5% has a present value of:

£1,000 x 2.723 = £2,723

Annuity factor formula

The general formula for the annuity discount factor, which is given in the exam, is as follows:

$$PV = \frac{1}{r}\left[1 - \frac{1}{(1+r)^n}\right]$$

or, in a single line, $1 / r \times [1 - (1 / (1 + r)^n]$

where r = discount rate (as a decimal)

n = number of years for which the annuity continues

This can also be expressed as:

$$PV = \frac{1-(1+r)^{-n}}{r}$$

or, in a single line, $[1 - (1 + r)^{-n}] / r$

The annuity or cumulative discount factors for a range of values of r are given in a cumulative PV table, e.g. for n = 5, r = 4% the cumulative factor from the table = 4.452.

A priori probability

The probability of an event is calculated by a process of logical reasoning. This is a form of objective probability, but based on logic: 'A priori' means 'from what was before'.

* EXAMPLE *

There is a 0.5 probability of an unbiased coin landing 'heads'. This is deduced without reference to any experiment, but is confirmed from previous personal experience of the way coins behave.

Appropriation of profit

The net profit for the year is divided between stakeholders. In a limited company, some is paid out as tax, some is paid to the shareholders as a dividend and the remainder is retained as additional capital.

Architects' certificates

As the work on a contract proceeds, the client's architects (or surveyors) will issue certificates indicating that a certain amount of the contract price is now due to the contractor in respect of the work completed. In most cases at this stage the contractor will invoice the contractee with a progress payment.

Arithmetic mean

The best known type of average. It is defined as the total value of the items divided by the total number of items.

Arithmetic mean for grouped data

For grouped data it is assumed that in each class all items are spread evenly about the mid-value. Hence, mean = $\frac{\Sigma fx}{\Sigma f}$ where x is the mid-value.

* EXAMPLE *

The following table shows the frequency distribution of 100 articles. The arithmetic mean is calculated as shown beneath the table.

Class interval Weight (grams)	Mid-value x	Frequency f	fx
100 and less than 110	105	1	105
110 and less than 120	115	2	230
120 and less than 130	125	85	625
130 and less than 140	135	11	1,485
140 and less than 150	145	21	3,045
150 and less than 160	155	20	3,100
160 and less than 170	165	17	2,805
170 and less than 180	175	11	1,925
180 and less than 190	185	6	1,110
190 and less than 200	195	6	1,170
Totals		$\Sigma f = 100$	$\Sigma fx = 15{,}600$

$$\bar{x} = \frac{\Sigma fx}{\Sigma f} = \frac{15{,}600}{100} = 156 \text{ grams}$$

Arithmetic mean for ungrouped data

Ungrouped data is data that has not been summarised (grouped) in the form of a frequency distribution. Assuming a set of data consists of n items, $x_1, x_2, \ldots,$ xn, then the arithmetic mean (denoted by $\bar{x}$, pronounced 'x bar') is given by the formula:

$$\bar{x} = \frac{x_1 + x_2 + x_3 + \ldots + x_n}{n}$$

i.e. $$\bar{x} = \frac{\Sigma x}{n}$$

where Σx (sigma x) denotes the **sum of** the individual values of x.

*** EXAMPLE ***

The arithmetic mean of 3, 6, 10, 14, 17, 19 and 22 is calculated as follows:

$$\bar{x} = \frac{\Sigma x}{n}$$

where $x_1 = 3, x_2 = 6, \ldots$ etc, and $n = 7$

$$= \frac{3 + 6 + 10 + 14 + 17 + 19 + 22}{7}$$

$$= \frac{91}{7}$$

$$= 13$$

Arithmetic mean of combined data

If one group of 10 people has a mean height of 175cm, and another group of 15 people has a mean height of 172cm, the mean of the whole group is found as:

$$\text{Mean} = \frac{\text{Sum of heights of all people in combined groups}}{\text{Total number of people in combined groups}}$$

This is an example of a weighted average.

Arithmetical and accounting controls

Control procedures which involve checking the arithmetical accuracy of the records, the maintenance and checking of reconciliations, control accounts and trial balances, and accounting for documents, e.g. preparation of a bank reconciliation statement as a check on the accuracy of the entries in the cash book.

Arithmetical progressions

Each term is formed from the preceding one by adding or subtracting a constant number called the common difference, e.g.

- 2, 3, 4, 5, ...
- −7, 3, 13, 23, ...

Arithmetical progression can be written in general terms as:

$a, a + d, a + 2d, \ldots$

where a is the first term and d is the common difference.

The nth term is:

$a + (n - 1)d$

The sum of the first n terms of an arithmetical progression (S_n) is given by the following formulae:

$$S_n = \frac{n}{2}[\text{First term - } n^{th} \text{ term}] = \frac{n}{2}[2a+(n-1)d]$$

*** EXAMPLE ***

Find the tenth term and the sum of the first ten terms of the series 22, 20.5, 19 ...

$a = 22, d = -1.5$

10th term $= a + 9d = 22 + (9 \times -1.5)$

$= 8.5$

$S_{10} = 10/2\ [2 \times 22 + (9 \times -1.5)]$

$= 152.5$

Asset

A resource controlled by the entity as a result of past events and from which future economic benefits are expected to flow to the entity. (Note that ownership is not necessarily a condition of something being an asset.)

Asset turnover

A measure of how well the assets of a business are being used to generate sales. Usually expressed as a ratio (Sales ÷ Operating assets).

Asset valuation

The balance sheet expresses a book value for each asset that is recognised in the financial statements.

Asset valuation methods

The most commonly used valuation method is historical cost, less depreciation in the case of non-current assets. The most common alternative is valuation, less depreciation where appropriate. More theoretical alternatives include replacement cost, net realisable value, economic value and constant money cost.

Attainable standard

A standard that assumes efficient levels of operation, but which includes allowances for normal loss, waste and machine downtime.

Attributable profit on uncompleted contracts (interim profit)

Where a contract extends over a long period SSAP 9 *(Stocks and Long-term Contracts)* allows the contractor to take credit for part of the profit **attributable** to the contract in each year's accounts. In deciding to what extent profit can be taken on uncompleted contracts, the following matters are important considerations:

- the successful outcome of the contract should be certain before any interim profit is taken
- any profit should only be taken in proportion to the work completed to date on the contract
- any anticipated overall loss on the contract should be provided for as soon as it is recognised.

The calculation of the profit to be taken on an uncompleted contract involves five steps:

Step 1	Determine the total sales value of the contract (for a fixed price contract this will be the contract price). Call this (a).
Step 2	Compute the total expected costs to complete the contract. Call this (b).
Step 3	The expected overall profit, or notional profit, on the contract is given by (a) minus (b).

Step 4	The attributable profit to date on the contract should reflect the amount of work that has been completed so far. It can be calculated as follows. Based on work complete: Attributable profit to date = $\frac{\text{Value of work certified to date}}{\text{Total sales value of contract}} \times \text{Expected overall profit}$ Based on costs incurred: Attributable profit to date = Costs incurred to date/total expected cost × Expected overall profit It is important to realise that the attributable profit thus calculated is the cumulative figure to date.
Step 5	The profit to be taken this year is the cumulative attributable profit calculated at Step 4 less the profit on the contract already recognised in previous years.

Audit The means by which one person is assured by another of the quality, condition or status of some subject matter which the latter has examined.

Audit process The approach taken by the auditor in order to gather evidence in support of the audit opinion.

Audit trail The flow of transactions through the bookkeeping system. The auditor follows transactions through the audit trail, checking that each stage of the calculation and recording is correct.

Authorisation and approval controls All transactions should be approved or authorised by a responsible official whose duties and authorisation limits are clearly defined.

Authorised share capital The maximum number of shares a company may issue.

Average A measure of location sometimes called a measure of central tendency.

Average cost/Weighted average A system of valuing inventory where it is assumed that the cost of each unit issued is the weighted average cost of the inventory on hand.

* EXAMPLE *

If there are 50 units on hand costing \$10 each and 150 units costing \$14, then each unit used would be assumed to cost ¼ × \$10 + ¾ × \$14 = \$13.

Average period of credit allowed by suppliers A ratio used to measure how well a business is managing its relationship with suppliers. To give the average number of days it takes to pay a supplier, it is expressed as:

$$\frac{\text{Trade payables}}{\text{Purchases}} \times 365$$

Too short a period suggests that the company is throwing away an opportunity to take advantage of this source of finance. Too long suggests that it is unable to pay its debts when they fall due.

B

Bad debts (receivables written off)

Amounts due from credit customers that have been written off because their recovery has been deemed unlikely.

Balance of payments

Records all of the transactions that have taken place between residents of a country and overseas residents during the period of a year.

- Inflows of money from overseas are recorded as positive items (credits), e.g. the sale of a Landrover to a French national.
- Outflows of money to overseas residents are recorded as negative items (debits), e.g. purchase of batteries from a Chinese supplier.

The balance of payments has three separate accounts, together with a balancing figure (net errors and omissions):

- The current account records trade in goods and services, together with income and current transfers.
- The capital account records transfer of capital, e.g. to and from the EU and the World Bank.
- The financial account contains investments in external assets and liabilities.

The current and capital accounts record flows into and out of the country. The financial account records where the money came from to fund these flows. The current and capital accounts added together should balance with the financial account. Any balancing figure required to achieve this is due to omissions or errors in calculations and is officially referred to as net errors and omissions.

Balance of payments deficits

If a country is said to have a deficit on its balance of payments, this means that there is a net outflow on the current and capital accounts. If there is a deficit in a particular year, this means that there has been a net outflow of funds from the country. Clearly, this outflow cannot continue as a country cannot keep spending more than it earns in foreign currency – eventually it will run out of reserves and other countries will cease to be willing to loan it money.
Government can seek to reduce a balance of payments deficit in a number of ways. Traditionally the strategies that can be used are divided into:

- expenditure reducing strategies
- expenditure switching strategies.

Balance of trade

The balance between imports and exports. Historically, this is a negative figure for the UK, i.e. its imports of goods are greater than exports.

Balance sheet

A statement showing the balances on the various asset, liability and capital accounts. It shows the business' financial position at a point in time.

Balanced budget

Government income = expenditure = a balanced budget

Bank of England

Has the following roles in the UK banking system:

- It is the only body with the authority to issues notes and coins into circulation.
- It sets interests rates through the Monetary Policy Committee by adjusting the repo rate – the rate at which it is prepared to repurchase Treasury bills. The main factor considered here is forecast inflation. The Bank will increase interest rates to reduce inflationary pressure if necessary.
- It provides advice and assistance to the Debt Management Office, a part of the Treasury, in connection with the issue and redemption of government securities such as Treasury bills and gilts.
- It acts as the bank for other banks, i.e. it holds accounts for all the UK Clearing Banks that are used to settle up cheque payments between the banks at the end of each day.
- It manages the Exchange Equalisation Account and the country's reserves of foreign currency.
- It represents the UK in overseas trade negotiations.

Bank reconciliations

It is important to check that the information in the cash book is both complete and accurate. One way to do this is to compare the balance according to the cash book with that according to the bank statement as at the end of each month. This comparison is not, however, a simple matter of agreeing the balances because there are often delays between a transaction being entered in the company's cash book and it appearing in the bank's records. For instance, a cheque might be written on the 25th of the month, but it will not appear as a payment until the payee has received it through the post, submitted it to the bank and the cheque processed through the bank's systems. This might not happen until well into the next month. A bank reconciliation statement involves adjusting the bank's balance for lodgements and withdrawals that occurred before the end of the month but that have not yet been processed by the bank. Once this has been done the two balances should agree.

Banks

The main business of banks includes offering financial services, taking deposits and extending credit. In the UK their activities are regulated by the Financial Services Authority (FSA). Banking activities are traditionally split between the following:

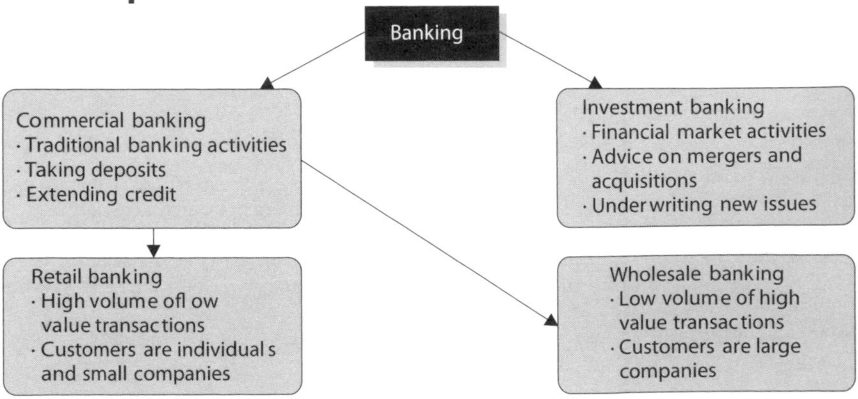

Bank statement

A record provided by the bank of the transactions that occurred according to its records during the month concerned and also the balance according to its records as at the end of the month. It is sent to customers as a routine service to enable them to check their records against the bank's.

Bar chart

Bars of equal width, either vertical or horizontal, are constructed with their lengths proportional of the value of the variable.

Barriers to entry into markets

Can take a number of forms, including:

- legal barriers, e.g. patents, award of a state monopoly to a utility company
- natural barriers reflecting the cost structure of an industry, e.g. high start-up costs
- integration in which monopolists control production, distribution and retail aspects of the industry making it very difficult for a new entrant to become established.

Basic mathematical tools

The basic tools of mathematics are addition, subtraction, multiplication and division.

- The addition of two or more numbers results in an answer which is termed the sum.
- When two numbers are multiplied together the result is termed the product.
- When one number is divided by another the result is termed the quotient.

Basic standard

A standard established for use over a long period from which a current standard can be developed.

Batch costing

A form of specific order costing in which costs are attributed to batches of products. (CIMA *Official Terminology*) Very similar to job costing.

- Each batch is a separately identifiable cost unit which is given a batch number in the same way that each job is given a job number.
- Costs can then be identified against each batch number, e.g. materials requisitions will be coded to a batch number to ensure that the cost of materials used is charged to the correct batch.

$$\text{Cost per unit in batch} = \frac{\text{Total production cost of batch}}{\text{Number of units in batch}}$$

Bilateral contract

A contract whereby both parties make promises and are bound. This is the usual type of contract.

* EXAMPLE *

A contract for the sale of goods, where the seller promises to transfer legal title to the buyer and the buyer promises to pay.

Bi-lateral trade agreements

Agreements between two countries to eliminate quotas and tariffs on the trade of most (if not all) goods between them, e.g. the Closer Economic Relations (CER) agreement between Australia and New Zealand.

Bills of exchange

Usually issued by companies to finance trade and promises to pay a certain sum at a fixed future date to the other party. In many respects it is very similar to a post-dated cheque. Characteristics of bills of exchange:

Returns	The bill is sold for less than the face value but is paid in full on maturity No interest
Risks	Varies – bills may be guaranteed by banks
Timescales	Usually short term – 3 to 6 months
Liquidity	Can be resold in the money markets

Block codes/ Hierarchical codes

Commonly form the basis of nominal ledger coding systems, for instance:
0000 to 0999 – Non-current assets
1000 to 1999 – Current assets
Etc.

Board meetings

Unless the Articles otherwise provide, any director may call a board meeting. The meeting must be called at a reasonable time and place. No minimum period of notice is required. The notice need not state the business to be transacted at the meeting. Minutes of board meetings must be kept. If signed by the chairman, the minutes are prima facie evidence of the proceedings.

Board structures

The term 'unitary' board structure refers to the situation where there is one board which is responsible for both management and governance. This is the type of structure usually found in the UK and the USA.
Under a two-tier system, there is:

- a supervisory board with a chairman, and
- a management board with a Chief Executive.

This type of system is commonly found in France and Germany.

Bonds

Loans may be broken down into smaller units e.g. one bond may have a nominal or par value of £100. Different varieties include debentures and loan stock and may be issued by companies, local authorities and governmental organisations. Characteristics of bonds:

Returns	Interest is expressed as the coupon rate and is usually fixed Gain on redemption (bonds are usually redeemed at par, though may be issued at a discount)
Risks	Default (though most bonds are secured) Increase in interest rates if variable rate
Time-scales	The maturity is defined on the bond Varies from very short term (e.g. government gilt-edged bonds) to long term (e.g. 25-year corporate bonds) May be irredeemable
Liquidity	If unquoted then no choice except to wait for redemption If quoted then easier to liquidate Note: high risk bonds will be sold at a large discount on face value

* EXAMPLE *

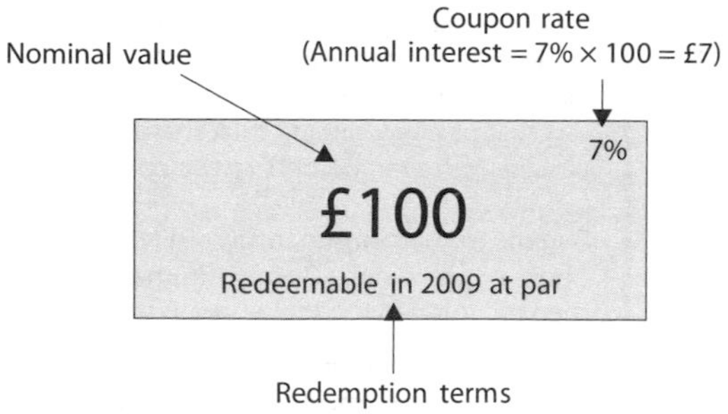

Bonds – returns (yields)

* EXAMPLE *

Consider a bond with the following characteristics:

- nominal value £100
- coupon rate 8%
- redemption terms – to be redeemed at par in 5 years' time
- current market value – £108.40.

* EXAMPLE *

The following yields can be calculated:

- The *bill rate* – this is just another name for the coupon rate, here 8%. This rate does not consider the market value of the bond or the capital gain/loss on redemption.
- The *running yield*, also known as the 'interest yield', given by:
  Running yield = (Annual interest/Market value) × 100%
  = 8/108.40 × 100%
  = 7.38%
  If you bought the bond for £108.40, then annual interest of £8 gives a return of 7.38% on your investment each year. Note that this approach takes into account the market value of the bond but ignores the impact of a capital gain or loss on redemption.
- The *gross redemption yield* gives the annualised overall return to the investor and incorporates both interest and capital gains and losses. For the above bond the gross redemption yield is 6%. (Calculation of this figure is outside the syllabus.)

Bonus issue

Carried out by using some of the company's reserves to issue fully paid shares to existing shareholders in proportion to their shareholdings. It does not raise any new funds.

Bonus shares / Capitalisation issue / Scrip issue

The issue of bonus shares (a bonus, scrip or capitalisation issue) represents the issue of shares to existing shareholders in proportion to their existing holdings, using the reserves of the company. It is effectively the conversion of part of the reserves of the company into share capital. No cash or other consideration is passed from shareholders to the company.

Books of prime entry / Day books

Routine transactions such as credit sales and purchases are recorded initially in books of prime entry. Totals summarising the transactions in these books are then recorded as a single entry in the relevant nominal ledger accounts.

* EXAMPLE *

Individual net sales, Value Added Tax (VAT) and gross sales are listed in the sales day book. At the end of every month the sales ledger control account is debited with total gross sales, the sales account is credited with total net sales and the VAT account is credited with the VAT on those sales.

Book values

The amounts attributed to assets by the accounting system. They may not be closely related to any of the values that might be useful for making specific economic or business decisions (e.g. how much could the asset be sold for or how much would it cost to replace?).

Breach of contract

Occurs when:

- a party fails to perform, or performs defectively, an obligation under the contract (actual breach)
- before the time fixed to perform an obligation, a party shows an intention not to perform (anticipatory breach).

Breakeven chart

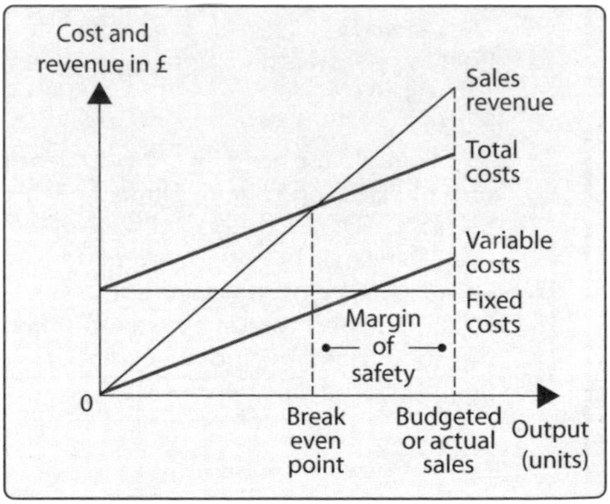

Breakeven point

The activity level at which there is neither a profit nor a loss.

$$\text{Breakeven volume (in units)} = \frac{\text{Total fixed costs}}{\text{Unit contribution}}$$

Breakeven point with a profit target

$$\text{Target (units)} = \frac{\text{Contribution target}}{\text{Unit contribution}} = \frac{\text{Profit target + fixed costs}}{\text{Unit contribution}}$$

Breakeven volume (in \$) = Total fixed cost/ C/S ratio

Budget

A quantitative statement, for a defined period of time, which may include planned revenues, expenses, assets, liabilities and cash flows.

Budget centre

A section of an entity for which control may be exercised and budgets prepared.

Budget committee

Typically comprises the chief executive, the management accountant (acting as budget officer) and functional heads. The functions of the committee are to:

- agree policy with regard to budgets
- co-ordinate budgets
- suggest amendments to budgets (e.g. because there is inadequate profit)
- approve budgets after amendment, as necessary.

Budget deficit

Government income < expenditure = budget deficit

Budget period

The period for which a budget is prepared and used which may then be subdivided into control periods.

Budget preparation

Assuming sales to be the principal budget factor:

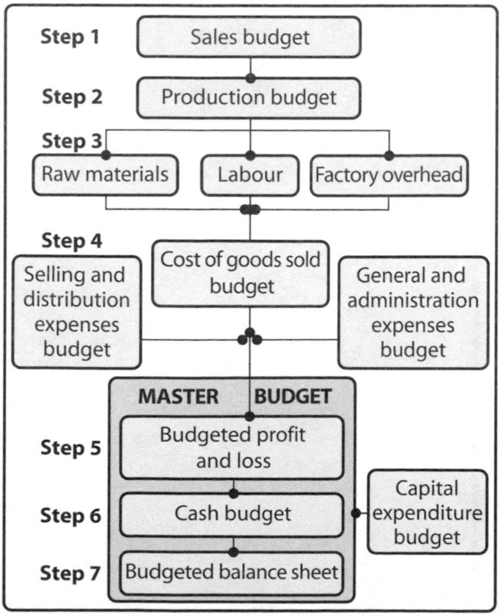

Budget surplus

Government income > expenditure = budget surplus

Budget variances

Original (flexed) budget	→	budget activity level	→	differences **volume variances**
Flexed budget	→	actual activity level	→	differences **expenditure variances**
Actual	→	actual activity level	→	

Budgetary control cycle

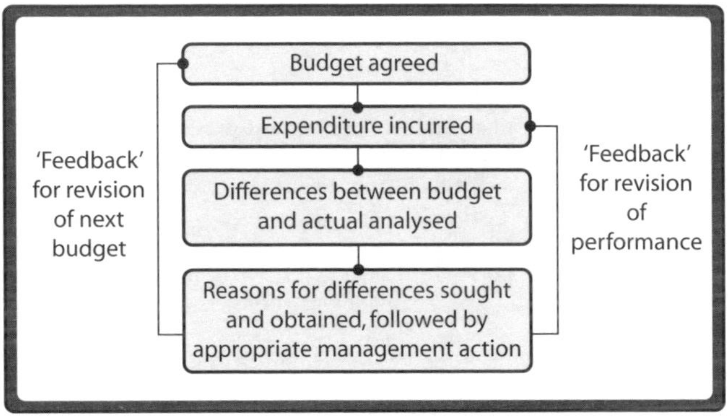

Budgeted balance sheet

The budgeted balance sheet represents the balances of revenue transactions that have not yet been realised in cash (inventory, receivables, payables, etc) as well as capital items.

Budgeting aims

- Planning and co-ordination.
- Authorising and delegating.
- Evaluating performance.
- Discerning trends.
- Communicating and motivating.
- Control.

C

Cadbury Report (1992)

Its objective was to help raise the standards of corporate governance and the level of confidence in financial reporting and auditing by setting out clearly the respective responsibilities of those involved and what is expected of them. In summary:

- appointment of non-executive directors (at least three)
- appointment of an audit committee
- non-executive directors to set remuneration of executive directors
- imposition of a three-year maximum term on executive directors' service contracts.

The Stock Exchange required all listed companies, as a continuing obligation of listing, to state whether or not they complied with the Combined Code and to give reasons for any areas of non-compliance. It also required the company's statement of compliance to be reviewed by the auditors before publication.

Called up share capital

The amount of nominal value paid by shareholders on their issued shares, plus further amounts agreed to be paid by shareholders on set dates in the future.

Captial account

The equity provided by the owner(s) is recorded in one or more capital accounts. In the case of a limited company, these will comprise share capital and reserves.

The capital account includes:

- transfers of capital
- the acquisition and disposal of non-financial, non-produced assets such as land, patents, brand names, copyrights, leases, etc
- transfers of capital by government, for example to the EU
- foreign aid by businesses
- transfers of capital by individuals including migrant workers.

Capital and money markets

For trading securities. Capital markets include the stock exchange and the AIM. Money markets include the inter-bank market. The time to maturity has traditionally been used to make a distinction between capital and money markets:

	Capital markets	Money markets
Maturities	>1 year	<1 year
Examples	Equities Bonds Mortgages	Certificates of deposit Bills of exchange

Capital and revenue

The acquisition of non-current assets is referred to as 'capital expenditure', whereas incurring expenses is referred to as 'revenue expenditure'. Sometimes payments have to be reviewed carefully in order to determine which category they should fall into.

> * EXAMPLE *
>
> Extensive refurbishment of a property might have the effect of improving a non-current asset and should be treated as capital expenditure. Alternatively, it might be argued that the expenditure was effectively a repair that should be treated as revenue expenditure.

Capital maintenance

The concept that a profit has only been earned if the owners' capital has been maintained. Different valuation methods lead to different values being attributed to profit because of this.

> * EXAMPLE *
>
> If a business purchased a piece of inventory for \$1, sold it for \$1.20 and then paid \$1.05 to replace it, we would then have two potential profit figures. Under historical cost accounting we sold an asset which cost \$1 and the profit is \$0.20. Under replacement cost accounting we sold an asset which cost \$1.05 to replace and so the profit is \$0.15.

Capital maintenance

Once capital has been raised it must be maintained. The law attempts to achieve this by forbidding a company from:

- acquiring its own shares
- giving financial assistance for the acquisition of its own sharesError! Bookmark not defined..
- making distributions except out of distributable profits.

Capital receipts

One that relates to an item that would be regarded as capital on the balance sheet.

Carriage inwards

Delivery costs associated with purchasing inventory. Treated as part of cost of sales.

Carriage outwards

Delivery costs associated with making sales. Treated as a distribution cost.

Cartel

When companies get together to share information, fix prices and agree market shares. It is illegal in most countries.

Cash book

To record a business' bank deposits and withdrawals. It may have a number of columns to enable analysis of receipts and payments, e.g. cash from trade payables or payments for wages.

Cash equivalents

Short-term highly liquid investments that are readily convertible to known amounts of cash and which are subject to an insignificant risk of changes in value. Investments are thus not cash equivalents unless they have these two attributes of being readily convertible and with little or no risk of change in value.

Cash flow statement

A detailed budget of cash inflows and outflows incorporating both revenue and capital items. Method of preparation:
- forecast sales
- forecast time-lag on converting debtors to cash, and hence forecast cash receipts from credit sales
- determine inventory levels, and hence purchase requirements
- forecast time-lag on paying suppliers, and thus cash payments for purchases
- incorporate other cash payments and receipts, including such items as capital expenditure and tax payments
- collate all this cash flow information to determine the net cash flows.

Cash flows

Absolute and relative cash flows
When deciding between two projects (known as mutually exclusive projects) two approaches are possible:
- discount the cash flows of each project separately and compare NPVs
- find the differential cash flow year by year, i.e. the difference between the cash flows of the two projects. Then discount those differential cash flows.

Why cash flows rather than profits?
- Cash is what ultimately counts – profits are only a guide to cash availability, they cannot actually be spent.
- Profit measurement is subjective – which time period income or expenses are recorded in, and so on.
- Cash is used to pay dividends – the ultimate method of transferring wealth to equity investors.

Cash payments book / Cash receipts book

Larger business might have separate cash books for keeping track of payments and receipts, in order to make it possible for more than one cashier to work on different parts of the cash book independently.

Cash transactions

Transactions involving receipts or payments of cash, or sometimes those involving receipts and payments through the bank.

Causal forecasting using correlation and regression

Used where there is a causal relationship between the variable whose value is to be forecast and another variable whose value can be ascertained for the period for which the forecast is to be made.

* EXAMPLE *

If there is correlation between the demand for sun roofs in a given year and the sales of new cars in the previous year, then this year's car sales could be used to predict sun roof demand for next year.

Certificates of deposit (CD)

A CD states that a deposit has been made with a bank for a fixed period of time, at the end of which it will be repaid with interest. The minimum amount invested is £50,000. Characteristics of CDs:

Returns	Interest
Risks	Very low risk but low interest rates as well
Timescales	3 and 6 month maturities are the most common
Liquidity	Can be readily sold on money markets

Certificate of incorporation

If the Registrar is satisfied that the registration requirements have been complied with, he must issue a certificate of incorporation which is conclusive evidence that:

- the relevant requirements of the Companies Act have been complied with
- the company is either a private or a public company as stated in the certificate.

The Registrar's certificate is conclusive evidence that the company has been validly incorporated on the date stated in the certificate.

Chain base index numbers

If a series of index numbers are required for different years, such that the rate of change of the variable from one year to the next can be studied, the chain base method is used. A chain base index number expresses each year's value as a percentage of the value for the previous year.

$$\text{Chain base index} = \frac{\text{This year's value}}{\text{Last year's value}} \times 100$$

Chart of accounts

When an accounting system is coded using the block/hierarchical method it is called a chart of accounts.

Circular flow of income for an open economy

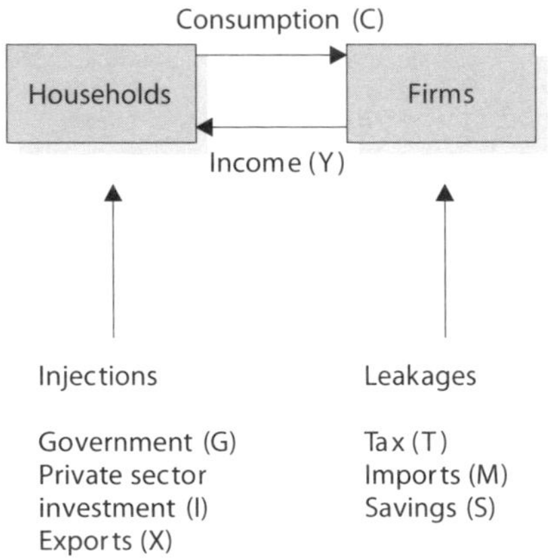

Total income plans will be (Y) = C + S + T + M

Total spending or demand plans (E) = C + I + G + X

In this model, for the circular flow to be in equilibrium (neither growing nor shrinking):

$$\text{Expenditure plans (E)} = \text{Income plans (Y)}$$
$$C + I + G + X = C + S + T + M$$
$$G + I + X = S + T + M$$
$$\text{Injections} = \text{Leakages}$$

Civil law

A civil action is brought by an individual (the claimant) who sues another individual (the defendant) to obtain redress, usually in the form of damages, for a wrong done to him personally. The primary purpose of the action is to compensate the injured party (or confirm the existence of his rights), and not to punish the offender. The court hearing is called litigation. The case against the defendant must be proved on a balance of probabilities.

Classical economic theory

Advocates that the economy has in-built mechanisms to establish and maintain equilibrium.

* EXAMPLE *

In the event of a depression the price of factors of production would fall. This would increase demand for them, leading to their utilisation and the re-establishment of economic growth.

Classification by behaviour

Classifying by behaviour explains how the total cost varies with changes in levels of activity (units produced or sold).

Classification by element

This identifies costs as being materials, labour or expenses.

Classification by function

Costs are identified by the function of the business responsible for incurring them e.g. production, sales, administration, distribution, research.

Classification by responsibility

Groups costs or revenues by the manager responsible for their control.

Classification of data

Bringing together items with a common characteristic.

Class intervals and class limits

The following points should be carefully noted when constructing a frequency distribution:

- Number of classes should be relatively few so that the information given is easily grasped and retained.
- Class intervals (or width) should all be equal if possible.
- Open-ended class intervals are classes such as '78 and over' or 'less than 60', which have only one boundary specified. For the purpose of statistical calculations, each such class is assumed to have the same interval as the class next to it.
- Class limits indicate what values from the original data will be included in each class.

Closing inventory

Inventory on hand at the year end. Closing inventory is valued by conducting a physical stock count and determining the lower of cost or net realisable of each item listed.

Cobweb theory

Attempts to explain why prices in some markets, particularly those in primary goods, are subject to periodic fluctuation. This type of cyclical fluctuation is common in markets where there is a lag between a change in prices and producers' response to that change.

Codes

Used to speed up data entry and processing all the main elements in the system, e.g. each supplier's record may be entered as a code rather than in full to save time.

Codified law

Sometimes referred to as civil law. Under this type of system, there are comprehensive written codes setting out the entire law on a particular topic. Codified law systems tend to be found in Continental Europe, Latin America and large parts of Africa.

Coding systems

Include sequential codes, faceted codes, mnemonic codes, significant digit codes, block codes and hierarchical codes.

Coefficient of determination, r^2

The coefficient of determination (r^2) is a measure of the explanatory power of a regression model, i.e. how much of the variation in the dependent variable can be explained by variation in the independent variable.

Coefficient of variation

A measure expressing the standard deviation as a percentage of the mean. It is a way of comparing variability between data sets:

$$\text{Coefficient of variation} = \frac{\text{Standard deviation}}{\text{Arithmetic mean}} \times 100$$

* EXAMPLE *

Two machines are used for filling bags of fertiliser. One machine is set to deliver a nominal weight of 1 kilo, and the other machine, 7 kilos. Tests on the actual amounts delivered gave the following results:

Machine	*Mean weight (kilo)*	*Standard deviation (kilo)*
1	1.05	0.062
2	7.13	0.384

Which machine varies most in weight delivered?
In absolute terms the answer is clearly machine 2, but:
Machine 1:

$$\text{Coefficient of variation} = \frac{0.062 \times 100}{1.05} = 5.9\%$$

Machine 2:

$$\text{Coefficient of variation} = \frac{0.384 \times 100}{7.13} = 5.4\%$$

Therefore machine 1 has a slightly greater variation in weight of output than machine 2, relatively speaking.

Collectability of debts/receivables

The amount owed by credit customers is not necessarily a reliable indication of the amount that will eventually be received. The company must consider the possibility that some customers will default. Only debts that are considered collectable should be carried forward in the balance sheet.

Combined Code

The Principles of Good Governance and Code of Best Practice (the 'Combined Code') was published in 1998 and slightly amended in July 2003. A new version of the code was issued on 27 June 2006. The Combined Code applies to all listed companies, whether they are large or small. The Stock Exchange Listing Rules require a listed company in the UK to include the following in its annual report and accounts:

- a narrative statement of how it has applied the principles set out in the Combined Code
- a statement as to whether or not it has complied throughout the accounting period with the Combined Code provisions. If it has not complied, it must specify the provisions with which it has not complied, and give reasons for any non-compliance.

The Combined Code covers the following topics:

- **Directors:** The roles of Chairman and Chief Executive should be split:
  - the Chairman should be responsible for the working of the board and the agenda for board meetings
  - the Chief Executive should have full operational control and authority to carry out the policies determined by the board.
- **Directors' remuneration:** A significant proportion of executive directors' remuneration should be structured so as to link rewards to corporate and individual performance.
- **Accountability and audit:** The board should, at least annually, conduct a review of the effectiveness of the company's system of internal controls.
- **Relations with shareholders:** A senior director should be identified and made available as a contact for shareholders.

Common Agricultural Policy (CAP)

A system of agricultural subsidies which work by guaranteeing a minimum price to producers and by direct payment of a subsidy for crops planted. This provides some economic certainty for EU farmers and production of a certain quantity of agricultural goods.

Common law

That which applies throughout England and Wales, declared by judges on the basis of fundamental legal principles. It developed through custom and case law. The only remedy available under the common law is damages.

Community Interest Companies (CICs)

Intended to be used primarily by non-profit distributing enterprises providing benefit to a community, such as childcare, social housing, leisure and community transport. To ensure that they use their assets and profits for the interest of the community, CICs are restricted from distributing profits and assets to their members. This is known as an 'asset lock'.

Company legislation

Companies are normally subject to a variety of legislation that is designed to protect both those who invest in them and those who deal with them. In the UK, most of this legislation is contained in the Companies Acts.

Comparability of information

Accounts should be comparable with those of other similar enterprises, and from one period to the next.

Comparative information

Financial statements often show the figures from the previous year alongside the latest information, so that readers can see whether there has been any significant change since last year.

Compensating errors

Occur where two or more errors cancel out each other. They are difficult to locate and fortunately tend not to occur frequently. They can be serious if they lead to significant errors being overlooked.

* EXAMPLE *

An unexplained difference of $10 on a reconciliation could be due to an undiscovered error of $10,000 overstatement being offset against a $10,010 understatement.

Compensation for unfair dismissal

Consists of three components:

Basic award

18 to 21 years of age	½ week's pay for each year of service
22 to 40 years of age	1 week's pay for each year of service
41 to 65 years of age	1½ week's pay for each year of service
Maximum	20 years' service at £290 a week

Compensatory award

- Discretionary award of up to £58,400. Based on employee's losses and expenses.
- Reduced if complainant contributed to his dismissal.

Additional award, given where:

- Employer ignores an order for reinstatement or re-engagement.
- Dismissal is unfair because of race, sex or disability discrimination.
- The reason cited for dismissal is an inadmissible one.

Complementary goods

When buying one good is likely to lead to the buying of another good, e.g. buying a new shirt could lead to a new tie being bought.

Complementary probabilities: at least one event occurs

When several events are being considered, then the probability that at least one of them occurs is given by:

P(at least one) = 1 – P(none of them)

* EXAMPLE *

If a coin is tossed five times, then the probability of obtaining at least one head is calculated as follows:

$P(\text{head}) = \frac{1}{2}$ and $P(\text{tail}) = \frac{1}{2}$

P(at least one head) = 1 – P(no heads)

$$= 1 - (\frac{1}{2} \times \frac{1}{2} \times \frac{1}{2} \times \frac{1}{2} \times \frac{1}{2})$$

$$= 1 - 1/32$$
$$= 31/32 \text{ (or } 0.97)$$

Complementary probabilities: two possible outcomes

When a single event has only two possible outcomes, usually denoted as success and failure, then, if p and q are the probabilities of success and failure respectively, it follows that:

$$p = 1 - q$$

This is because $p + q = 1$, since they are the only possible outcomes of the event.

* EXAMPLE *

When an unbiased die is thrown, a six is regarded as success and any other number as failure.

∴ $p = P(\text{success}) = 1/6$

And $q = P(\text{failure}) = 1 - 1/6 = 5/6$

The event 'A does not occur' is called the negation of A and is denoted by $\bar{A}$ or A'. Hence:

$$P(\bar{A}) = 1 - P(A)$$

$P(\bar{A})$ is called the complement of P(A)

In a Venn diagram, the complement is shown as the rest of the diagram – if A is represented by a circle as usual, then $\bar{A}$ is shown by the shaded area:

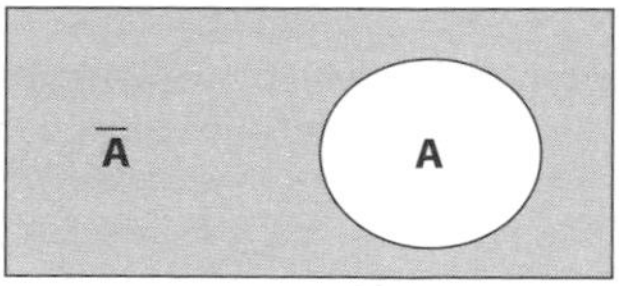

Compliance tests

Tests that seek to provide reasonable evidence that internal control procedures are being applied as prescribed.

Component bar chart

A component bar chart is drawn when each total figure is built up from several component parts.

* EXAMPLE *

The following bar chart represents the grain production (rye, barley and wheat) in the UK for the years 20X4 to 20X6:

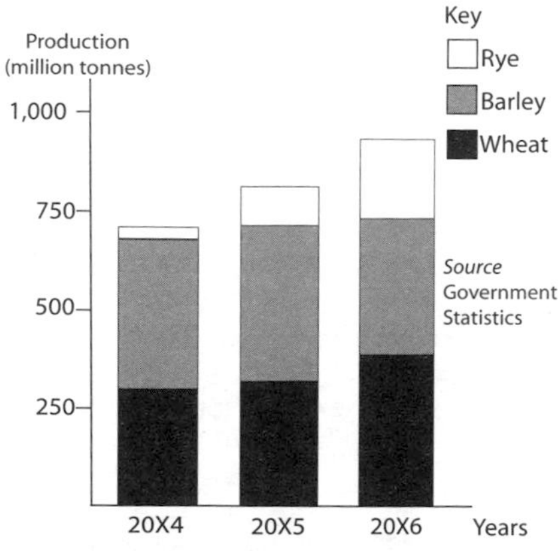

Composite cost units

Where output is measured as a combination of two factors, e.g. a passenger kilometre.

Compound depreciation

Similar to compound interest except that, instead of adding interest, depreciation is subtracted. The law is therefore:

$D = X(1 - r)^n$ where D = the depreciated value
X = the initial value
r = rate of depreciation
n = number of periods

Compound interest

With compound interest, the interest is added each year to the principal and for the following year the interest is calculated on their sum. So the value (V) at the end of the nth year is given by:

$V = X(1 + r)^n$

where r is the rate of interest

So the amounts at the end of successive years form a geometrical progression with common ratio (l + r):

i.e. $(1 + r), (1 + r)^2, (1 + r)^3 \ldots$

* EXAMPLE *

Calculate the compound interest on £624 at 4% pa for 10 years.

Using $V = X(1 + r)^n$ with X = £624
r = 0.04
n = 10

then $V = £624\,(1 + 0.04)^{10}$
$= £624\,(1.04)^{10}$
$= £923.67$

So the compound interest = (923.67 – 624)
= £299.67

Computerised accounting systems

Most accounting systems used computers to keep the records up to date. These vary in complexity from major corporate databases to simple PC-based systems using off-the-shelf software packages.

Conditional probability

The probability of an event whose calculation is based on the knowledge that some other event has occurred:

$$P(A \mid B) = \frac{P(A \text{ and } B)}{P(B)}$$

Connected persons

The connected persons of a director include:

- spouse, children (under 18) or stepchildren
- a company in which the director or their connections control at least 20% of the equity or votes
- a trustee of a trust from which the director or their connections may benefit
- a partner or director of any of their connections.

Consistency

A business should be consistent in its accounting treatment of similar items, both within a particular accounting period and between one accounting period and the next.

Constant money (or real) cost

The constant money cost is the equivalent of the original cost, but expressed in current money terms after allowing for the decline in the value of money. In other words, figures are restated to reflect the effects of general inflation.

Constructive dismissal

An employee is entitled to treat himself as constructively dismissed if the employer is guilty of conduct which:

- is a significant breach going to the root of the contract of employment, or
- shows that the employer no longer intends to be bound by one or more of the essential terms of the contract.

Whether the employee leaves with or without notice, the conduct must be sufficiently serious to entitle him to leave at once. However, he must act quickly for, if he continues for any length of time without leaving, he will be regarded as having elected to affirm the contract and will lose his right to treat himself as discharged.

Consumption function

Keynesian economists view consumption, an important component of aggregate demand, as being a function of national income:

$C = a + bY$

where

C = desired level of consumption (backed by purchasing power)

a = that part of desired consumption that is independent of income

b = marginal propensity to consume

Y = national income

Graph showing the consumption function

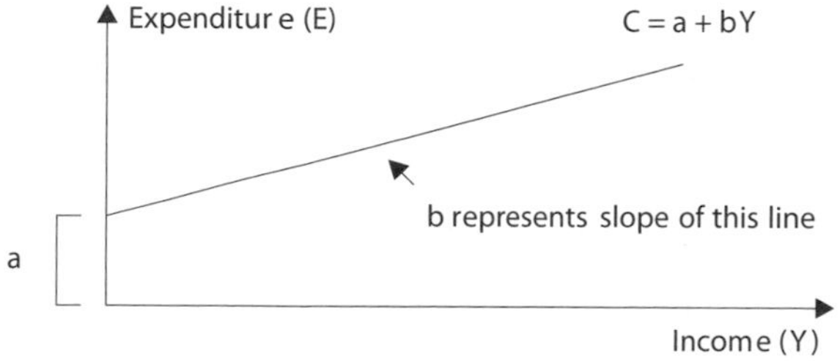

Contingency tables

Created by taking the given probabilities, multiplying by some convenient number, typically 100 or 1,000 (to make the numbers easy to work with), then drawing a table to show the various combinations of factors that may exist.

* EXAMPLE *

40% of the output of a factory is produced in Workshop A and 60% in Workshop B. Fourteen out of every 1,000 components from A are defective and six out of every 1,000 components from B are defective. After the outputs from A and B have been thoroughly mixed, a component drawn at random is found to be defective. The probability that it came from Workshop B is calculated in the following way.

* EXAMPLE *

The contingency table looks like this:

	Workshop A	*Workshop B*	*Total*
Defective	56	36	92
Non-defective	3,944	5,964	3,308
Total	4,000	6,000	10,000

Hence P(came from Workshop B given that it is defective)

$= \frac{36}{92}$

= 0.39

Continuous operation costing

Applicable where goods or services result from a sequence of continuous or repetitive operations or processes.

Contract

An agreement between two or more parties that is enforceable by law.

Contract account

A separate contract account is kept for each contract to record the costs incurred on the contract and the work certified (completed) to date. A contract account is a form of WIP account. Features of contract accounts are that:

- they contain a high proportion of direct costs
- plant may be debited to the account at cost and credited with the written down value at the end of the accounting period. Alternatively the depreciation charge may be debited to the account.

* EXAMPLE *

Contract number 412

	$		$
Materials, wages and subcontractors' costs	90,000	Client account (certified work)	100,000
Plant (at cost)	20,000	Materials c/d	19,000
Income statement	25,000	Plant c/d	15,000
		Work-in-progress c/d	1,000
	135,000		135,000
Work-in-progress b/d	1,000		
Materials b/d	19,000		
Plant b/d	15,000		

Contract costing

Used for large jobs produced to the customers specification, often of a constructional nature, which take a long time to complete.

Contract for the sale of goods

Defined in the Sale of Goods Act 1979 as a contract whereby the seller transfers or agrees to transfer the property in goods to the buyer for a money consideration called the price.

Contractionary fiscal policy

By running a budget surplus, i.e. planned expenditure is less than planned tax receipts, the government is running a tight or contractionary fiscal policy. This may be used to try to reduce inflation.

Contras

Offsetting two interrelated balances, e.g. a bank and a customer might agree that an overdraft balance ought to be offset against a positive balance in another account to leave a net balance.

Contribution

Contribution is sales value less variable cost of sales. This can be in total or per unit.

Contribution/Sales ratio (C/S ratio or P/V ratio)

$$\text{C/S ratio} = \frac{\text{Contribution}}{\text{Sales revenue}}$$

This can either be in total or per unit.

Contributory negligence

If a claimant is partly responsible for his own injuries, the defendant can plead the defence of contributory negligence. The court may then reduce any damages it awards to the claimant, depending on the degree to which they are judged responsible for their loss.

Control

Control is the comparison of the results of the plans and the stated objectives to assess the company's performance, and the taking of action to remedy any differences in performance.

Control account reconciliations

The payables ledger control account should be agreed to the payables ledger on a regular basis, as should the sales ledger control account with the sales ledger. Any difference should be investigated and dealt with.

Control accounts

Used to simplify the double entry system. The balance on a control account keeps track of the total balance on a large number of individual accounts (e.g. the total due from all trade payables or the total due to all suppliers). The balance on a control account is broken down into individual sums by a supporting ledger (e.g. the payables ledger or the sales ledger). The supporting ledgers are not part of the double entry system.

Control test

A person is an employee if the employer can tell him not only what to do but also how, when and where to do it.

Convergence criteria

Countries that wish to use the Euro as their main currency have to satisfy convergence criteria, in order to maintain the price stability within the Euro zone even with the inclusion of new member states. These include:

- Inflation: The inflation rate must be no more than 1.5 percentage points higher than the three best-performing member states of the EU (based on inflation).

- Government finance: The annual government deficit must not exceed 3% of the Gross Domestic Product (GDP). Gross government debt must not exceed 60% of GDP.
- Exchange rates: Applicant countries should have joined the exchange-rate mechanism (ERM II) under the European Monetary System (EMS) for two consecutive years and should not have devalued their currency during the period.
- Long-term interest rates: The nominal long-term interest rate must not be more than 2 percentage points higher than the three best-performing member states (based on inflation).

Corporate governance

Concerned with improving the way companies are governed and run. In particular, it seeks to address the principal-agent problem. The main objectives are to:

- control the managers/directors by increasing the amount of reporting and disclosure
- increase level of confidence and transparency in company activities for all investors (existing and potential) and thus promote growth in the company
- increase disclosure to all stakeholders
- ensure that the company is run in a legal and ethical manner
- build in control at the top that will 'cascade' down the organisation.

Corporate governance – benefits

The benefits of corporate governance include:

- risk reduction
- leadership improvement
- performance enhancement
- improving access to capital markets
- enhancing stakeholder support by showing transparency, accountability and social responsibility.

Corporate governance – mechanisms

Recommendations concerning corporate governance include:

- the UK combined code arising from the Cadbury (1992), Greenbury (1995) and Hampel (1998) reports
- the Turnball Report (1999)
- the Higgs Report (2003)
- the Smith Report (2003)
- the Sarbanes-Oxley Act (2002) in the USA.

The main areas covered by these reports include:

- detailed disclosure and reporting requirements
- the design and implementation of internal control structures and systems, especially those dealing with risk management
- the composition of boards, including the separation of CEO and chief executive
- the need for and responsibilities of non-executive directors, e.g. to represent shareholders' interests
- remuneration committees to set directors' pay
- audit committees
- nomination committees to control board appointments
- the management of Annual General Meetings (AGMs).

Corporate governance – OECD principles

The Organisation of Economic Co-operation and Development (OECD) identifies five principles of corporate governance:

- the rights of shareholders
- the equitable treatment of shareholders
- the role of stakeholders
- disclosure and transparency
- the responsibility of the board.

Corporate planning

Essentially a long-run activity that seeks to determine the direction in which the company should be moving in the future.

Correlation

A measure of how strong the connection is between two variables. Positive correlation exists where the values of the variables increase together (direct relationship). Negative correlation exists where one variable increases as the other decreases in value (inverse relationship).

Correlation coefficient, r

Pearson's correlation coefficient, r, is defined as:

$$r = \frac{n\Sigma xy - \Sigma x \Sigma y}{\sqrt{(n\Sigma x^2 - (\Sigma x)^2)(n\Sigma y^2 - (\Sigma y)^2)}}$$

where x and y represent pairs of data for two variables x and y, and n is the number of pairs of data used in the analysis.

Having calculated the value of r, it is necessary to interpret this result. Does r = 0.98 mean that there is high correlation, low correlation or no correlation? The coefficient of linear correlation (r) is a numerical measure of the degree of linear correlation between two variables. It has a range of values between −1 and +1.

r	=	+1	means perfect positive linear correlation
r	=	0	means no correlation, and
r	=	−1	means perfect negative linear correlation

Cost centre

A production or service location, function, activity or item of equipment for which costs are accumulated, e.g. machine shop, personnel department.

* EXAMPLE *

Types of correlation

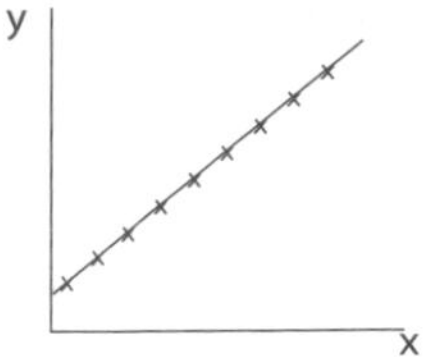

Perfect positive linear

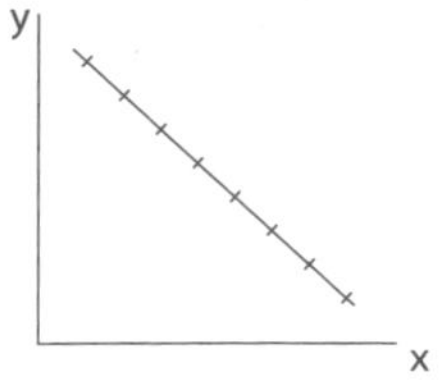

Perfect negative linear

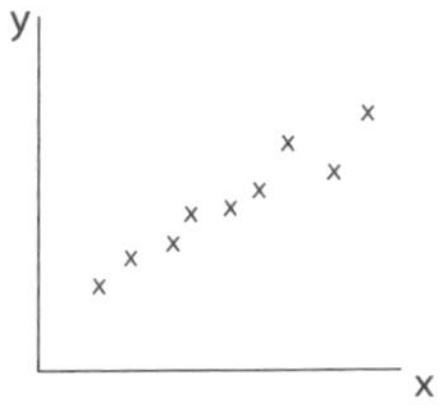

High positive

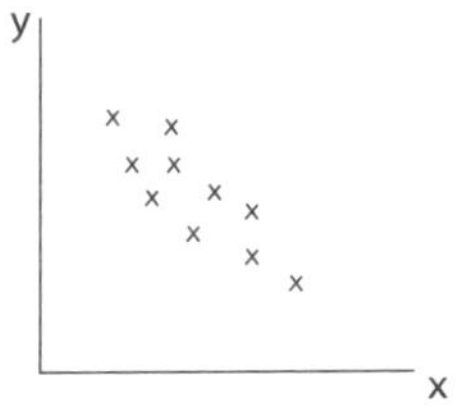

Moderate negative

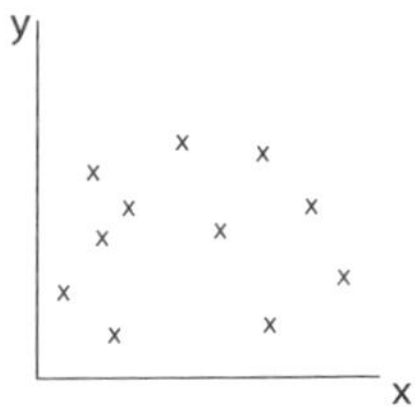

None

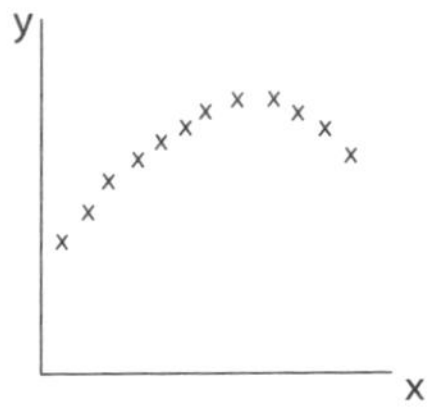

Non-linear or curvilinear

Cost curves

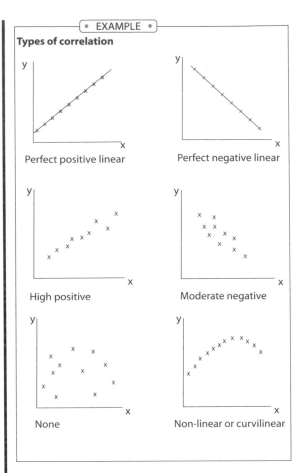

Variable costs (VC)
Costs that vary with output quantity.
Fixed costs (FC)
Costs that do not vary with output quantity.
Total costs (TC)
Fixed plus variable costs.
Marginal cost (MC)
Change in total cost as a result of producing an extra unit of output.
Average cost (AC)
The average unit cost of producing a good or service.
Graph showing average total, variable and fixed costs and marginal costs.

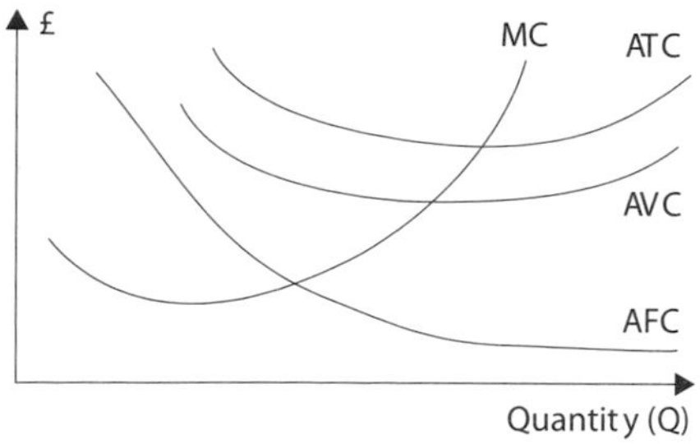

Note: The marginal cost curve crosses the average variable and total cost curves at their lowest points.

Cost classification

The logical grouping of similar costs, so that they may be accumulated to produce meaningful information.

Cost code

A code is a system of symbols designed to be applied to a classified set of items to give a brief, accurate reference, facilitating entry, collation and analysis. (CIMA *Official Terminology*)

Cost forecasts

Past costs can be used to predict future costs. Once a cost function has been identified using the high-low method or line of best fit method, this can be used to forecast future costs

* EXAMPLE *

Cost type	*Cost for 100 units*	*Cost for 200 units*
A	400	800
B	800	1,100
C	1,000	1,000

To forecast costs for 300 units, first identify whether the costs are fixed or variable.

- Cost A is variable because it changes in direct proportion to output. Cost is $4 per unit.
- Cost C is fixed because the cost is the same at all levels of output.
- Cost B is neither fixed nor variable and must therefore be semi-variable.

Using the high-low method variable cost is:

$$\frac{\$1,100 - \$800}{100} = \$3 \text{ per unit}$$

Total variable cost at 100 units is	$300
Total cost is	$800
So total fixed cost is	$500

The total fixed cost is therefore $1,500 (cost C + part cost B).
The total variable cost is $7 per unit (cost A + part cost B).

Then, prepare forecast at 300 units = 300 × $7 + $1,500 = $3,600

Cost object

Any activity for which costs are collected including products, services, customers, and processes.

Cost (of inventory)

Cost is the amount of expenditure (actual or notional) incurred on, or attributable to, a specified item or activity.

Cost of conversion

Comprises: costs that are specifically attributable to units of production, e.g. direct labour, direct expenses and sub-contracted work; production overheads; and other overheads, if any, attributable in the particular circumstances of the business to bringing the product or service to its present location and condition.

Cost of goods produced

Costs incurred in manufacturing finished goods completed during the year. Comprises prime cost plus factory overheads, adjusted for opening and closing inventories of raw materials and partly completed goods.

Cost per equivalent unit

Used to value finished output and closing work-in-progress.

Cost-push inflation

If the underlying cost of factors of production increase, this is likely to be reflected in an increase in output prices as companies seek to maintain their profit margins.

Cost unit

A unit of the product or service in relation to which costs may be ascertained.

* EXAMPLE *

For a farmer- a tonne of wheat; for brick making - a batch of 1,000 bricks; for passenger transport - passenger/kilometer.

Cost variance

The difference between a planned, budgeted or standard cost and the actual cost incurred. (CIMA *Official Terminology*)

Counter offer

An offer made in response to an offer. This has the effect of rejecting the original offer and the original offer is therefore no longer capable of acceptance.

Credit agreements

An arrangement where one party borrows or takes possession of something in return for future payment, e.g. credit cards, store hire purchase contracts. Characteristics of credit agreements:

Returns	High interest rate
Risks	Default
Timescales	Usually short term
Liquidity	Cannot be resold by the lender. The borrower may be able to repay early if funds permit

Credit multiplier

An initial deposit will increase the money supply by an amount determined by the credit multiplier:

Change in money supply = $1/\text{Liquidity ratio} \times \text{initial cash deposit}$

Credit risk

Collecting debts can be difficult if the customer is in another country, possibly with different time zones and who may speak a different language. Credit risk can be managed by a mixture of the following:

Advances
The exporter's (seller's) bank may agree to advance cash against the instrument by which the payment is to be made by the customer. The instrument might be a cheque payment or a bill of exchange.

Letters of credit
Provided all conditions are fulfilled within the time specified, letters of credit guarantee payment to the exporter and formally establish the payment period, which ranges from immediately upon presentation to the designated paying bank, to an unlimited period. A letter of credit also protects the customer against being pressed for payment before being presented with documentation, which conforms with the conditions originally set out with the exporter.

Export factoring
In essence, no different from the factoring of domestic trade debts. The service provided by the factor is effectively one of underwriting the client's debt; if the client's debtors fail to meet their debt obligations, the factor rather than the client bears the financial loss.

Export credit guarantees
A form of insurance for exporters.

Criminal law

Intended to punish or deter wrongdoers and, in principle, to correct and reform them. Criminal proceedings are usually brought by the Crown. This is known as a prosecution, which may result in conviction and sentence (e.g. a fine or imprisonment) if the accused is found guilty, or an acquittal if the case is not proved. The parties are known as the prosecution and the accused or defendant, and the court hearing is called a trial. The case against the accused must be proved beyond reasonable doubt.

Critical mass

If companies grow to a sufficient size to enable them to operate at the lowest point of the long-run average cost curve, they have achieved 'critical mass'. The low costs that result allow the company to set its prices below those of smaller competitors and can act as a serious barrier to new companies trying to enter the industry. Obtaining such a scale of production can result from organic growth and/or acquisition.

Cross Elasticity of Demand (XED)

Measures the relationship between the price of one good and demand for another good. XED is positive for substitutes and negative for complements.

Cumulative frequency curves (ogives)

If the cumulative frequencies are plotted against the upper class limits the resulting graph is called an ogive or a cumulative frequency curve.

* EXAMPLE *

The following is the frequency distribution of the weights (to the nearest gram) of 100 articles. They have been grouped into intervals of 10 grams.

Class interval	*Frequency*	*Cumulative frequency*
Weight (grams)	*Number of articles*	
100 and less than 110	1	
110 and less than 120	2	1
120 and less than 130	5	1 + 2 = 3
130 and less than 140	11	3 + 5 = 8
140 and less than 150	21	8 + 11 = 19
150 and less than 160	20	19 + 21 = 40
160 and less than 170	17	40 + 20 = 60
170 and less than 180	11	60 + 17 = 77
180 and less than 190	6	77 + 11 = 88
190 and less than 200	6	88 + 6 = 94
		96 + 6 = 100

- The cumulative frequencies are plotted against the upper class limits because:
  1 article weighs less than 110g
- 1 + 2 = 3 articles weigh less than 120g
- 1 + 2 + 5 = 8 articles weigh less than 130g
- 1 + 2 + 5 + 11 = 19 articles weigh less than 140g, etc.

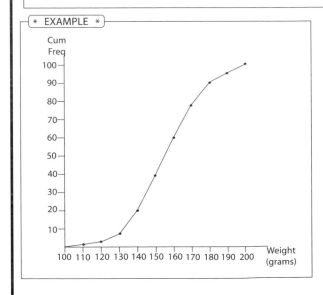

* EXAMPLE *

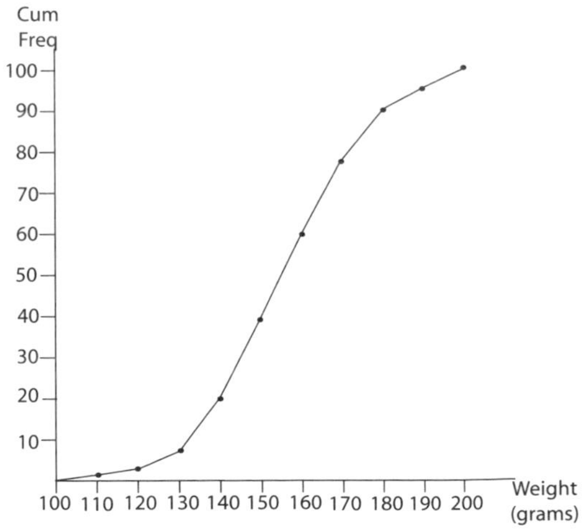

Currency – demand

Demand for sterling comes from a number of sources:

- It is required to pay for UK exports, e.g. a French supermarket buying English food will need to pay its suppliers in sterling.
- Overseas investors making investments in the UK will need sterling, e.g. an American property company buying a factory building in the UK will have to pay in sterling.
- Speculators may buy sterling if they feel it is about to increase (appreciate) in value relative to other currencies.
- The government may wish to buy sterling to manipulate the exchange rate.
- For some currencies there may be a demand for it to be held as an international medium of exchange as is the case with the US dollar.

Currency – supply

Supply of sterling is derived from a number of sources:

- UK residents wishing to buy imports will need to sell sterling and buy foreign currency.
- UK residents making overseas investments will need to sell sterling and buy foreign currency.
- Speculators may sell sterling if they feel its value is about to decrease (depreciate) relative to other currencies.
- The UK government may sell currency on the international markets to weaken the currency to improve export performance.

Current account

Records the exports and imports of goods and services.

- Visibles refers to tangible goods imported into and exported from the UK.
- Invisibles refers to services such as financial services and tourism.

Traditionally, the positive balance on invisibles was sufficiently large to outweigh the negative balance on visibles. More recently, however, the visibles trade gap has widened and invisibles have not increased sufficiently, leading to a negative balance on the current account.

Current assets

Cash or other assets e.g. inventory held for conversion into cash in the normal course of trading, e.g. inventory or trade receivables.

Current liabilities

Those liabilities that fall due for payment within one year, e.g. trade payables.

Current ratio

A measure of liquidity, calculated by dividing current liabilities into current assets. This is usually expressed as a ratio (e.g. 2.0:1). Too low a ratio may indicate liquidity problems. Too high a ratio indicates inefficiency owing to too much tied up in working capital.
The systematic allocation of the depreciable amount of an asset over its useful life.

Customs unions

A free trade area with a common external tariff. The participant countries set up common external trade policy but, in some cases, they use different import quotas, e.g. Mercosur is a customs union between Brazil, Argentina, Uruguay, Paraguay and Venezuela in South America.

Cyclical unemployment

Sometimes referred to as demand deficient, persistent or Keynesian unemployment. In this case unemployment is caused by the fact that aggregate demand in the economy is too small to create employment opportunities for all those wishing and able to work.

D

Damages in contract

The aim of damages in contract is usually to put the injured party into the position he would have been in if the contract had been properly performed. The parties may include a term in the contract which states the amount of damages to be paid in the event of a breach of contract.

- If the amount specified is a genuine attempt to pre-estimate the loss that will be suffered in the event of a breach of contract, the clause will be enforceable by either party to the contract.
- However, if the amount which is specified is much greater than the greatest loss which the innocent party could suffer, and the intention is to deter a breach and to punish in the event of a breach, the clause will be void and unenforceable.

Data and information

Data means facts. It consists of numbers, letters, symbols, raw facts, events and transactions that have been recorded but not yet processed into a form which is suitable for making decisions. Information is data that has been processed in such a way that it has a meaning to the person who receives it, who may then use it to improve the quality of decision making.

Data + meaning = information

Day books

See books of prime entry.

Debenture

Defined in company law as including debenture stock, bonds or other securities of a company, whether constituting a charge on the assets of the company or not, i.e. it may be secured or unsecured.

Decimal exponents and logarithms

It is, of course, possible to express a number to a decimal exponent. This means that any number can be expressed as 10 to a power, e.g. number 2 can be expressed as $10^{0.3010}$. When used in this way (with the number 10) the exponent 0.3010 is known as a logarithm. The logarithm of any number can be looked up in log tables. Logarithms can also be used to work out the value of numbers that are tedious or impossible to work out on an ordinary calculator.

* EXAMPLE *

5^{12} or $\sqrt[6]{56,257}$

$$5^{12} = (10^{0.6990})^{12} = 10^{(0.6990 \times 12)} = 10^{8.388} = 244,140,625$$

$$\sqrt[6]{56,257} = (10^{4.7502})^{1/6} = 10^{(4.7502/6)} = 10^{0.7917} = 6.19$$

You may have noticed that when your calculator returns a result that is a very small number, it shows you the result in a form such as: 5.214×10^{-3}. The number is really 0.005214. The notation $\times 10^{-x}$ tells you to move the decimal place x places to the left. This will also happen if you calculate a very large number (e.g. it might be shown as 5.6×10^{11}, which means move the decimal place 11 places to the right).

Decisions made under uncertainty

The essential features of making a decision under uncertain conditions are:

- the decision maker is faced with a choice between several alternative courses of action
- each course of action may have several possible outcomes, dependent on a number of uncertain factors
- which choice is made will depend upon the criteria used by the decision maker in judging between the outcomes.

Deflating a monetary series

Deflating a monetary series shows the 'real term' effect of price changes.

$$\text{Deflated value} = \frac{\text{Actual value}}{\text{Index value (e.g. RPI)}} \times 100$$

* EXAMPLE *

The following example illustrates the method, using the Retail Prices Index as the measure of inflation to deflate a set of sales values:

Year	Actual sales (£000)	RPI	Deflated sales (£000)
1	275	100	$\frac{275}{100} \times 100 = 275$
2	305	112	$\frac{305}{112} \times 100 = 272$
3	336	122	$\frac{336}{122} \times 100 = 275$
4	344	127	$\frac{344}{127} \times 100 = 271$
5	363	133	$\frac{363}{133} \times 100 = 273$

It will be seen that, although actual sales have increased in value by a fairly large amount, in real terms there has been a slight decrease.

Deflationary gap

Where there is insufficient aggregate demand to provide full employment. There are number of ways that aggregate demand could be boosted:

- a direct increase in government spending
- encouragement of business investment
- encourage consumer spending
- encourage exports
- discourage imports.

Increasing aggregate demand may be an effective remedy for cyclical unemployment, but is unlikely to be effective for structural unemployment.

* EXAMPLE *

Assuming aggregate demand is currently at AD_1, the equilibrium national income is at Y_1, requiring employment of Q_1 workers. However, for full employment Q_f to occur, national income has to be boosted to Y_2, requiring an increase in aggregate demand to AD_2.

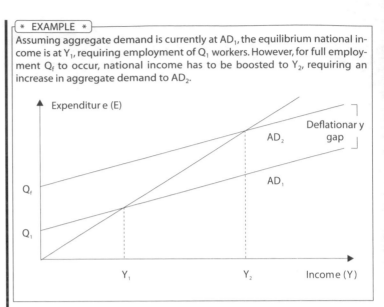

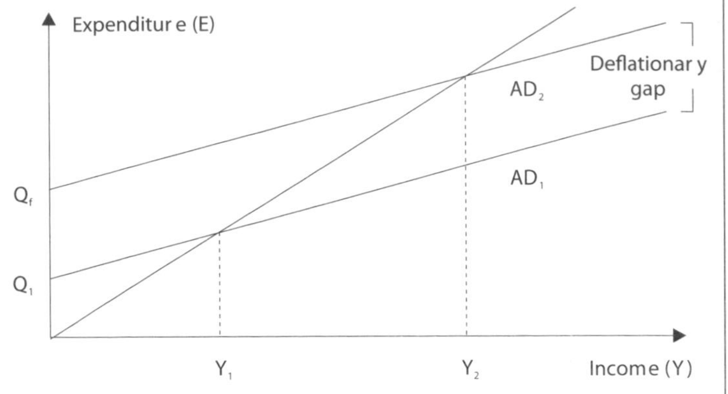

Delegated legislation

Legislation-making powers may be delegated to bodies outside Parliament, usually to save Parliamentary time. The different types of delegated legislation are:

- Orders in Council
- Statutory Instruments
- Bye-laws.

Demand curve

Shows quantities that consumers are willing and able to buy at each price, assuming that all other variables are constant. For a normal good the demand curve is downward sloping. A change in price thus causes a movement along the demand curve.

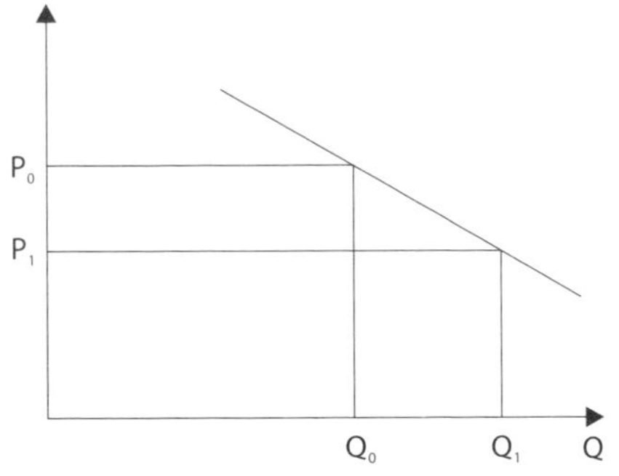

Factors that can cause the whole demand curve to shift include:

- taste/fashion
- income
- price of complements
- price of substitutes
- expectations of price movements.

Demand-pull inflation

If aggregate demand exceeds full employment income, then there is an inflationary gap. There is too much money chasing too few goods and prices rise.

Demerit goods

Goods that can be provided by the private sector and have significant negative externalities.

Direct costs

Items of expenditure which can be economically identified with and specifically measured in respect to a relevant cost object.

* EXAMPLE *

The raw material used in making a piece of furniture (direct materials); carpentry work (direct labour) and design royalty (direct expense).

Direct expenses

Expenses that can be identified directly with units of production. A patent royalty paid in respect of each unit produced would be classified as a direct expense.

Direct labour

All payroll expenses that can be identified directly with units of production. Payroll costs that relate to production generally but which cannot be identified with particular units of production (e.g. the salary of the works manager) are regarded as factory overheads.

Direct materials

The materials consumed by the manufacturing process during the accounting period. Purchases of materials must therefore be adjusted for opening and closing inventories, to give the cost of materials consumed in the period.

Direct method (cash flow statement)

A method of calculating cash flows from operations for the cash flow statement which presents gross trading cash flows. That is, it starts with cash collected from customers and deducts the cash payments associated with trading expenses to arrive at the net cash flow from operations. This method yields the same end result as the indirect method.

Direct taxes

These are taxes on wealth or income, e.g. income tax.

Discharge

The parties may agree to discharge (i.e. end) the contract. This agreement will be binding only if it is under seal or supported by consideration. The discharge may be bilateral or unilateral.

- Bilateral discharge – where both parties still have contractual obligations to perform. Any agreement to discharge the contract relieves both parties from further performance. Each party's promise to release the other party from further performance is his consideration for the release from his own obligations.
- Unilateral discharge – where one party has performed all his obligations but the other has not. Any promise by the party who has performed his obligation to release the other ('accord') will not be binding on him unless the other party has given consideration ('satisfaction') or the agreement to discharge is made by deed.

Discount factor

Discount factors can be found in two ways:

1 Use the tables provided, e.g. the discount factor for a future cash flow received in one year's time at an interest rate of 10% is found by using
   - the column for a rate of 10%, and
   - the row for a cash flow in one year's time.

   This gives a factor of 0.909.

2 Use the formula:
   discount factor = $1 / (1+r)^n$, where r is the discount rate and n relates to the timing of the cash flow.

Discounting

Discounting is the reverse of compounding.

Discounting and business problems

One of the difficulties in many business problems is to evaluate, on a common scale, cash flows occurring at different points in time. Since businesses normally are either borrowing or lending money, interest is the cost/benefit to the business of cash at different points in time. Therefore, discounting provides a method of adjusting cash flows to a common base through the device of the notional interest charges. For this reason discounting is widely used for financial evaluations, especially of new capital investment projects.

Discounts (C03)

A percentage or an amount deducted from the price, cost, etc.

Discounts (C02)

An amount given to reduce a price or a balance. This might be used to simplify price lists (e.g. business customers might be given a 10% discount from the retail customer price list to avoid having two separate lists) or to encourage prompt payment (e.g. customers might be given a 1% discount if they pay early).

Dishonoured cheques

Cheques that have been accepted in payment from a customer might 'bounce' when they are presented to the bank. This could be because the person writing the cheque has insufficient funds in the account or because the cheque has not been completed properly.

Diseconomies of scale

Diseconomies can arise as a company grows very large. These often reflect the difficulty of communicating within a large organisation, together with a decline in management control.

Dismissal – fair reasons

There are five reasons on which the employer may rely in order to justify the dismissal as fair:

- the capabilities/qualifications of the employee
- the conduct of the employee
- redundancy
- the fact that continued employment would contravene statute
- some other substantial reason.

Dismissal for one of these reasons is fair unless the employer acted unreasonably in dismissing for the reason given.

Dismissal – inadmissible reasons

Dismissal for one of these reasons is automatically unfair. There is no need to meet the length of employment condition. They also entitle the complainant to an additional award of compensation:

- victimisation of health and safety complainants
- pregnancy or childbirth
- trade union membership/non-membership/activities
- assertion of a statutory right
- unfair selection for redundancy.

Distributions

A company can only make a distribution (e.g. pay a dividend) out of distributable profits. Distributable profits are accumulated realised profits less accumulated realised losses. Plcs can only declare a dividend if their net assets will not fall below the total of their called up share capital and undistributable reserves.

Dividend

An amount paid to the shareholders, usually at the discretion of the directors. The dividend for the year is shown in the statement of changes in equity.

Donations and legacies

Clubs and societies may treat large donations and legacies as injections of capital, although there are unlikely to be any specific rules that require them to do so.

Doubtful debts

Amounts due from customers that may not be collectable. If there is a serious doubt about any given balance, then it should be written off immediately as a bad debt/receivables written off. Otherwise, the doubt should be taken into account in calculating the allowance for receivables.

Drill down

Computerised record-keeping systems often make it possible to work down a hierarchy of records, so that more detail can be obtained for an entry if required.

Duality

Underpins double entry and the balance sheet. For each entry in the accounting records, there is both a debit entry and a credit entry, both of exactly the same amount.

Duties of employee

An employee is required to:

- obey lawful and reasonable orders
- exercise care and skill
- perform duties personally
- act in good faith, i.e. not make secret profit/misappropriate property; not compete with the employer; not disclose confidential information or trade secrets
- act in a reasonable manner.

Duties of employer

An employer is required to:

- pay agreed wages (whether work is available or not)
- indemnify employees for liabilities properly incurred
- take reasonable care for the safety of their employees
- behave in a way that does not damage the relationship of trust and confidence.

There is no duty to provide work, unless:

- payment is by commission or piecework
- the employee relies on publicity or needs to maintain skills.

There is also no duty to provide a reference.

E

Earnings per share (EPS)

The profit available to shareholders expressed per share:

$$\text{ROCE} = \frac{\text{Profits after interest and tax}}{\text{Number of shares}}$$

EC Directives

Instruments used by the EU to ensure that the law is consistent throughout member states. The two directives which have the most impact on the preparation of financial statements are the Fourth Directive, governing formats and disclosure requirements, and the Seventh Directive, relating to group accounts. The Eighth Directive deals with the audit of financial statements.

Economic costs

These are current values, e.g. replacement costs for regularly used material or opportunity cost. LIFO approximates an economic cost method of stock pricing as it uses the latest prices to issues materials to production.

Economic growth

This is normally measured as an increase in the level of Gross Domestic Product (GDP) or Gross National Product (GNP) in an economy. Growth should result in an improved standard of living in a country. However, growth is not without its problems:

- Is economic growth fast enough to keep up with population growth?
- Growth rates have to exceed inflation rates for benefits to arise (i.e. real growth has to occur).
- Growth may be in demerit goods.
- Growth may be at the expense of the environment or through exploitation of the poor.
- The gap between rich and poor may grow, as the benefits from growth are not evenly distributed.
- Measurement of growth is difficult given the black market and goods that are excluded from national income calculations.
- Rapid growth, means rising incomes and this often 'sucks in' imports, worsening the balance of trade.

Economic reality test

Looks at the economic reality behind the relationship. It is also sometimes called the multiple test. The list of factors to be considered includes:

- the degree of control by the 'employer'
- the degree to which the worker risks loss or stands to gain from their work
- the ownership of tools and equipment
- the degree to which the worker's work is an integral part of the business
- the regularity and method of payment
- the regularity of hours
- whether there is a mutuality of obligations, i.e. is the employer under a duty to provide work and the worker under a duty to accept it
- the ability to provide a substitute, i.e. ability to delegate the performance of the contract)

- the terms used by the parties – although this is not a decisive factor. The court will consider the substance not the form, and will not be persuaded by a label which is clearly inconsistent with the facts of the relationship.

Economic unions

An economic and monetary union is a single market with a common currency, e.g. the Eurozone. The Eurozone consists of the European Union member states that have adopted the Euro and is the largest economic and monetary union at present.

Economic value

The value of an asset's future earnings discounted to present value. This is another way of saying that the economic value is the wealth that the asset will create for the company.

Economic welfare

A measure of the overall satisfaction or happiness in an economy. Thus industrial growth may lead to improved economic growth but welfare may be affected by pollution, stress, congestion, etc.

Economies of scale

Economies of scale reduce the average total cost per unit and can be either internal or external.

Internal economies of scale – arising from the size of the company	External economies of scale – arising from the size of the industry in which the company operates
Technical economies – the law of increased dimensions, indivisibilities in inputs	Specialisation in the local labour force that reduces training costs
Specialisation and the division of labour	Agglomeration economies, i.e. provision of ancillary or back-up service industries
Integration/utilisation of waste products	
Financial economies/risk spreading – risk-bearing economies of scale	

Elastic demand

PED>1

Demand changes more in proportion to price.

* EXAMPLE *

If a petrol station increases the price of fuel by 5%, demand will change by more than 5% as all customers buy their fuel at a different petrol station. Total revenue will fall.

Embargoes

The prohibition of commerce and trade with a certain country.

Empirical probability

Where a particular situation can be repeated a large number of times, an experimental approach may be used to derive probabilities. This is a form of objective probability, based on the relative frequency in a large number of experiments, i.e. 'empirical probability

* EXAMPLE *

Using meteorological records, the probability of rain on the 30 June can be estimated.

Employee	Someone who works under a contract of service.
Employer's National Insurance contributions	National Insurance is a tax deducted from UK employees' wages and salaries by their employers. Employers have to supplement this deduction with an additional amount paid to HM Revenue & Customs. The Employer's National Insurance contribution is accounted for as an additional component of wages.
Employer's pension contributions	UK law requires most employees to pay a proportion of their wages or salaries into a pension fund. These payments are supplemented by additional amounts paid by the company. Accounting for pensions is a complex area, and so it is sufficient at this stage to know simply that the employer must calculate the total amount due and remit that to the pension fund at regular intervals.
Employment Act 2002	Gives parents of children under the age of six the right to request flexible working arrangements. The employer must give serious consideration to such a request and can only reject it for clear business reasons. The Act also introduced paternity and adoption leave.
Employment Equality (Age) Regulations 2006	Make age-related discrimination and harassment unlawful. The regulations impose a default retirement age of 65. Compulsory retirement at an earlier age is still possible, but only if justifiable. Employees have the right to request to work beyond their normal retirement date. The employer is not legally bound to agree to these requests, but has to give them reasonable consideration.
Employment Rights Act 1996	Gives employees certain rights, such as a right not to be unfairly dismissed, a right to a redundancy payment if made redundant and a right to a minimum period of notice to terminate the contract.
Equations	A statement of the equality of two quantities.

Equation of a straight line

As an example, the relationship between costs, y, and activity, x, may be of the form:

$$y = a + bx$$

where	y	=	total costs
	x	=	activity level
	a	=	fixed costs
	b	=	variable cost per unit

Equations with one unknown

Where an equation contains only one unknown figure, say x, its solution may be found by simply manipulating the equation until x appears on the left-hand side only, and then evaluating the right-hand side.

* EXAMPLE *

3x – 4	=	2 – 6x
Adding 6x to both sides gives:		
9x – 4	=	2
Adding 4 to both sides gives:		
9x	=	6
x	=	$\frac{2}{3}$

Equity

The body of discretionary rules and remedies devised by the courts on the basis of fairness and good conscience to remedy the defects of the common law.

Equity gearing

A measure of gearing calculated using the formula:

$$\frac{\text{Debt (including preferences shares)}}{\text{Equity (excluding preference shares)}}$$

Equity securities

Shares other than shares which with respect to dividends and capital carry a right to participate only up to a specified amount in a distribution. In short, equity shares are generally the ordinary shares.

Equivalent units

Uncompleted units in process must be valued and this is done by the equivalent units concept which is based upon the principle that costs are incurred at an even rate throughout processing. So, for example, two units both 50% complete will have incurred the same amount of cost as one completed unit.

Equivalent units = physical units × %

Equivalent units table

Used to accumulate the finished units of each cost element, with the equivalent number of units of work-in-process for each cost element in order to show the output for the period in respect of each cost element.

* EXAMPLE *

Opening work-in-process	Nil
Input of raw materials	12,000 units @ $4.50
Conversion costs	$45,000
Normal loss expected	1% input
Output of finished goods	11,200 units
Closing work-in-process	600 units

(Fully complete for materials, 75% complete for conversion costs)

Scrapped units are identified at the end of the process and can be sold for $2 per unit.

Equivalent unit table

	Raw material		*Conversion*	
Good output	11,200		11,200	
Abnormal loss (to balance)	80	(100%)	80	(100%)
Closing work-in-process	600	(100%)	400	(75%)
	______		______	
(99% × 12,000)	11,880		11,730	
	______		______	

Errors

Irregularities in the bookkeeping records that are not deliberate.

Errors of commission

Where an amount has been correctly posted but to the wrong account, although it is the right type of account, e.g. a payment received from the debtor B Smith is incorrectly posted to the credit of the account of R Smith, another customer. The trial balance would still balance despite this error.

Errors of entry

Where an incorrect amount is posted to both the accounts in question, e.g. \$2.00 is misread as \$200 and so entered on both debit and credit sides of the correct accounts. Provided the error in the amounts is consistent, the trial balance will still balance.

Errors of omission

Where a transaction has been omitted from bookkeeping records. The trial balance would still balance under these circumstances.

Errors of principle

Where an item is incorrectly classified by the bookkeeper and posted to the wrong type of account, e.g. the sale of surplus office equipment has been classified as sales of goods. This could lead to a serious error in the financial statements, but the trial balance would still balance.

European Central Bank (ECB)

The central bank for the Euro currency area, it is the sole issuer of the Euro. Based in Frankfurt, its main objective, as defined by the Maastricht Treaty, is price stability. It therefore has the power to set short-term interest rates.

European Union (EU)

The EU is an example of a single market and, within the Eurozone, an economic union. It has its origins in the Treaty of Rome (1957). The aims of the treaty were as follows:

- the elimination of customs duties and quotas on imports and exports between member states
- the establishment of a common customs tariff and a common commercial policy towards non-member states
- the abolition of obstacles to the free movement of persons, services and capital between member states
- the establishment of common policies on transport and agriculture
- the prohibition of business practices that restrict or distort competition
- the association of overseas countries in order to increase trade and development.

European Union institutions

- Council of Ministers: Consists of one representative from each member state and has law-making powers.
- European Commission: A non-elected secretariat based in Brussels, making policy proposals that must either be accepted or rejected by the Council of Ministers.
- European Parliament: An elected body based in Strasbourg. Every member state elects a number of representatives to the European Parliament. Directives are debated here before being passed for final consideration to the Council of Ministers.
- European Court of Justice (ECJ): Its jurisdiction includes:
  - actions between the Commission and member states where it is alleged that a member state has failed to comply with its obligations as laid down in the Treaty of Rome
  - the giving of rulings on the inter pretation of EU law or national laws passed to implement directives.

European Union law

- Regulations: Directly applicable in all member states without the need for national legislation.
- Directives: Require member states to alter their national laws to implement them within a certain period of time.
- Decisions: Made by the European Commission and the Council of Ministers and addressed to a particular member state and binding on the recipient.

Exchange controls

Domestic companies wishing to buy foreign goods will have to pay in the currency of the exporter's country. To do this they will need to buy the currency involved by selling sterling. If the government controls the sale of sterling, it can control the level of imports purchased.

Exchange rates

If a currency is treated like a good or service, it becomes possible to determine exchange rates by considering the supply and demand for a particular currency.

* EXAMPLE *

From the diagram the current quantity of £ demanded is Q, with an exchange rate of $1.45 to the £.

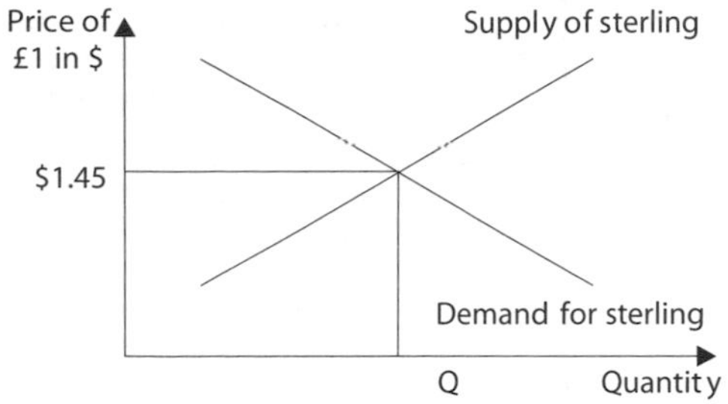

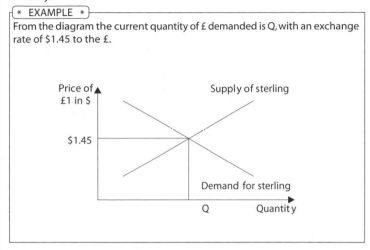

Exclusion clause (exemption clause)

Applied both to clauses that totally exclude one party from the liability which would otherwise arise from some breach of contract and to clauses that restrict liability in some way. In order to be valid, the exclusion clause must:

- be incorporated into the contract and not added after the contract is complete
- be clear and precise; any vagueness will be construed against the party who is attempting to rely on it
- meet the statutory test laid down by The Unfair Contract Terms Act 1977
- meet the test set out in The Unfair Terms in Consumer Contracts Regulations 1999.

Exempt supplies

Traders in exempt supplies do not charge VAT on their sales but are not allowed (unlike the zero-rated situation) to recover VAT on their purchases. In such cases the irrecoverable VAT will be added to the trader's costs, and there will be no VAT account.

Expanding brackets

To get rid of brackets, re-express a mathematical statement without them and follow the usual order of operations. Great care is needed.

- Numbers outside brackets multiply (or divide) everything within.
- Signs outside brackets multiply (or divide) everything within.
- Each element within a bracket containing items linked by addition or subtraction signs multiplies each element in another such bracket, and then the elements are added together.

Expansionary fiscal policy

By running a budget deficit, i.e. planned expenditure is greater than planned tax receipts, the government is running a loose or expansionary fiscal policy. This may be used to try to stimulate economic growth and reduce unemployment.

Expectations effect

If anticipated levels of inflation are built into wage negotiations and pricing decisions, then it is likely that the expected rate of inflation will arise. Whilst the expectations effect is not the root cause of inflation, it can contribute significantly to an inflationary spiral, particularly when underlying levels of inflation are high and rising.

Expected value (EV)

The expected value of a particular action is the sum of the values of the possible outcomes each multiplied by their respective probabilities. If the probability of winning £x is p, then the expectation (or expected value) is: p × £x
Where there is more than one possible outcome, each with a probability attached, the expected value of the outcome E(x) will be the sum of the expected values of the individual outcomes: $E(x) = \sum px$

* EXAMPLE *

On the throw of a dice £5 is to be paid for a 6, £4 for a 5, £3 for a 4, and nothing for a 1, 2 or 3. The expectation is calculated as follows:

P(6)	= 1/6 ∴ expectation = 1/6 × £5 =	£0.83
P(5)	= 1/6 ∴ expectation = 1/6 × £4 =	£0.67
P(4)	= 1/6 ∴ expectation = 1/6 × £3 =	£0.50
P(1, 2 or 3)	= 3/6 ∴ expectation = 3/6 × £0 =	£0.00
	Total	£2.00

The expectation is £2.

The criterion of expected value is only valid where the decision being made is either:

(a) one that is repeated regularly over a period of time, or
(b) a one-off decision, but where its size is fairly small in relation to the total assets of the company and it is one of many, in terms of the sums of money involved, that face the company over a period of time.

In other words, the law of averages will apply in the long run.

Expenditure reducing strategies

The government deliberately shrinks the domestic economy by using contractionary monetary or fiscal policies. By reducing overall demand in the domestic economy a government will be able to reduce demand for imports. Reducing demand in the home economy should also reduce inflationary pressures, thus reducing export prices and making them more competitive.

Expenditure switching strategies

The government seeks to change expenditure patterns of consumers by encouraging expenditure on domestically produced rather than imported goods.

Export Credit Guarantee Department (ECGD)

A department of the UK government established in 1930 to provide an insurance service for exporters to recompense them in the event of non-payment by their overseas customers. The ECGD was to achieve the objective of insuring exporters by:

- selling credit insurance to exporters
- providing guarantees to banks on behalf of exporters in order to encourage the banks to grant credit to either the exporter or the exporter's customer.

The former function is now provided by a private company NCM UK, which purchased the credit insurance division of the ECGD when it was privatised in 1991. The ECGD retained the function of providing guarantees to banks for exporting companies.

External audit

The independent examination of, and expression of opinion on, the financial statements of an enterprise.

Externalities

Social costs or benefits that are not automatically included in the supply and demand curves for a product or service.

- Social costs arising from production and consumption of a good or service are described as negative externalities, e.g. pollution.
- Social benefits are positive externalities, e.g. education.

Extraordinary General Meeting (EGM)

Any general meeting that is not an AGM is an EGM.

F

Faceted codes

One that is broken down into a number of facets or fields, each of which signifies a unit of information, e.g. in a three-digit code each of the digits could signify something – the first digit could be location, the second age and the third identifies the specific item.

Factorisation

Factorisation is the reverse of multiplying out brackets.

* EXAMPLE *

$3x(x + 2) = 3x^2 + 6x$

hence:

$3x^2 + 6x$ factorises to $3x(x + 2)$

Three important factorisations that must be memorised are:

$a^2 + 2ab + b^2 = (a + b)(a + b) = (a + b)^2$

$a^2 - 2ab + b^2 = (a - b)(a - b) = (a - b)^2$

$a^2 - b^2 = (a + b)(a - b)$

Factors of production

Factor	Reward
Land (all natural resources)	Rent
Labour	Wages
Capital (e.g. factories, machinery)	Interest
Enterprise/entrepreneurship	Profit

Factory overheads

Overheads that cannot be identified with particular units of production. The overheads are expense headings that are accounted for in the same ways as any other expense accounts.

Fair presentation

Financial statements prepared under IFRSs must 'present fairly' the financial position, financial performance and cash flows of an entity. Fair presentation requires the faithful representation of the effects of transactions, other events and conditions.

Fiduciary duty of directors

Every director has a fiduciary duty to act in good faith for the benefit of the company as a whole. This duty encompasses a number of aspects:

- duty to exercise their powers for the proper purpose
- duty to avoid a conflict of interest
- duty not to compete with the company.

Fiduciary relationship

A relationship of trust and confidence.

Financial account

The financial account records flows of capital, both short- and long-term investment. It includes:

- investments made overseas by UK entities
- investments made in the UK by overseas entities
- movements on assets held in reserve by the UK government.

Financial capital maintenance

The concept that profit is earned only if the financial (or money) amount of the owners' capital at the end of the period exceeds the financial (or money) amount of the owners' capital at the beginning of the period, after excluding any distributions to (e.g. dividend payments) and contributions (e.g. share issues or increases in capital) from owners during the period.

Financial controls

Systems or procedures within the bookkeeping system that are designed to secure as far as possible the completeness and accuracy of the records.

Financial intermediaries

Lenders and borrowers are brought together through a process known as financial intermediation. It is common to split financial intermediaries into two types:

- deposit-taking institutions (DTIs), such as banks and building societies
- non-deposit-taking institutions (NDTIs), such as insurance companies, pension funds, unit trusts and investment trusts.

They have a number of important roles:

- *Risk reduction:* By lending to a wide variety of individuals and businesses, financial intermediaries reduce the risk of a single default resulting in total loss of assets.
- *Aggregation:* By pooling many small deposits, financial intermediaries are able to make much larger advances than would be possible for most individuals.
- *Maturity transformation:* Most borrowers wish to borrow in the long-term while most savers are unwilling to lock up their money for the long-term. By developing a floating pool of deposits, financial intermediaries are able to satisfy both the needs of lenders and borrowers.

Financial management

The management of all the processes associated with the efficient acquisition and deployment of both short- and long-term financial resources.

Financial statements

Usually comprise the income statement, balance sheet and cash flow statement. They are normally supplemented by additional statements, such as a statement of changes in equity, and by notes providing additional monetary and non-monetary disclosures.

First-in-first-out (FIFO)

A method of valuing inventory that assumes that the oldest stock is issued each time inventory is used. It tends to provide a smaller cost of sales and higher profit during periods when prices are rising.

First In, First Out (FIFO) inventory pricing

Each issue is valued at the price paid for the material first taken into the inventory from which the issue could have been drawn.

* EXAMPLE *

1 November bought 300 kgs costing $1 each
6 November bought 200 kgs costing $1.20 each
8 November used 100 kgs
Using FIFO, materials used on 8 November would be valued at $1 per kg.

Fiscal policy

Refers to a government's taxation and spending plans to support achievement of its macroeconomic policy objectives.

Fixed costs

Do **not** change when activity levels change, e.g. supervisory costs, depreciation costs, rent.

Graph showing relationship between rent and output

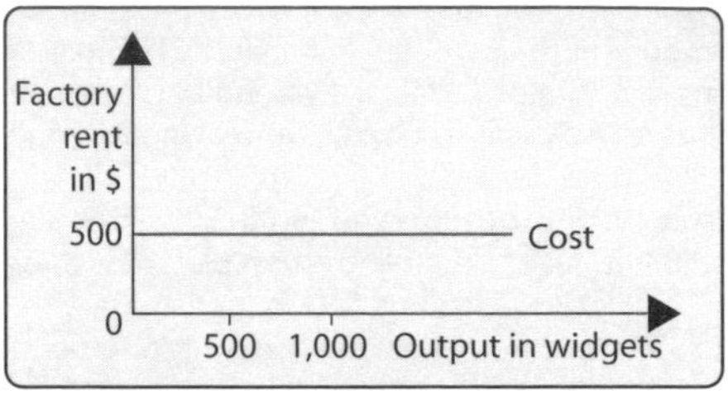

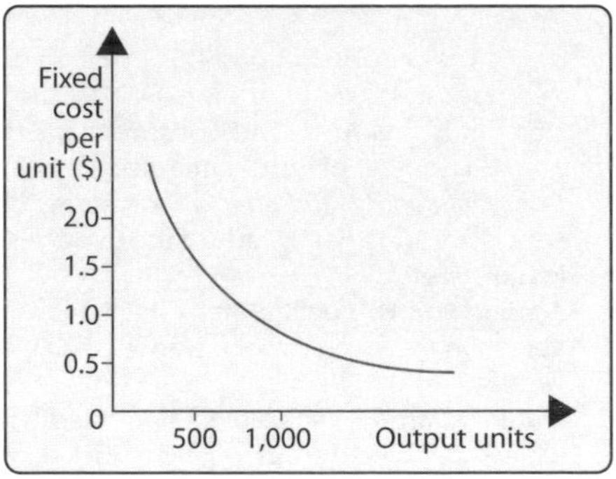

Fixed charge

Created by the procedure appropriate for mortgaging property of that particular type.

* EXAMPLE *

- A mortgage of land by deed.
- A mortgage of shares of another company by transfer to the mortgagee.

Fixed exchange rates

Under this regime the government sets a precise exchange rate and then intervenes in the foreign exchange markets as necessary to maintain the currency at this level. This is a highly interventionist policy and can only be successful if there is co-operation between the central banks of different countries. Periodically, underlying economic pressures, either national or international, may require a country to revalue or devalue its currency, leading to a step-change in the exchange rate. While a fixed exchange rate gives exchange rate stability for companies trading internationally, it does not allow automatic correction of balance of payments disequilibria, and it is costly and time-consuming to maintain.

Flexible budget

A budget which, by recognising different cost behaviour patterns, is designed to change as volume of activity changes. (CIMA *Official Terminology*) The procedure to flex a budget is as follows:

- identify whether each budgeted cost or revenue is fixed or variable
- adjust all variable costs and revenues to reflect the actual activity level
- do not adjust any fixed costs.

* EXAMPLE *

	Original budget	*Actual*	*Variance*
Units	100	120	
Sales ($)	1,000	1,100	100 F
Material cost ($)	200	250	50 A
Labour cost ($)	300	320	20 A
Fixed overhead ($)	100	120	20 A
Profit ($)	400	410	10 F

Restate the budgetary control report using a flexible budgeting approach:

	Original budget	*Flexed budget*	*Actual*	*Variance*
Units	100		120	
Sales ($)	1,000	1,200	1,100	100 A
Material cost ($)	200	240	250	10 A
Labour cost ($)	300	360	320	40 F
Fixed overhead ($)	100	100	120	20 A
Profit ($)	400	500	410	90 A

Floating charge

Defined in Re Yorkshire Woolcombers Association date? as having three characteristics:

- It is a charge on a class of assets present and future, e.g. if it applies to stock in trade or book debts it comprises whatever assets of that class the company may own at the moment of crystallisation.
- The class of assets will change from time to time in the ordinary course of the company's business.
- The company may carry on its business and dispose of the assets in the course of business until the charge crystallises.

Floating exchange rates

A country's currency is said to be freely floating when exchange rates are simply determined by the interaction of supply and demand. This should lead to the automatic correction of a balance of payments deficit. In practice, free floating does not exist as all governments tend to 'smooth the course of exchange rate adjustment'. In part this is because of the effect of the government's day-to-day actions which would impact on the exchange rate.

> * EXAMPLE *
>
> If imports exceed exports, then:
> - In sterling terms, this means that more sterling is being sold to buy imports than is being bought to purchase UK exports.
> - This excess of supply of sterling over demand for sterling will lead to a weakening of the currency.
> - This makes imports more expensive and exports from the UK cheaper.
> - As a result, export volumes should start to rise and import volumes fall, gradually removing the balance of payment deficit.

Forecasting using time series

Forecasting using additive model:
Forecast = Estimated trend + Seasonal variation

Forecasting using multiplicative model:
Forecast = Estimated trend × Seasonal variation

Foreign exchange risks

Firms dealing with more than one currency are exposed to risks due to exchange rate movements. There are three main aspects of this.

- *Economic risk:* Long-term movements in exchange rates can undermine a company's competitive advantage, e.g. a strengthening currency will make an exporter's products more expensive to overseas customers.
- *Transaction risk:* In the time period between an order being agreed and payment received, the exchange rate can move causing the final value of the transaction to be more or less than originally envisaged. Transaction risk can be hedged by fixing the exchange rate with a bank in advance, i.e. arranging a forward contract.
- *Translation risk:* If a company has foreign assets (e.g. a factory) denoted in another currency, then their value in its home currency will depend on the exchange rate at the time, e.g. if its domestic currency strengthens, then foreign assets will appear to fall in value. This risk, however, is not realised unless the asset is sold, so is of less commercial importance.

Foss v Harbottle

The rule in Foss v Harbottle has two principles:

- In order to redress a wrong done to a company or to recover money or damages alleged to be due to the company, the action should be brought by the company itself.
- Where the majority does not wish the company to sue, the court will not generally permit the minority to sue on its behalf, nor interfere in the internal management of the company.

These principles represent different aspects of the majority rule in company law, i.e. if the majority can do something, the minority cannot interfere.

Fractional exponents

When a number is expressed to a fractional exponent, that is the same as expressing the number, to the power of the numerator, to the root indicated by the denominator. This is easier to understand in maths notation than in words.

> * EXAMPLE *
>
> $10^{2/3} = \sqrt[3]{10^2}$

Fractional reserve system

Typically banks operate a fractional reserve system, i.e. only a part of their deposits are kept in cash on the assumption that not all customers will want their money back at the same time. The proportion of deposits retained in cash is known as the reserve asset ratio or liquidity ratio.

Fractions

It is essential to understand simple fractions in order to manipulate equations and formulae properly. The number on the top is called the numerator and the number on the bottom is called the denominator:

$$\frac{\text{Numerator}}{\text{Denominator}}$$

Fractions – adding or subtracting

If the fractions have the same denominator, simply add (or subtract) the numerators:

$$\frac{1}{3} + \frac{1}{3} = \frac{1+1}{3} = \frac{2}{3}$$

To add (or subtract) two fractions that have different denominators, find a common denominator. The quickest way of doing this is to multiply the existing denominators together. Then, to find the new numerators, multiply each fraction's existing numerator by the other fraction's denominator:

$$\frac{1}{4} + \frac{1}{2} = \frac{(1 \times 2) + (1 \times 4)}{(4 \times 2)} = \frac{2+4}{8} = \frac{6}{8}$$

Fractions – dividing

When dividing fractions, invert the one you are dividing by (the 'divisor') and multiply them instead:

$$\frac{1}{2} \div \frac{1}{4} = \frac{1}{2} \times \frac{4}{1} = \frac{4}{2} = 2$$

Fractions – lowest common denominator

It is usually desirable to reduce fractions to their lowest common denominator because they are easier to understand and manipulate in that form.

* EXAMPLE *

If your calculations give an answer of 147/1,617 it might be useful to know that this is the same as 1/11.

Fractions – multiplying

Numerators and denominators are dealt with separately:

$$\frac{1}{4} \times \frac{1}{2} = \frac{1 \times 1}{4 \times 2} = \frac{1}{8}$$

Fraud

Errors are irregularities in the bookkeeping records that are deliberate. The motives for doing so may be to conceal theft or otherwise to mislead.

Fraudulent trading

Errors are irregularities in the bookkeeping records that are deliberate. The motives for doing so may be to conceal theft or otherwise to mislead.

Free trade areas

If the members of a multi-lateral free trade agreement are all in the same geographical area, then it is sometimes described as a free trade area, e.g. the ASEAN Free Trade Area (AFTA) is an agreement by the Association of Southeast Asian Nations (Brunei, Indonesia, Malaysia, Philippines, Singapore, Thailand, Vietnam, Laos, Myanmar and Cambodia).

Frequency curves

A smooth, freehand curve is drawn rather than joining up the mid-points with straight lines.

Frequency polygons

If the mid-points of the tops of the rectangles in the histogram are joined by straight lines, the figure is known as a frequency polygon. Compared to the histogram, some areas are cut off when the polygon is drawn and some extra areas are enclosed. The area of the frequency polygon is equal to the area of the histogram because the areas of the cut-off triangle and of the additional triangle (shaded areas) are equal at each stage.

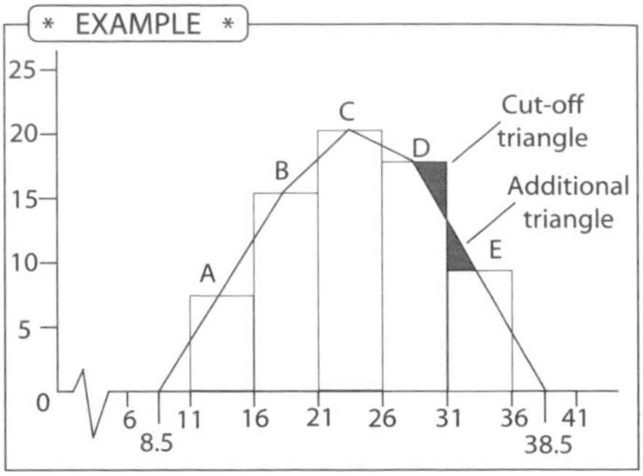

Frictional unemployment

Refers to those people who are short-term unemployed as they move from one job to another.

Frustration

A contract is frustrated where, although possible to perform when made, it subsequently becomes impossible through the happening of a supervening event that was the fault of neither party.

Full cost pricing

This occurs when a profit margin is added to the full cost of the product to arrive at a price. This is the minimum price acceptable to the company in the long run as any price less than this will result in a loss.

Full product cost

Direct materials
\+ Direct labour
\+ Direct expense

= Prime Cost
\+ Share of production overhead (Indirect costs)

= Full production cost
\+ Share of non-production overhead

= **Full cost**

Functional budget

A budget of income and/or expenditure applicable to a particular function.

Fundamental economic problem

There are scarce resources but unlimited wants. All societies are thus faced with a fundamental economic problem:

- What goods and services should be produced?
- In what quantities?
- Who should make them?
- Who gets the output?

Fundamental principles

CIMA's Code of Ethical practice lists five fundamental principles, with which its members are expected to comply:

- Integrity: Accountants should be straight forward and honest in all their professional and business relationships.
- Objectivity: Accountants should not allow bias, conflict of interest or the undue influence of others to override their professional or business judgements.

G

Gearing

An important measure that reflects the long-term financial stability of a business. It is the proportion of a business' long-term funding that has been obtained from fixed return capital (i.e. loans and preference shares). The more a business raises in this way, the higher the risk that the associated finance costs will lead to a loss or that the business will be unable to make the loan repayments.
Gearing can be measured as either:

$$\frac{\text{Debt (including preferences shares)}}{\text{Equity (excluding preference shares)}}$$

or

$$\frac{\text{Debt (including preferences shares)}}{\text{Debt + Equity}}$$

General Agreement on Tariffs and Trade (GATT)

Implemented in 1948 to agree trading patterns around the world and to negotiate removal of trade barriers. Replaced by the World Trade Organisation (WTO) in 1995.

General allowance for receivables

An allowance for receivables that is calculated by taking a percentage of the gross amount due from customers as the estimate of the balances that will default. This percentage is based on past experiences of bad debts/receivables written off.

General equation of a straight line

$y = a + bx$ where a is the intercept on the y axis and b is the gradient.

General ledger/ Nominal ledger

The record that contains all of the accounts that are part of the double entry bookkeeping system.

General meeting

As a rule, a general meeting is one in which all shareholders may take part and which decides on matters binding the whole membership.

General reserve

A balance created by transferring some of the balance on retained profits. This transfer does not have any particular significance in itself, although it is usually treated as a signal that the directors do not intend to distribute that sum as a dividend.

Geometrical progressions

A series in which each term is found by multiplying the previous term by a constant number. The constant is known as the common ratio, e.g.:

- 1, 2, 4, 8, 16 ... common ratio = 2
- 1/3, 1/9, 1/27, 1/81... common ratio = 1/3

A geometrical progression may be written in general terms as:
$A, AR, AR^2, AR^3, \ldots$
where A = the first term and R = common ratio.
The nth term is AR^{n-1}
R can be calculated by dividing the second term by the first.

The formula for calculating the sum of the first n terms of a geometrical progression is:

$$S_n = \frac{A\,(1-R^n)}{1-R} \qquad \text{for } R < 1$$

$$S_n = \frac{A\,(R^n-1)}{R-1} \qquad \text{for } R > 1$$

* EXAMPLE *

Calculate the sixth term and sum of the first six terms of the series: 5, 2.5, 1.25 ...

Here A = 5

R = (2.5 ÷ 5) = 0.5

Hence 6th term = $AR^{n-1} = 5 \times 0.5^5$

$= 5 \times 0.03125 = 0.15625$

$$S_6 = \frac{5x(1-0.5^6)}{1-0.5} = \frac{5x(1-0.015625)}{1-0.5}$$

$= 9.84375$

Globalisation

No universally agreed definition. The International Monetary Fund (IMF) defines globalisation as 'the growing economic interdependence of countries worldwide through increasing volume and variety of cross-border transactions in goods and services, free international capital flows, and more rapid and widespread diffusion of technology'. Factors driving globalisation include:

- improved communications, e.g. internet, mobile phones
- political realignments.

Going concern concept

Assumes that a business (or entity) will continue in operational existence for the foreseeable future. Where the going concern assumption is not valid (e.g. because shortage of finance is likely to force the business into liquidation), the financial statements are prepared on a basis that takes the likely consequences into account – e.g. non-current assets might be written down to their resale value instead of carrying them at cost less depreciation.

Government policy objectives

- Economic growth – how can productive capacity be increased?
- Inflation – how can we ensure that general price levels do not increase?
- Unemployment – how can we ensure that everyone who wants a job has one?
- Balance of payments – how should we manage our relationship and trade with other countries?

Gradient

The gradient of the line of best fit gives an estimate of the variable cost.
To calculate the gradient pick two points on the line, e.g.:

Y = $2,400x = 420

Y = $2,160 x = 300

The gradient is given by $\frac{\text{Differences in y values}}{\text{Differences in x values}} = \frac{240}{120} = 2$

Graphical representation of data

May take the following forms:
- histograms and ogives (cumulative frequency curve)
- frequency polygons
- frequency curves.

Graphics

A major advantage of using a spreadsheet package is the ease with which graphs and charts can be generated.

Greenbury Report (1995)

Its objective was to draw up guidelines on directors' remuneration. All listed companies registered in the UK were required to comply with the Code. They had to include a statement about their remuneration committee. Any areas of non-compliance had to be explained and justified.

Gross Domestic Product (GDP)

Measures the value of all output within the country and excludes any income generated by assets held overseas by the country's residents.
- GDP can be calculated by adding up the sales value of all goods finished during the year. This gives a value known as GDP at market prices.
- This value is affected by expenditure taxes and subsidies. If these are removed from the calculation, the total figure is known as GDP at factor cost.
- Mathematically: GDP at market prices + subsidies – expenditure taxes = GDP at factor cost.

* EXAMPLE *

The following information is available for a country:

	£billion	
Consumers' expenditure		10
General government consumption	20	
Gross domestic fixed capital formation		4
Increase in stocks and work in progress	5	
Exports of goods and services		3
Imports of goods and services		2
Expenditure taxes		3
Subsidies		1

So, GDP at market prices and factor cost is:

	£billion	
Consumers' expenditure		10
General government consumption	20	
Gross domestic fixed capital formation		4
Increase in stocks and work in progress	5	
Exports of goods and services		3
	42	
Imports of goods and services		(2)
GDP at market prices		40
Taxes		(3)
Subsidies		1
GDP at factor prices	38	

Gross margin

Gross margin = Sales revenue – Purchasing cost or production cost. Indirect costs are deducted from gross margin to arrive at net profit.

Gross margin percentage

Gross margin percentage = Gross margin/Sales revenue × 100%.

Gross National Product (GNP)

GNP is calculated as GDP plus income earned by domestic residents on assets held abroad less income earned by overseas residents on assets held in the UK. The difference between income earned by UK residents on assets abroad and income earned by foreign residents on assets in the UK is known as the net property income from abroad. GNP like GDP can be calculated at market prices or factor cost.

Gross profit percentage /Gross profit margin

An important measure of performance, expressed as (Gross profit ÷ Sales) × 100. This ratio gives an indication of the business' pricing policies. A higher ratio indicates that the profit per sale is higher, although it could also indicate that the company is overpricing its products compared to its competitors.

Group incentive schemes

These involve the payment of a bonus for excess group production over the standard within a given time (or time saved for a given level of production). This will then be split between the members of the group on a given basis.

Group of Eight (G8)

Consists of Canada, France, Germany, Italy, Japan, Russia, the United Kingdom and the United States. Together, these countries represent about 65% of the world economy. The agenda of G8 meetings is usually about controversial global issues such as global warming, poverty in Africa, fair trade policies and AIDS, but has implications for global trade. The 31st G8 summit in 2005 resulted in a stated commitment to reduce subsidies and tariffs that inhibit trade.

H

Hampel Report (1998)

Its objective was to restrict the regulatory burden facing companies and substitute broad principles where practicable. A board must not approach the various corporate governance requirements in a compliance mentality – the so-called 'tick-box' approach. Good corporate governance is not achieved by satisfying a checklist. Directors must comply with the substance as well as the letter of all best practice pronouncements. After publishing its report, the Hampel Committee drew up a single Combined Code of Best Practice, incorporating the Cadbury, Greenbury and Hampel recommendations.

Health and Safety at Work Act 1974

Every employer has a general duty to ensure the health, safety and welfare at work of all his employees, so far as is reasonably practicable.

Health and Safety Executive (HSE)

The HSE has the power to enter premises and make examinations and investigations, take pictures or samples, and require people to give information. Where appropriate, it serves notices on the employer to ensure that they carry out their duties under the legislation. Two types of notice:

- Improvement notice: An inspector may serve such a notice calling for the remedying of contraventions within a specified period. During the period specified in such a notice, work may be carried on but, if at the end of a specified period of time the remedial work has not been done, the inspector may prosecute or serve a prohibition notice.
- Prohibition notice: An inspector may serve notice which will prevent any activities at all being carried on, should an employer contravene the relevant statutory provisions and involve the risk of serious personal injury.

Inspectors also have the duty of instituting criminal proceedings against any person who fails to discharge his legislative duties (including failure to comply with an improvement or prohibition notice). The sanctions include fines and imprisonment and, in the case of directors and managers of companies, disqualification. Inspectors may also prosecute common law offences such as manslaughter.

Hierarchical codes/Block codes

Commonly form the basis of nominal ledger coding systems, for instance:
0000 to 0999 – Non-current assets
1000 to 1999 – Current assets
etc.

Hierarchy of courts

European Court of Justice – decisions bind all UK courts

↓

House of Lords – binds all lower courts, but does not bind itself

↓

Court of Appeal – binds all lower courts and itself, unless earlier decision over-ruled or inconsistent with European law

↓

High Court – not bound by its own decisions, but strong persuasive authority

High-low (or range) method

This method is based on an analysis of historical information about costs at different activity levels.

* EXAMPLE *

The data for the three months to 31 October 20X8 is as follows:

Month	*Units*	*Inspection costs*
		$
August	300	2,160
September	380	2,320
October	420	2,400

The variable element of a cost item may be estimated by calculating the unit cost between high and low volumes during a period.

Three months to 31/10/X8	*Unit produced*	*Inspection costs*
		$
Highest month	420	2,400
Lowest month	300	2,160
Range	120	240

The additional cost per unit between high and low is $\frac{\$240}{120 \text{ units}} = \$2$ per unit

which is used as an estimate of the variable content of inspection costs.
Fixed inspection costs are, therefore:
$2,400 - (420 units × $2) = $1,560 per month
or $2,160 - (300 units × $2) = $1,560 per month
i.e. the relationship is of the form y = $1,560 + $2x

Higgs Report (2003)

Commissioned in response to the collapse of the American company Enron. It made the following recommendations:

- The role of Chairman and Chief Executive should not be combined.
- A Chief Executive should not become Chairman of the same company.
- A nomination committee (with a majority of independent non-executive directors) should recommend future executive and non-executive directors.
- At least half the board of the top 350 listed companies must be independent non-executive directors.
- Smaller listed companies must have at least two independent non-executives.

Histograms

A special form of column or bar chart that is used to represent data given in the form of a grouped frequency distribution. The important difference is that the area of each rectangle rather than the height represents the frequency of a particular class interval.

Histograms – equal class intervals

If the class intervals are all equal, then the heights of the rectangles are proportional to the frequencies.

Histograms – unequal class intervals

If the distribution has unequal class intervals, adjust the heights of the bars to compensate for the fact that the rectangles do not have all the same length of base. Only by doing this will the area of the rectangle represent the frequency.

Historic cost

A company's assets and liabilities are valued at historic cost for financial accounting purposes. This means that they are valued at the cost paid by the business. FIFO is a histories cost method as it values issues to production at the earliest possible price.

Historical cost accounting convention

A system of accounting in which all values are based on the historical costs incurred (in other words, the actual amount paid). It has the advantage of simplicity and so it is the basis for much of actual accounting practice.

HM Revenue & Customs

The branch of the UK government that is responsible for assessing and collecting tax from businesses and individuals.

Human Rights Act 1998

- What is its purpose? The Human Rights Act 1998 incorporates the European Convention for the Protection of Human Rights and Fundamental Freedoms into UK domestic law.
- How does it affect judicial interpretation? UK courts must take Convention law into account when deciding a question that has arisen in connection with a Convention right.
- What is convention law? Convention law means the Convention and the decisions of the European Court of Human Rights.
- Any impact on the doctrine of precedence? Judges will not be bound by a previous interpretation of existing legislation where it did not take into account Convention rights.
- What if legislation is incompatible with the Convention? The courts cannot declare primary legislation to be invalid. They can only make a declaration of incompatibility and leave it to Parliament to remedy the situation through new legislation. However, the courts do have the power to declare secondary legislation (e.g. statutory instruments) to be invalid.
- What is derogation? Derogation allows a state to opt out of some rights.

I

Ideal standard

A standard that makes no allowance for normal losses, waste and machine downtime, and is only attainable under the most favourable conditions.

Illegal contract

Illegal here is not confined to what is criminally illegal. Some agreements are declared illegal by statute or by the common law. They are a nullity, i.e. absolutely void of legal effect, and therefore no action can be based on them.

Imported inflation

In an economy in which imports are significant, a weakening of the national currency will increase the cost of imports and could lead to domestic inflation.

Imprest system for petty cash

Under this efficient system of organising and controlling petty cash payments, the cashier in charge of the petty cash box is given a fixed amount of cash (the 'imprest') at the start of every period. Vouchers supporting cash payments are put in the box whenever a payment is made. At any given time it should be possible to total the remaining cash plus the value of all of the vouchers and the resulting totals should together add up to the imprest.

Incentive schemes

These operate by comparing the standard time allowed with the actual time taken.

* EXAMPLE *

Basic rate = $10 per hour
Standard time = 20 mins per unit
Time taken for 100 units = 28 hours

If bonus is paid at half the time saved then:

Bonus = 50% × time saved × time rate
Bonus = 50% × ($33^1/_3$ - 28) × $10 = $26.67
Total pay = 28 × $10 + $26.67 = $4,306.67

Income and expenditure account

A club or other non-profit making organisation's equivalent of the income statement for a business.

Income Elasticity (YED)

Measures how responsive demand is to change in income.

Normal goods
Have a positive YED (people buy more of them as incomes rise).

Inferior goods
Have a negative YED (people buy less of them as income rises), e.g. basic foodstuffs – as income rises more expensive food may be bought instead.

Income statement

A financial statement that is used to bring together all of the revenue and expense account balances as at the end of each financial year. The resulting balance is the net profit for the year.
To prepare the budgeted income statement:

- compute values for opening and closing inventories
- use these and the functional cost budgets to compute budgeted cost of sales
- compute any other non-production cost budgets
- combine sales, cost of sales, and any other non-production cost budgets into a budgeted income statement.

* EXAMPLE *

	$	$
Sales		605,000
Cost of sales:		
Opening inventories	24,448	
Raw materials	123,600	
Direct labour	312,000	
Production overhead	124,800	
	584,848	
Closing inventories	95,168	
		489,680
Operating margin		115,320
Marketing/administration		45,000
Operating profit		70,320

Incomplete records

A misleading title for an accounting system that is not based on double entry bookkeeping. It is possible to prepare a set of financial statements from a cash book and sales and payables ledgers.

Incremental cash flows

For any decision, managers should consider what difference the project concerned makes to the company, i.e. future incremental cash flows:

Cash position if the project is accepted	£A
Cash position if the project is not accepted	£B
Relevant incremental cash flow =	A – B

Independent contractor

Works under a contract for services.

Independent non-executive directors

The following persons cannot be regarded as independent:

- anyone who has been an employee of the company in the previous five years
- anyone who has had a material business relationship with the company in the previous three years
- anyone who has served on the board for more than nine years.

Index numbers

A single value that measures change in a series. Types of index number:

- simple indices
- weighted indices
- chain base indices.

Index numbers and inflation

When measuring UK inflation, the RPI and CPI measure the percentage changes month by month in the average level of prices of goods and services purchased by most households in the UK. Within each year, the RPI and CPI are calculated as fixed quantity price indices – only the prices of goods affect the index from month to month. However, the contents of the baskets of goods and services and their associated weights are updated annually.

Indirect costs

Also known as overhead costs, indirect costs are items of expenditure on labour, materials or services which cannot be economically identified with a specific saleable cost unit, e.g. factory rent, supervisory and management salaries and service departments.

Indirect method (cash flow statement)

A method of calculating cash flows from operations for the cash flow statement which presents gross trading cash flows. That is, it starts with operating profit, and adjusts for the non-cash expense of depreciation and for the movements in working capital. This method yields the same end result as the direct method.

Indirect taxes

These are levied on expenditure.

- An ad valorem indirect tax takes the form of a fixed percentage on expenditure, e.g. VAT.
- A specific indirect tax is charged at a fixed amount per unit of product, e.g. duty per packet of cigarettes.

In the event of an indirect tax being levied, the tax is payable to the government by the vendor of the goods. The vendor will plan to pass all the tax on to the customer in the form of a higher price. Whether they are able to depends on market conditions, specifically the elasticity of demand in relation to the elasticity of supply.

- If a product has a highly elastic demand, then the customer is likely only to pay a small proportion of the tax – increasing prices will significantly reduce sales volumes.
- If a product has a highly inelastic demand, then the customer is likely to pay a large proportion of the tax – increasing prices will have little effect on sales volumes.

* EXAMPLE *

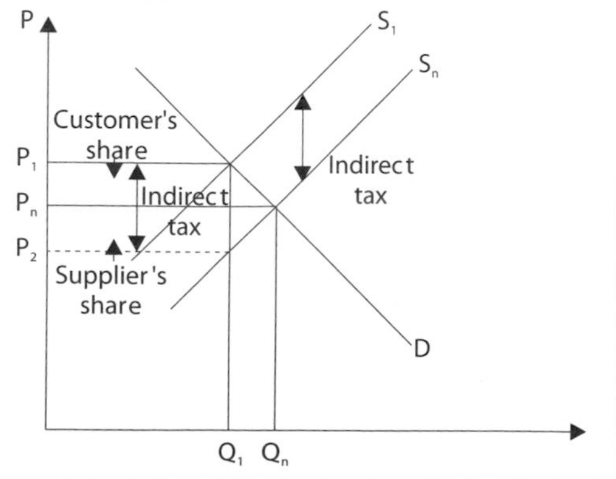

* EXAMPLE *

Prior to imposition of an indirect tax, the equilibrium market price was P_0, with quantity Q_0 being demanded and supplied (intersection of supply curve S_0 and the demand curve D). In the absence of any indirect tax, the supplier keeps all of P_0.

If an indirect tax is imposed per unit of output, this in effect increases the cost of production to the supplier and the supply curve will move upwards by an amount equal to the tax (S_1).

The new equilibrium price is P_1 with quantity Q_1 being demanded and supplied. Consumers are now paying a higher price P_1 – their contribution to the tax is the difference between P_0 and P_1.

The supplier is now receiving a higher price, P1. However, after they have paid the tax to the government they keep P_2, which is lower than the original price of P_0 – their contribution to the tax is the difference between P_0 and P_2.

Inelastic demand

PED<1
Demand changes less in proportion to price.

* EXAMPLE *

Commuter train fares – if prices rise by 5%, demand will change by less than 5% and total revenue increases.

Inequalities – rules for manipulating inequalities

Addition and subtraction
Addition and subtraction always preserve the original direction of the inequality:
If a>b, then a+c > b+c
If a>b, then a–c > b-c

* EXAMPLE *

- Adding 5 to each side of 3>2 gives 8>7
- Subtracting 1 from each side of 3>2 gives 2>1

Multiplication and division
Multiplying or dividing by a positive number preserves the direction of an inequality but multiplying or dividing by a negative number reverses it:

If a>b, then
- a×c > b×c for positive c
- a×c < b×c for negative c
- a/c > b/c for positive c
- a/c < b/c for negative c

* EXAMPLE *

- Multiplying both sides of 3>2 by 5 gives 15>10
- Multiplying both sides of 3>2 by –5 gives –15<–10
- Dividing both sides of 3>2 by 5 gives 0.6>0.4
- Dividing both sides of 3>2 by -5 gives – 0.6<–0.4

Reciprocals

Taking the reciprocal of an expression reverses the direction of the inequality:

If a>b, then 1/a < 1/b

> * EXAMPLE *
>
> 3>2 but 1/3<1/2

Inequalities – graphical interpretation

When a line or curve is drawn on a graph it usually defines three areas – on the line, above the line or below the line. Being on the line reflects equality in the original equation but to specify being above or below the lines requires inequalities.

> * EXAMPLE *
>
> Take the equation y = 10 + 0.1x:

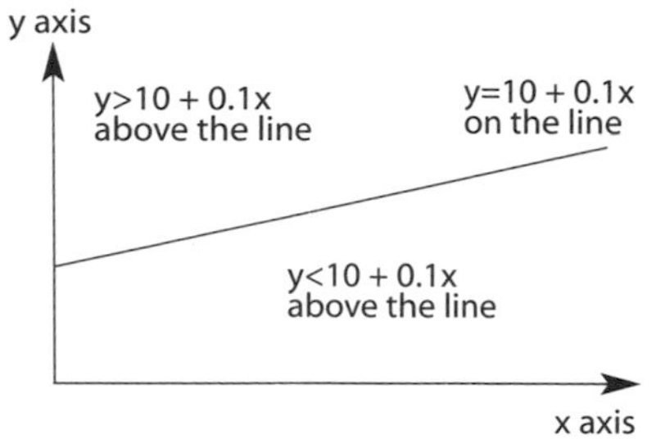

Inflation

Defined as a sustained rise in general prices. In theory, if wages keep up with inflation, it can have minimal economic impact. In reality it can have a number of damaging effects:

- loss of business confidence
- erosion of living standards
- discouragement of saving
- damages exports and encourages imports
- loss of faith in currency by international community
- uneven effect within the economy.

Information

Good information should be:

- complete
- relevant
- timely
- as accurate as is required
- understandable
- significant
- communicated to the right person
- communicated via an appropriate channel.

Three further properties may be added:

- good information commands the confidence of the user
- information is only useful as long as its value is higher than the cost of generating it
- if information is inaccurate, the probability and level of inaccuracy are known.

The mnemonic RC Cactus helps to remember what makes management information useful:
R elevant
C omplete
C ommunicated to the right person
A s accurate as is required
C ommunicated via an appropriate channel
T imely
U nderstandable
S ignificant

Information – cost

- The cost of designing and setting up the system that produces the information.
- The day-to-day running costs of the system providing the information.
- Storage costs.

Information – value

The value of information results from actions by decision makers who use the information to improve profitability.

* EXAMPLE *
- Reducing unnecessary costs
- Adopting better marketing strategies
- Better analysis of 'cost drivers'
- Optimising techniques

Injections

Injections boost the circular flow of income in the form of exports (X), government investment (G) and private sector investment (I).

Input tax

Value Added Tax paid on purchases.

Insurance companies

Perform the important role of enabling individuals and firms to reduce their risk exposure. All insurance companies share the following characteristics:
- They provide insurance against financial loss.
- They collect 'premiums' from customers.
- They agree to compensate the policyholder in the event of a specified event occurring within a specified time period (e.g. death, fire, theft).
- The amount and terms of compensation are detailed in the policy.
- The level of premiums is determined by the risk (likelihood of payout) and the sum insured. This is often discussed via the 'premium: benefit' ratio.
- The premiums are collected into a pool of funds. Provided sufficient funds are available to meet unexpected claims, the rest can be invested to earn a return.

Integrated accounting using standard costs

If integrated accounts are prepared using standard costs this means that:
- the price/rate variances are extracted within the relevant production cost ledger accounts (materials, labour, overheads), so that
- the work-in-progress account is charged with standard costs of actual resources used
- efficiency and usage variances are extracted in the work-in-progress account, so that
- the finished goods stock account carries inventory at standard cost
- the variances are written off to the income statement.

Sales price and volume variances are not recorded in the accounts as sales are recorded at actual value.

Integrated accounts

A set of accounting records that provides both financial and cost accounts using a common input of data for all accounting purposes. (CIMA *Official Terminology*)

Integration test

Under a contract of service the work done is an integral part of the business; whereas under a contract for services the work done is not integrated into it but only accessory to it and is being done by the worker as a person in business on his own account.

Intention to create legal relations

In domestic and social arrangements, there is a rebuttable presumption that there was no intention that the agreement should be legally binding. In the case of ordinary commercial dealings (e.g. buying goods in a shop), there is a strong presumption that the parties intended it to be legally binding.

Inter-bank market

The sterling inter-bank market (SIBM) is a market in short-term sterling funds in which the banks are the main participants, either lending to other banks or borrowing from them. Recently they have been joined by the larger building societies. The SIBM has become such an important source of funds to banks that the London Inter-Bank Offered Rate (LIBOR) is now used instead of base rate to determine the interest payable on some types of company borrowing.

Interdependence of variances

Different variances may be related. For instance, a favourable sales price variance may result in an adverse sales volume variance if increases in price result in a fall in demand for a product.

Interest cover

An alternative approach to measuring gearing. Dividing interest payable into earnings before interest and tax gives an indication of the number of times that the company can pay its interest without making a loss. The higher the resulting figure, the smaller the interest burden on the company.

Internal audit

An appraisal activity established within an entity as a service to the entity. Its functions include, among other things, examining, evaluating and monitoring the adequacy and effectiveness of internal control.

Internal control system

May be defined as the whole system of controls, financial and otherwise, established by the management in order to carry on the business of the enterprise in an orderly and efficient manner, ensure adherence to management policies, safeguard the assets and secure as far as possible the completeness and accuracy of the records.

Internal control techniques

Include pre-numbering of documents and the creation of other procedures so that transactions and balances are adequately controlled.

Internal rate of return (IRR)

The annual percentage return achieved by a project, at which the sum of the discounted cash inflows over the life of the project is equal to the sum of the discounted cash outflows. In general, it is necessary to compute the IRR by trial and error; that is to compute NPVs at various discount rates until the discount rate which gives an NPV of zero is found.

If A is the lower discount rate (15%)
B is the higher discount rate (20%)
N_A is the NPV at rate A (£36)
N_B is the NPV at rate B (– £33)

The IRR is given by:

$$IRR \quad A + (B - A) \times \frac{N_A}{N_A - N_B}$$

Note that this is only an approximate relationship (as indicated by the ≈ sign). Also note that N_B is negative, which means that care must be taken with the signs. This formula is not given in the exam. A useful mnemonic is that it spells out 'A BANANA – N.B.', but you still have to remember what the letters stand for and what to add, subtract, multiply and divide!

International Federation of Accountants (IFAC)

The global organisation for the accountancy profession. The IFAC Code of Ethics was developed with the help of input from the global accountancy profession. The IFAC code applies to all bodies that are members of IFAC.

International law

Derived from a number of sources:

- International treaties/conventions: Obligations expressly and voluntarily accepted between states.
- Custom: Derived from the consistent practices of states. Judgements of international tribunals and scholarly works are persuasive sources of custom.
- General principles of law: Refers to those principles that are commonly recognised by the major legal systems of the world.
- International bodies: May establish collective agreements on defined areas, e.g. the International Federation of Accountants.

International Monetary Fund (IMF)

Founded in 1944 at Bretton Woods in the USA, the IMF became responsible for:

- promoting international financial co-operation and establishing a system of stable exchange rates and freely convertible currencies
- providing a source of credit for members with balance of payments deficits while corrective policies were adopted
- managing the growth of international liquidity.

International trade – benefits

- *Choice:* The diversity of goods available in a domestic economy is increased through the import of goods that could be uneconomic or impossible to produce at home.
- *Competition:* International trade will increase competition in domestic markets, which is likely to lead to both a reduction in price, together with increasing pressure for new products and innovation.
- *Economies of scale:* By producing both for the home and international markets, companies can produce at a larger scale and therefore take advantage of economies of scale.
- *Specialisation:* If a country specialises in producing the goods and services at which it is most efficient, it can maximise its economic output.

Internationalisation

Internationalisation refers to the increasing spread of economic activities across geographical boundaries.

* EXAMPLE *

- Many companies are taking advantage of the internet to sell to new countries overseas.
- Setting up production facilities overseas.

Interpolation and extrapolation

Regression lines can be used to calculate intermediate values of variables, i.e. values within the known range. This is known as interpolation and it is one of the main uses of regression lines. It is also possible to extend regression lines beyond the range of values used in their calculation, and then to calculate values of the variables that are outside the limits of the original data; this is known as extrapolation. Generally speaking, extrapolation must be treated with caution since, once outside the range of known values, other factors may influence the situation, and the relationship which has been approximated as linear over a limited range may not be linear outside that range.

* EXAMPLE *

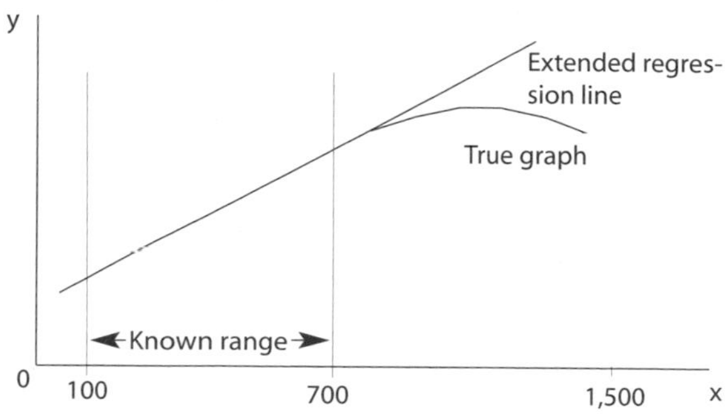

Inventory

Goods intended for resale. Comprises raw materials, work-in-progress and finished goods.

Inventory account

Entries are only ever made to the inventory account at the end of the accounting period when the opening inventory is transferred to the income statement and the closing inventory is entered into the inventory account.

Inventory replacement reserve

During a period of increasing prices, measuring the cost of inventory consumed using the FIFO assumption can overstate profits. Making a transfer into an inventory replacement reserve reminds shareholders that some of the reported profit might not be distributable profits (although such a transfer has no more effect than a transfer into general reserve).

Inventory turnover ratio

Measures how well a business is managing its inventory. To give the average number of days it takes to use an item of inventory, it is expressed as:

$$\frac{\text{Inventory}}{\text{Cost of sales}} \times 365$$

Too long a period suggests that the company is holding excessive stocks and is tying up too much capital as a result. Too short a period suggests that it might be holding too little inventory to meet its commitments.

Inventory valuation

Inventory should be valued at the lower of cost and net realisable value.

Investment centre

The manager is responsible for costs, revenues and assets. Performance is measured by ROCE or other measures.

Investment decisions

There are two possible approaches:

- Internal rate of return approach - is the IRR on the project greater than the borrowing rate? If so, accept.
- Net present value (NPV) approach - at the borrowing rate, is present value of cash inflows less initial cash outflows (i.e. the net present value) positive? If so, accept.

Invitation to treat

Not an offer in itself, but an invitation to others to make an offer. Examples of invitations to treat include advertisements and shop displays.

Issued share capital

The actual number of shares in issue at any point in time. It is the issued share capital that appears on a company's balance sheet.

J

Job cost sheet (or card)

Each job will be given a unique job number and a separate sheet will be opened for each job, on which will be recorded:

- materials purchased specifically for the job (from GRNs or suppliers' invoices)
- materials drawn from inventory (from requisitions)
- direct wages (from time sheets/job cards)
- direct expenses (from invoices, etc).

* EXAMPLE *

Job card

Customer:	Green & Co Ltd	Job No:	342
Description:	Transfer machine	Promised delivery date:	3.11.X1
Date commenced:	25.9.X1	Actual delivery date:	13.11.X1
Price quoted:	$2,400	Despatch note no:	7147

		Materials Estimate $1,250		*Labour Estimate $100*			*Overhead Estimate $176*		*Other charges Estimate $25*	
Date	**Ref**						*Hourly rate $11*			
20X1		*Cost $*	*Cum $*	*Hrs*	*Cost $*	*Cum $*	*Cost $*	*Cum $*	*Cost $*	*Cum $*
	b/f		1,200	17		110		187		13
6 Nov	MR 1714	182	1,382							
7 Nov	Consultant's test fee								10	23
8 Nov	MR 1937	19	1,401							
9 Nov	MRN 213	(26)	1,375							
10 Nov	Labour analysis			5	28	138	55	242		

Summary	$	**Comments**
Materials	1,375	
Labour	138	
Overhead	242	
Other charges	23	
	1,778	
Invoice price (invoice number 7147 dated 12.12.X1)	2,400	
Profit	622	

Job costing

Used where unique products or services are provided to a customer. The volume of individual jobs undertaken is large, with the value of those in progress at the financial year-end being small relative to the value of work completed. Each job is a separate cost unit which is given a code number. This code is used to identify the direct material and direct labour cost incurred on the job and this is recorded on a job cost sheet designed for the purpose. Overhead cost is attributed to the job using pre-determined absorption rates. When the job is completed its total costs may be used as the basis of the selling price or, if a fixed price has been agreed, the profitability of the job may be determined.

Journal entries

Any entry made in the double entry bookkeeping system that does not come directly from a day book. These are non-routine transactions, such as the correction of errors or entries made at the year end when the books are being closed off.

Journals

Journals comprise the various days books that are used to record routine transactions, along with the journal, which is used as a diary to record any non-routine journal entries.

Judicial precedent

The system, adopted by the judges, of following previous decisions is called the 'doctrine of judicial precedent'. Some precedents are binding (meaning they must be followed in later cases) whereas others are merely persuasive (meaning that a judge in a later case may choose to follow it but is not bound to do so).

'Just and equitable' winding up

A person complaining of the behaviour of the majority may apply for the company to be wound up completely and their capital returned to them. This is a final and extreme remedy and the court will not grant it unless nothing else is available. Situations that may incline the court to wind up include:

- changes in personal relationships that have rendered the operation of a small company unfair to the petitioner
- where the principal object or objects of the company cannot ever or can no longer be achieved
- where a state of deadlock exists in the management of the company.

K

Keynesian equilibrium

From a Keynesian perspective, equilibrium occurs when aggregate demand is equal to national output, i.e. the point at which the aggregate demand line crosses the 45° line. In the diagram below, if aggregate demand is shown by AD_1, then the equilibrium national income will be Y_1.

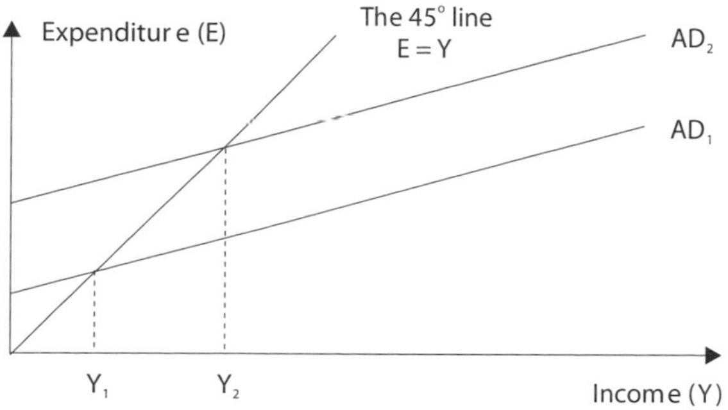

If government can boost aggregate demand to AD_2 by injecting money into the circular flow, then it is possible to boost national income from Y_1 to Y_5, i.e. the government has stimulated economic growth.

Keynesian theory

Based on manipulation and management of aggregate demand in the economy (demand-side economics). Keynes argued that it was government's role to move the economy to a better equilibrium, i.e. one closer to full employment. This involves government borrowing money and injecting it into the economy to stimulate economic growth. Increased future tax revenues would then allow the government to repay this money. Conversely, if an economy were growing too fast and experiencing inflation, government could slow the economy down by increasing levels of taxation, thus reducing the amount of money in the economy.

Kinked demand curve

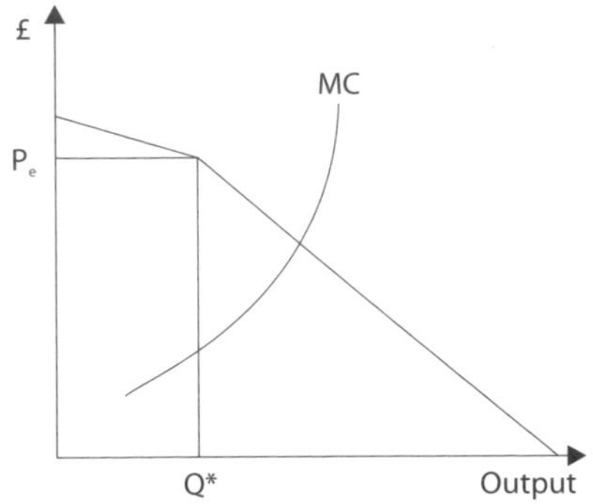

Demand curve is kinked at current price (Pe) since:

- an increase in price by one cartel member is not followed by competitors, leading to a large loss of sales
- a reduction in price by one cartel member is copied by competitors, leading to only minor sales increases.

L

Labour budget

Production budget × labour hours per unit = labour budget in hours × budgeted wage rate = labour budget in $.

Labour control account

The accounting entries for labour costs are as follows:

- Actual labour costs are recorded at gross cost before deductions for tax and national insurance (debit entry).
- The labour cost is analysed according to whether it is a direct or indirect cost and by function (credit entry).
- Any balance at the end of the period represents labour paid in advance or in arrears.

Labour variances

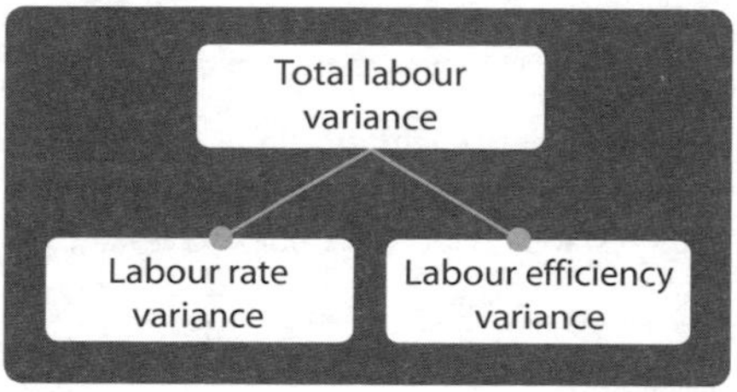

Total labour cost variance
Standard labour cost of actual output should have been:
(units of actual output × standard labour cost per unit)
But was:
(actual cost)
Difference is the total labour cost variance
If the actual cost is greater than the standard cost, then the variance is adverse.

Labour rate variance
Actual labour hours should have cost:
(actual hours × standard rate)
But did cost:
(actual cost)
Difference is the **labour rate variance**

Labour efficiency variance
Actual units produced should have used:
(actual units × standard hours per unit)
But did use:
(actual hours)
Difference is the labour efficiency variance in hours
Value at standard rate per hour to give **labour efficiency variance in $.**

* EXAMPLE *

Standard labour cost/unit	= 2 hours @ $5/hr = $10/unit
Actual production	4,600 units
Hours worked	9,400 hours, cost $45,120
4,600 units should have cost × $10	$46,000
But did cost	$45,120
Total labour cost variance	$880 F
The variance is favourable since the cost of labour content was less than expected.	
9,400 hours should cost × $5.00/hour	$47,000
But did cost	$45,120
Labour rate variance	$1,880 (F)
The variance is favourable because the actual rate is less than expected.	
4,600 units should use 2 hours each	9,200 hours
But did use	9,400 hours
Labour efficiency variance in hours	200 (A)
Value at standard rate per hour × $5 per hour	$1,000 A
The variance is adverse because the actual hours used were more than expected.	

Lapse of an offer (in law)

An offer can lapse in a number of situations:

- If the offer is stated only to be open for a specific time period, it will end after the expiration of this time.
- If there is no specific period of time mentioned by the offeror, the offer will lapse after a reasonable length of time. If there is a dispute about the time period, the court will decide what is reasonable. It is a question of fact to be decided in each case.
- If the offer were made subject to a condition, it will lapse on failure of that condition.
- If the offeror dies, the offer can no longer be accepted once the offeree knows of the death.
- If the offeree dies, the offer cannot be accepted by his personal representatives.

Last-in-first-out (LIFO)

A method of valuing inventory that assumes that the newest stock is issued each time inventory is used. It tends to provide a higher cost of sales and lower profit during periods when prices are rising. It is not permitted to use LIFO to value stock for external reporting purposes.

Last In, First Out (LIFO) inventory pricing

Each issue is valued at the price paid for the material last taken into the inventory from which the issue could have been drawn.

* EXAMPLE *

1 November bought 300 kgs costing $1 each
6 November bought 200 kgs costing $1.20 each
8 November used 100 kgs
Using LIFO, materials used on 8 November would be valued at $1.20 per kg.

Law of comparative advantage

All countries benefit if they concentrate on producing goods in which they have a comparative advantage.

* EXAMPLE *

Imagine a global economy with two countries and two products. Each country needs both products and at present all needs are met by domestic production. Each country has the same resources available to it and they are split equally between the two products. The current situation is as follows:

	Units of X per day	Units of Y per day
Country A	1,200	720
Country B	960	240
Total daily production	2,160	960

As the situation currently stands, country A has an absolute advantage in production of both X and Y. Given this what are the benefits of A trading with B? To answer this question we need to consider the opportunity costs incurred by producing X and Y:

- If country A were to focus on making X only, it would give up 720 units of Y to produce an extra 1,200 units of X, i.e. the opportunity cost of 1 unit of X is 720/1,200 = 0.6 units of Y.
- If country B were to focus on making X only, it would give up 240 units of Y to produce an extra 960 units of X, i.e. the opportunity cost of 1 unit of X is 240/960 = 0.25 units of Y.

The opportunity cost of producing X is lower for country B than it is for country A. It follows that B has a comparative advantage in production of X and should specialise in this product.
If country B is to make product X, it follows that country A should make product Y. An analysis of opportunity costs supports this conclusion.

- If country A were to focus on making Y only, it would give up 1,200 units of X to make 720 units of Y, i.e. the opportunity cost of 1 unit of Y is 1,200/720 = 1.67 units of X.
- If country B were to focus on making Y only, it would give up 960 units of X to make 240 units of Y, i.e. the opportunity cost of 1 unit of Y is 960/240 = 4 units of X.

Since country A has the lowest opportunity cost for production of Y, it should specialise in production of this product.

* EXAMPLE *

The impact of this decision by each country to specialise in production of the good for which they have the lowest opportunity cost on world output is shown below:

Specialisation based on lowest opportunity cost		
	Units of X per day	Units of Y per day
Country A	0	1,440
Country B	1,920	0
Total daily production	1,920	1,440

Law of Diminishing Returns

As equal quantities of one variable factor input are added to a fixed factor, output initially increases by a greater proportion (increasing returns), causing average cost to fall. A point will be reached beyond which the resulting addition to output will begin to decrease (diminishing returns), causing average costs to rise.

* EXAMPLE *

Suppose we increase the number of workers while fixing the number of machines. Initially the extra workers will allow specialisation and greater efficiency and so average costs fall. At a later point, however, staff are getting in each other's way and waiting to access machines. The system thus becomes less efficient and average costs rise.
The short-run average total cost curve (SRATC) is 'U'-shaped because of the law of diminishing marginal returns.

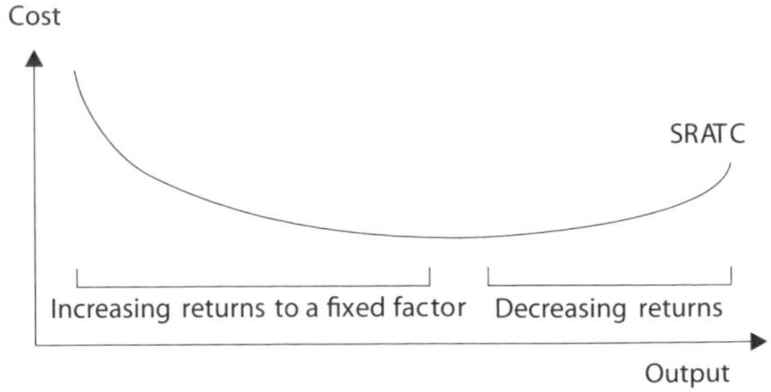

Leakages

Leakages reduce the circular flow of income in the form of imports (M), taxation (T) and savings (S).

Ledger accounts

Each asset, liability, capital, revenue and expense balance has its own account in the general ledger which keeps track of transactions and balances.

Legal person

An entity that the law recognises as having rights and as being subject to duties. Since rights and duties can only be enforced by legal proceedings, an alternative definition is 'an entity that can sue (to enforce its rights) and be sued (for the enforcement of its duties)'.

Legislation

The law created by Parliament and other bodies to whom it has delegated authority.

Liabilities

A present obligation of the entity arising from past events, the settlement of which is expected to result in an outflow from the entity of resources embodying economic benefits. Note that this definition is broader than that used in ordinary language – a liability might exist even if the business does not 'owe' anything.

Life membership fees

In theory these should be credited to a club's income and expenditure account over the number of years of estimated remaining life of the members concerned. The amount not recognised as income should be carried forward as unearned income (effectively a liability) in the balance sheet. (If such fees figure in an exam question, then the examiner will have to specify how they are to be dealt with.)

Lifting the veil of incorporation

There are a number of exceptions to the principle that a company is a person separate from its members. This means that, in certain circumstances, the courts can look through the company to the identity of the shareholders. For example:

- If a plc trades without acquiring a trading certificate, the directors may be personally liable with the company if it defaults on its debts.
- If the number of members of a plc falls to less than two for six months, the remaining member, if aware, becomes jointly and severally liable with the company, for debts arising after that time.
- If an officer signs a document on which the company's name is incorrectly stated or does not appear, he is personally liable if the company defaults.
- Under the Insolvency Act 1986, members and/or directors guilty of wrongful or fraudulent trading may be personally liable for losses arising as a result.
- Nationality – in times of war it is illegal to trade with the enemy. It may be possible to lift the veil of incorporation so as to impute to a company the same nationality as its members.
- Mere facade (sham or puppet companies).
- For the purpose of imposing criminal liability, the state of mind and acts of the company's employees and agents may be imputed to the company.

Limitation Act 1980

Provides that any action on a contract is 'barred' if not brought within the requisite period. Normally time runs from the date on which the breach occurred. In the case of simple contracts the limitation period is 6 years and in the case of contracts by deed it is 12 years. If the claim includes damages for personal injuries or death, however, the period is normally reduced to 3 years. (However, the Act provides that the 3-year period can be extended by the court if the injury does not become apparent within the period.)

Limited company (C05)

In the case of a company limited by shares, the liability of a member to contribute to the company's assets is limited to the amount, if any, unpaid on his shares. Once the shares are fully paid there is, in general, no further liability, i.e. if the company becomes insolvent, the shareholders are not required to make any further contribution to discharge its debts.

Limited company (C02)

A separate legal entity that has the ability to enter into contracts in its own right. The owners (shareholders) normally appoint managers (the board of directors) to manage the company for them. The shareholders are not personally liable for the company's debts and so they have a measure of protection from the risk of the company failing. These factors mean that a large number of formalities must be observed in creating and managing a company, including the preparation of financial statements.

Limited Liability Partnership (LLP)

Characteristics:

- It is an artificial person with unlimited capacity. This means it can do anything that a natural person can do.
- It can enter into contracts in its own name. Each member of the LLP is an agent of the LLP.
- It can own its own property.
- It will continue in existence despite any changes in membership.
- The members will be liable to contribute to its assets if it is wound up. The extent of their liability will be set out in its internal regulations.

Limiting factor analysis

Step 1	Identify the limiting factor.
Step 2	Calculate contribution per unit for each product.
Step 3	Calculate contribution per unit of limiting factor for each product.
Step 4	Rank.
Step 5	Allocate resource on the basis of the ranking.

* EXAMPLE *

Product	*A*	*B*
Selling price/unit	$20	$30
Variable cost/unit	$5	$15
Labour hours/unit	1	3
Maximum demand (units)	1,000	800

There are 2,500 labour hours available.

* EXAMPLE *

The number of products A and B that should be produced to maximise profit are calculated as follows:

Product	*A*	*B*
Contribution per unit	$12	$15
Units of limiting factor (labour)	1	3
Contribution per labour hour	$12	$5
Ranking	1	2

Produce maximum demand of A 1,000 units using 1,000 labour hours.
Use the remaining hours to produce B; 1,500 hours will produce 500 units of B.

Limiting factor analysis with minimum demand

Follow the same procedure as for limiting factor analysis to step 4 then:

Step 5	Allocate the minimum requirements.
Step 6	Allocate the remaining resource on the basis of the ranking calculated.

Linear correlation

When the points on a scatter diagram tend to lie in a narrow band, there is a strong correlation between the variables.

Linear equations

A linear equation (or 'equation of the first degree') is an equation containing no higher powers than the first of x and y, and is of the type $y = a + bx$ where a and b are both constants. By convention, values of x are plotted on the horizontal axis and values of y on the vertical axis. A good way of remembering this is via the x in the word relax: the axis that is 'relaxing' (lying down, horizontally) is the x axis.

Line of best fit (C03)

To obtain a description of the relationship between two variables in the form of an equation in order to forecast values, it is necessary to fit a straight line through the points on the scatter diagram which best represents all of the plotted points. There are several ways of accomplishing this:

- **Establishing trend lines by eye**
- **Equation of a straight line**
  The equation for any straight line is of the form:
  $y = a + bx$
  a is called the intercept on the y-axis and measures the point at which the line will cut the y-axis.
  b is called the gradient of the line and measures its degree of slope.
- **Least squares linear regression**
  The most mathematically acceptable method of fitting a line to a set of data. Instead of relying on our eyes to draw the line of best fit, mathematical techniques are used to derive the equation. It is possible to calculate two different regression lines for a set of data, depending on whether the horizontal deviations or the vertical deviations of the points from the line are considered. It is the sum of the squares of these deviations which is minimised; this overcomes problems that might arise because some deviations would be positive and some negative.

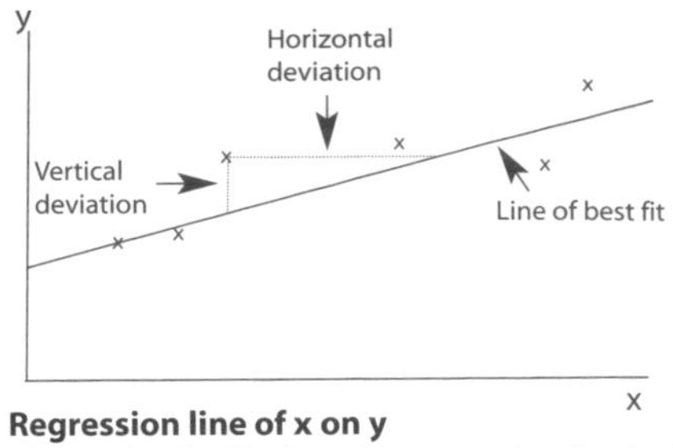

Regression line of x on y

The method of finding the regression line is the same as for the regression line of y on x, but with x and y interchanged. Thus the equation is:

$$x = a' + b'y$$

$$\text{where } a' = \bar{x} + b'\,\bar{y} = \frac{\Sigma x}{n} - \frac{b'\Sigma y}{n}$$

$$b' = \frac{n\Sigma xy - \Sigma x\Sigma y}{n\Sigma y^2 - (\Sigma y)^2}$$

Regression line of y on x

Assuming that the equation of the regression line of y on x is:

$$y = a + bx$$

it is necessary to calculate the values of a and b so that the equation can be completely determined. The following formulae may be used; a knowledge of their derivation is not necessary and they do not need to be memorised since they are supplied in the exams (using upper case X and Y):

$$a = \bar{y} - b\bar{x} = \frac{\Sigma y}{n} - \frac{b\Sigma x}{n}$$

$$b = \frac{n\Sigma xy - \Sigma x\Sigma y}{n\Sigma x^2 - (\Sigma x)^2}$$

n is the number of pairs of x, y values, i.e. the number of points on the scatter graph.

The value of b must be calculated first as it is needed to calculate a.

Line of best fit (C02)

The line which passes through the plotted points on a scatter chart to roughly equalise the number of points on each side and minimise the aggregate vertical distance from the line. For a scatter chart with units of output on the x axis and cost on the y axis, fixed cost will be given by the point at which the line of inspection crosses the y axis. Variable cost will be given by the gradient of the line.

Liquidity (C04)

The ease with which an asset can be sold to release funds early if required, e.g. shares in an unquoted company are much harder to sell to release funds than Treasury bills which have a recognised market.

Liquidity (C02)

The business' ability to pay its debts when they fall due.

Liquidity (or quick) ratio

A more cautious measure of liquidity than the current ratio. It excludes inventory from working capital and is measured as:

(Current assets – Inventory at end of period)/Current liabilities at end of period

The result is usually expressed as a ratio (e.g. 1.0:1).

Loans, mortgages and amortisation

Amortisation means the repaying of a debt by regular instalments, as with a mortgage. Such repayments consist partly of interest and partly repayment of some of the loan. The amount of each instalment remains constant, but as the amount of the outstanding debt decreases, the proportion of the instalment which goes to paying the interest decreases, and the proportion which goes to paying off the outstanding debt increases. From the point of view of the lender (mortgagee) this is equivalent to an annuity. The lender invests a lump sum in the borrower (mortgager) and receives a regular income in return.

* EXAMPLE *

Find the annual repayment on a building society loan of £40,000 over five years at 12% pa.
This is equivalent to an annual income derived from an investment of £40,000.
Let the amount of each repayment = £A.
The first repayment is made at the end of the first year, the second at the end of the second year, and so on, so that:

£40,000 = Present value of all repayments

$$= A\left[\frac{1}{1.12^1}+\frac{1}{1.12^2}+\frac{1}{1.12^3}+\frac{1}{1.12^4}+\frac{1}{1.12^5}\right]$$

$= A \times 3.605$ (from cumulative PV table)

$A = 40{,}000 / 3.605$

$= £11{,}096$

Lodgements

An amount deposited in the bank.

Log tables

A log of any number consists of two parts: the decimal part, called the mantissa, and a whole number, called the characteristic. The mantissa is obtained from log tables. Ignore the decimal point in a number and any leading zeros; just look up the first four digits, e.g. for either 56,253.0 or 56.253 or 0.0056253 you would look up 5625. The characteristic depends on the size of the original number:

		Example
0	if the number is greater than 1 but less than 10	Log 2 = 0.3010
1	if the number is greater than 10 but less than 100	Log 20 = 1.3010

and so on. This applies to numbers less than 1 as follows:

		Example
–1	if the number is greater than 0.1 but less than 1	Log 0.2 = –1 + 0.3010
–2	if the number is greater than 0.01 but less than 0.1	Log 0.02= –2 + 0.3010

There are antilog tables that can be used to convert back from the log to the number it represents or you can convert back by using the log tables backwards.

Long run

The time period during which all the factors of production are variable but the basic technology of an industry is unchanged. This implies that, in the long run, all costs are of a variable nature since it is now possible to vary the quantities of any factors that were fixed in the short run, e.g. in the long run we can buy more machinery, rent extra land, build more factories and employ more staff.

Long-run average cost curve

In the long run all factors of production can be varied. Companies can move to a different short-run cost curve – in fact the long-run cost curve is essentially a combination of different short-run cost curves. It is thus possible to ensure that a company always operates near the bottom of the short-run average total cost curve (SRATC).

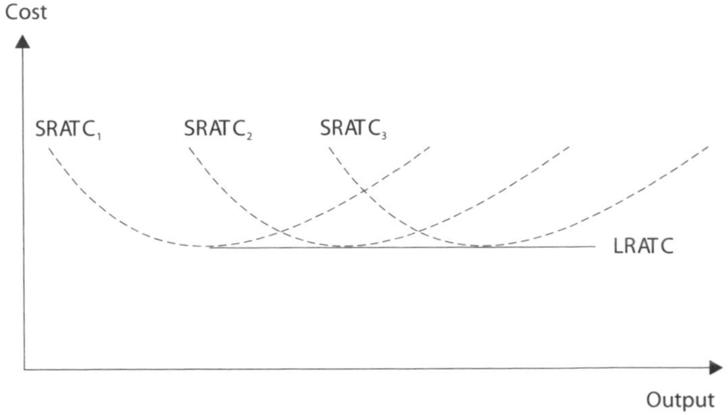

The existence of economies and diseconomies of scale ensures that the LRATC is 'U'-shaped:

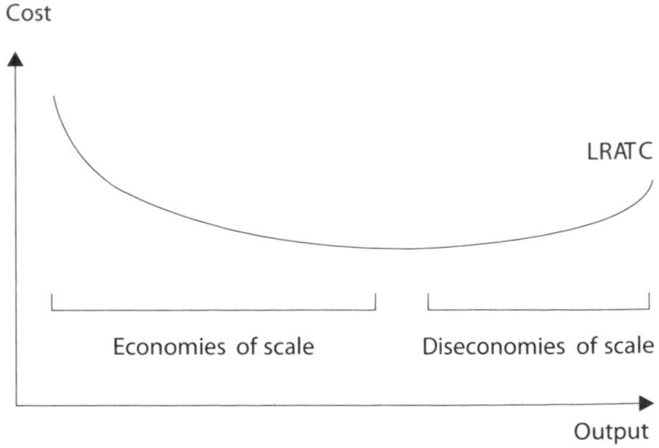

M

Macroeconomics

The study of the workings of the economy as a whole, analysing how national income and output are determined and the causes of and cures for unemployment and inflation.

Macros

If there is a process that you wish to repeat, such as reformatting financial statements to reflect International Accounting Standards, then one way of doing this is to use the macro function. This acts like a mini tape recorder and will record all of the actions specified. This can then be replayed to implement the actions on a new selection of cells, e.g. the financial statements on other worksheets. To set up a macro involves the following steps:

1. On the Tools menu, point to Macro, and then click Record New Macro.
2. In the Macro Name box, enter a name for the macro.
3. If you want to run the macro by pressing a keyboard shortcut key, enter a letter in the Shortcut Key box.
4. In the Store Macro In box, click the location where you want to store the macro.
5. Click OK.
6. If you want the macro to run relative to the position of the active cell, record it using relative cell references. On the Stop Recording toolbar, click Relative Reference so that it is selected. If this is not selected, then the macro will repeat the actions only on the original cell locations specified on each new sheet.
7. Carry out the actions you want to record.
8. On the Stop Recording toolbar, click Stop Recording .

To run the macro involves the following steps:

1. On the Tools menu, point to Macro, and then click Macros.
2. Highlight the macro you wish to run and click Run.

Make or buy decisions

If the relevant internal manufacturing cost is less than the buying price, the item should be manufactured; otherwise it should be bought. The relevant internal cost should take account of variable and avoidable fixed costs if the decision to buy would involve the closure of the manufacturing process altogether.

* EXAMPLE *

Variable manufacturing cost = \$5 per unit

Fixed costs	– avoidable	\$10,000
	– committed	\$20,000

No. of units required = 5,000

The maximum buy-in price that would make closure of internal manufacturing operations worthwhile is:

Total avoidable costs of internal manufacture = \$10,000 + \$5 × 5,000 = \$35,000

$$\text{Max. buy-in price} = \frac{\$35{,}000}{5{,}000} = \$7$$

Managed floating exchange rates

In this scenario the exchange rate is still fundamentally set by the interaction between supply and demand. However, the government may set upper and lower exchange rate limits and will intervene in the market to keep the currency within these bands. This manipulation is undertaken by the Bank of England through its Exchange Equalisation Account but it may involve co-ordinated action by a series of central banks in the international market.

* EXAMPLE *

Suppose that the government has set lower and upper limits for sterling against the dollar of $1.45 and $1.55. Sterling is in danger of falling below $1.45. What can the Bank of England do?

- It could put up interest rates to make sterling more attractive to boost demand for the currency.
- It could try to increase the demand for sterling through support buying of sterling, selling off foreign currency reserves.
- If when it buys sterling it sells dollars, it will also increase the supply of dollars, weakening the dollar on the international market.
- It could impose exchange controls, which directly limit the amount of sterling that can be traded – this would be hugely controversial, and the Bank of England would only use this policy as a last resort.

Management accounting

The application of the principles of accounting and financial management to create, protect, preserve and increase value so as to deliver that value to the stakeholders of profit and not-for-profit enterprises, both public and private. Management accounting is generally proactive and is concerned with planning and co-ordination.

Management by exception

The practice of focusing on activities that require attention and ignoring those that appear to be conforming to expectations. (CIMA *Official Terminology*)

Management controls

Operated outside the day-to-day routine of the system. They include regular review by directors of management accounts including comparisons with corresponding periods and budgets, the internal audit functions, and special review procedures e.g. relating to inventories and wages.

Manufacturing accounts

A section of the income statement that accumulates the costs of production in a logical sequence. The cost of finished production is then transferred to the income statement to be incorporated into the computation of cost of sales and gross profit.

Marginal cost pricing

This occurs when a profit margin is added to the variable (or marginal) cost of the product to arrive at a price. Any profit margin will contribute to fixed cost and then profit. It is generally used as a short run pricing strategy to generate contribution when there is spare capacity, e.g. standby tickets for air travel.

Marginal propensity to consume (mpc)

The proportion of every extra £ of income that individuals will spend rather than save. This is given by change in consumption/change in income.

* EXAMPLE *

If the mpc is 0.7, a £100 increase in national income (Y) would increase consumption by £70.

Marginal propensity to import (mpm) The proportion of every extra £ of income that individuals will spend on imports. This is given by change in imports/change in income.

Marginal propensity to save (mps) 1 – marginal propensity to consume (mpc)

Marginal propensity to tax (mpt) The proportion of every extra £ of income that individuals pay in tax. This is given by change in tax/change in income.

Margin of safety The difference between budgeted sales volume and breakeven sales volume. Often shown as a percentage of the budgeted sales volume.

Market concentration Market concentration measures the market share controlled by the largest companies in an industry. This typically involves working out the percentage of total sales generated by either the top three or five companies in a market.

Market equilibrium In a free market, the quantity and price of goods supplied are determined by the interaction between supply and demand. In the diagram below the equilibrium price is P_1 and the equilibrium quantity is Q_1.

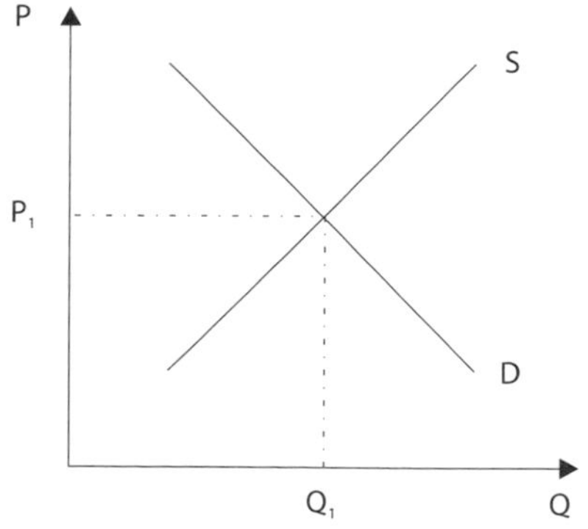

Market failure The inability of a market to allocate resources in a way that maximises utility.

Market structures

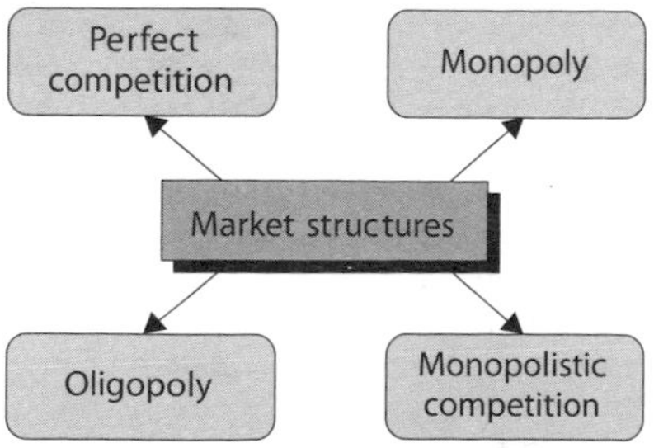

Market	Sellers	Products	Entry barriers	Pricing policies
Perfect competition	Many	Homogeneous	No	Price-takers
Monopoly	One	No close substitutes	Yes (high)	Price-setters
Monopolisti competition	Many	Differentiated	No	Price-setters
Oligopoly	Few	Similar	Yes	Price-setters

Market value of shares

The value of issued shares when they are bought and sold from one shareholder to another. If the company is quoted on the stock exchange, then its market value can be observed on a day-to-day basis. If it is not quoted, then the market value will have to be negotiated between buyers and sellers.

Master budget

Comprises:

- budgeted income statement
- cash flow statement
- budgeted balance sheet.

Materiality

An item is material if its omission or misstatement could influence the economic decisions of users taken on the basis of the financial statements. The significance of an item stems from its importance in the overall context of the financial statements. Only material items should be included in the financial statements in order to improve clarity.

Material variances

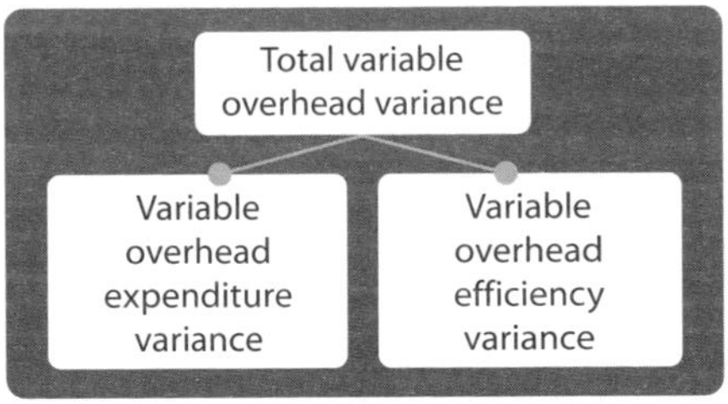

Total material cost variance

Standard material cost of actual output should have been:

(units of actual output × standard material cost per unit)

But was:

(actual cost)

Difference is the total material cost variance

If the actual cost is greater than the standard cost then the variance is adverse.

Material price variance
Actual quantity of material purchased should have cost:
(actual quantity purchased × standard price)
But did cost:
(actual cost)
Difference is the material price variance

Material usage variance
Actual units produced should have used:
(actual units × standard usage of material per unit)
But did use:
(actual material used)
Difference is the material usage variance in units
Value at standard price per unit gives the material usage variance in $.

* EXAMPLE *

Standard material cost/unit	= 3kg @ $8/kg = $24/unit
Actual production	= 4,600 units
Materials purchased	= 14,200 kg, cost $106,500
Total material cost variance:	
4,600 units should have cost × $24	$110,400
But did cost	$106,500
Total material cost variance	$3,900 F
The variance is favourable since the actual material cost per unit was less than $24, which will increase profits.	
Price variance:	
14,200 kg should have cost × $8	$113,600
But did cost	$106,500
Material price variance	$7,100 F
The variance is favourable since the lower cost per unit of material ($7.50) would increase profits.	
Usage variance:	
4,600 units should have used × 3kg	13,800 kg
But did use	14,200 kg
Usage variance in kg	400 kg A
Value at standard price of $8 per kg	$3,200 A

The variance is adverse because more materials were used than expected.

Material variances and inventories

If inventories are valued at standard price, price variances are calculated based on the quantity **purchased** rather than the quantity of materials **used**.

If inventories are valued at actual price (FIFO, LIFO), any price variance is recognised not at the time of purchase but at the time of issue. The price variance is calculated based upon the quantity **used**.

Materials purchase budget

The raw materials purchases budget will be derived from the usage budget as follows:

		Material A (kg)	*Material B (kg)*
Usage	Product X	2,100	525
	Product Y	180	180
		———	———
		2,280	705
Add:	closing inventory raw materials	500	100
Less:	opening inventory raw materials	(350)	(80)
		———	———
Materials purchases (kg)		2,430	725
		———	———
Cost per kg		$2	$1
Purchases		$4,860	$725

Materials usage budget

Multiplying production budgets by usage of materials per unit will give the raw materials usage budget (in units).

Maximisation of expected value

The expected value (EV) criterion of decision making consists of choosing the option giving the maximum expected return.

* EXAMPLE *

Using the following data, apply the criteria of maximisation of expected value to decide the best course of action for the company, assuming the following probabilities:

P (low demand)	0.1
P (medium demand)	0.6
P (high demand)	<u>0.3</u>
	<u>1.0</u>

A company has three new products A, B and C, of which it can introduce only one. The level of demand for each course of action might be low, medium or high. If the company decides to introduce product A, the net income that would result from the levels of demand possible are estimated at £20, £40 and £50 respectively. Similarly, if product B is chosen, net income is estimated at £80, £70 and – £10, and for product C £10, £100 and £40, respectively. The expected value of the decision to introduce product A is given by the following summation:

$0.1 \times £20 + 0.6 \times £40 + 0.3 \times £50 = £41$

* EXAMPLE *

The expected value of all the products may be calculated by means of a pay-off table:

Table of expected values

State of the world (demand)	Prob of state of the world	Product A Income	Product A Income x Prob	Product B Income	Product B Income x Prob	Product C Income	Product C Income x Prob
		£	£	£	£	£	£
Low	0.1	20	2	80	8	10	1
Medium	0.6	40	24	70	42	100	60
High	0.3	50	15	(10)	(3)	40	12
Total	1.0		41		47		73

Thus, if the criterion is to maximise the expected value, it means that the product with the highest expected value will be chosen, in this case product C.

Maximum price controls

Government may impose maximum price controls or price ceilings on certain goods or services, which should:

- benefit consumers on low incomes, so that they can afford the particular good (particularly important if dealing with merit goods)
- control inflation.

* EXAMPLE *

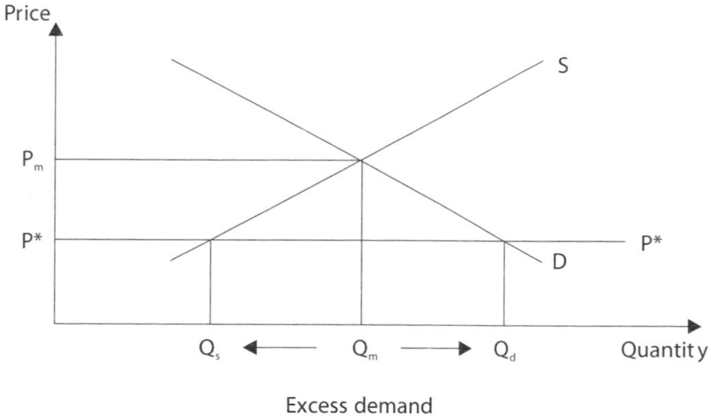

The equilibrium price and quantity are P_m and Q_m respectively. The government has imposed a price cap at P*. To be effective P* must be below P_m. At the lower price, demand has risen to Q_d but the amount suppliers are willing to supply at that price has fallen to Q_s. There is now excess demand in the market and so an alternative system of allocation has to be employed, such as:

- queuing - first come/first served
- suppliers' preferences
- proportion of past purchases/regular customers only
- rationing - may be fair but relatively inefficient.

The longer such controls are kept, the more likely it is that a black market will evolve.

Measure of damages

The amount that will put the claimant in the position in which he would have been had the contract been performed.

Measuring dispersion

Dispersion is a method of choosing a single number to measure the spread of the items.

Measuring inflation

The Retail Prices Index (RPI) was the UK's main indicator of inflation before 2003. Since then, the government has focused policy on the Consumer Prices Index (CPI), although RPI figures are still widely quoted and used.

Median

The value of the middle item in a distribution once all the items have been arranged in order of magnitude.

Median for ungrouped data

Once the items have been arranged in order, starting with either the largest or smallest, then, if the number of items is odd, the median is simply the value of the middle item. However, if the number of items is even, the median is the arithmetic mean of the two middle items.

* EXAMPLE *

The median of 3, 6, 10, 14, 17, 19 and 22 is 14 since this is the value of the middle item. Therefore, median = 14.

Median for grouped data

The median can be estimated from a cumulative frequency curve by going to the mid-point on the frequency range (on the y-axis) and then reading the corresponding value on the x-axis.
When data has been categorised into classes, each containing a range of values, then the median is the value of the n/2 th item.

n is taken rather than n + 1 because, for grouped data, n is always large, otherwise the data would not have been grouped, and when n is large, the difference between n and n + 1 is negligible. The median can be estimated from a cumulative frequency graph (ogive) as follows. The value of the middle item is read off the horizontal axis as M:

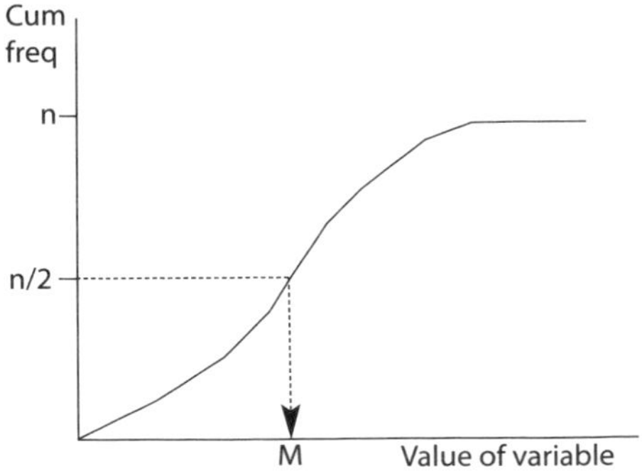

where n is the total frequency (Σf) and M is the median value.

Membership fees/Subscriptions

It may be necessary to adjust cash received from members in order to correct for the effects of fees paid in advance and in arrears on the club's fee income for the year.

Memorandum of Association

Defines the essential components of the structure of the company, partly for the information of those who do business with it. The mandatory clauses of the Memorandum of a public company limited by shares state the following matters:

- the name of the company, which must end with the words 'public limited company' (plc) or the Welsh equivalent
- that the company is a public company
- the situation of the company's registered office
- the objects of the company
- that the liability of the members is limited
- the nominal amount of the authorised share capital (at least £50,000) divided into a specific number of shares of a specific value.

After the main clauses of the Memorandum comes a declaration of association which must be signed by at least two subscribers; they must each agree to take one or more shares – their signatures must be witnessed and dated.

Merit goods

Goods that can be provided by the private sector and have significant positive externalities.

Minimum price controls

In certain markets government may seek to ensure a minimum price for different goods and services. It can do this in a number of ways such as providing subsidies direct to producers, e.g. the Common Agricultural Policy. Alternatively, it can set a legal minimum price which, to be effective, must be above the current market price.

* EXAMPLE *

Theoretically, imposition of a legal minimum wage by government should benefit individuals on low wages. In the diagram below, the market wage rate before imposition of a minimum wage is P_m with the number of people employed being Q_m.

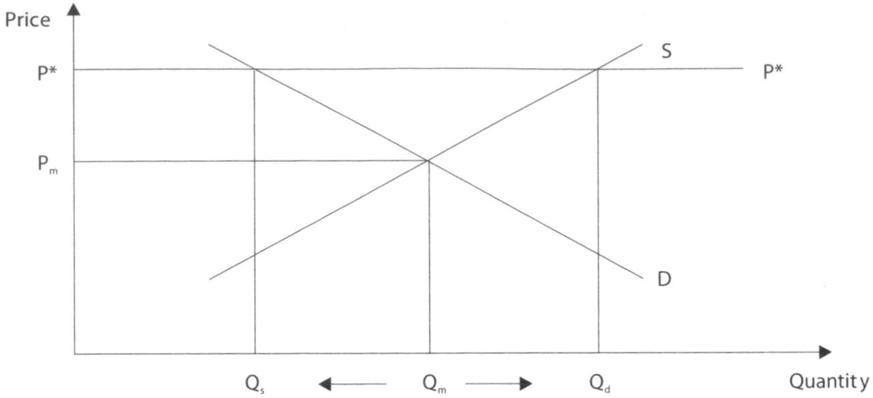

If the government imposes a minimum wage of P* (to be effective P* must be above P_m), then a number of things happen:

- those who remain in employment experience an increase in wages from Pm to P*
- the number of people employed falls from Q_m to Q_d.
- there is an excess supply of workers (unemployment) in the sector equivalent to $Q_s - Q_d$.

Misrepresentation (in law)

A false statement of material fact made by one of the contracting parties before or at the time of entering into the contract, which was intended to and did induce the other party to make the contract. Three types:

Fraudulent misrepresentation

Meaning: Deliberate or reckless statement.

Remedies: Rescission and/or damages based on the tort of deceit.

Negligent misrepresentation

Meaning: Statement made without reasonable care (this is easier to prove than fraudulent misrepresentation).

Remedies: Rescission and/or damages based on either the tort of negligence or s2(1) Misrepresentation Act 1967.

Innocent misrepresentation

Meaning: No fraud or negligence.

Remedies: The sole remedy is rescission; however, damages may be awarded in lieu of rescission, provided the right to rescission has not been lost.

Mnemonic codes

Usually in alphanumeric form, incorporating some descriptive element that makes it easy to find the correct code, e.g. a customer called 'Robertson' would have a code beginning ROB…, for instance ROB052.

Mode

The value that occurs most frequently among all the items in the distribution. When dealing with data grouped into class intervals, it is usual to refer to the modal class. It is possible for a distribution to have more than one mode or, indeed, no mode at all.

Mode for grouped data
In a grouped frequency distribution, the modal class is the class with the largest frequency. This can easily be found by observation. The value of the mode within the modal class can then be estimated from a histogram. Having located the modal class it is necessary to draw in the dotted lines shown in the following diagram:

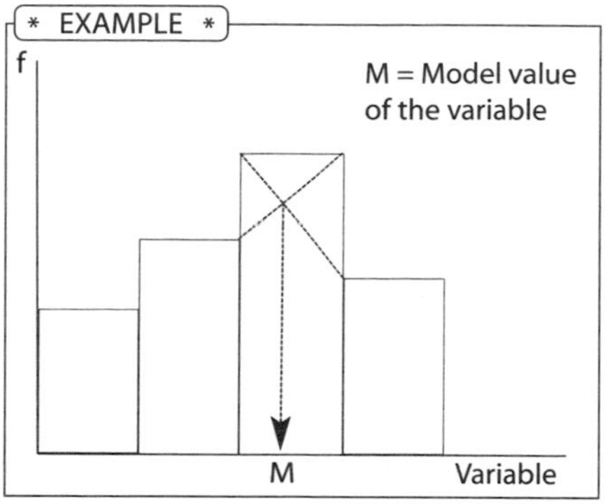

Monetarist theory

Monetarists revived the earlier classical view and believe that there is only one true equilibrium point in the national economy. Equilibrium will only occur when supply is equal to demand in all markets in an economy.
Monetarists believe that the economy will automatically gravitate towards this 'natural' equilibrium unless hindered by market imperfections. Thus it is the role of government to 'free up' the economy by removing these imperfections. Once this is done the role of government is minimal. Market imperfections include:

- inflation, as it distorts the market price mechanism
- government spending and taxation
- price fixing
- minimum wages
- regulation of markets
- abuses of monopoly power.

Monetarist solutions to economic problems are often described as supply-side economics as they focus on improving the supply of factors of production in an economy.

Monetary inflation

Monetarists argue that inflation can result from an over-expansion of the money supply. In effect, increasing the money supply increases purchasing power in the economy, boosting demand for goods and services. If this expansion occurs faster than expansion in the supply of goods and services, inflation can arise.

Money supply measures

The two most important measures currently monitored in the UK are:

- Mo Notes and coins in circulation and balances at the Bank of England
- M4 Notes and coins and all private sector sterling bank/building society deposits (96% of which deposits).

Monopolistic market in the long run

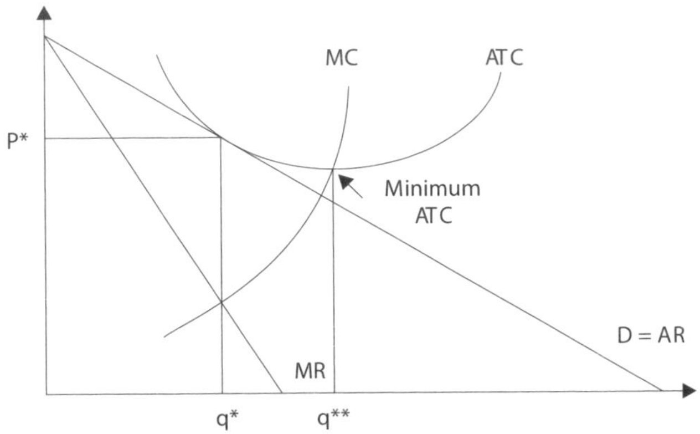

- Companies make quantity Q* where MC = MR for maximum profits. Company charges price P* and makes normal profits as ATC = AR.
- Companies produce at a cost above minimum ATC and are therefore inefficient.
- Companies supply less at higher price than equivalent company in perfect competition (which would supply Q**). Company has excess capacity Q** – Q*.

Monopolistic market in the short run

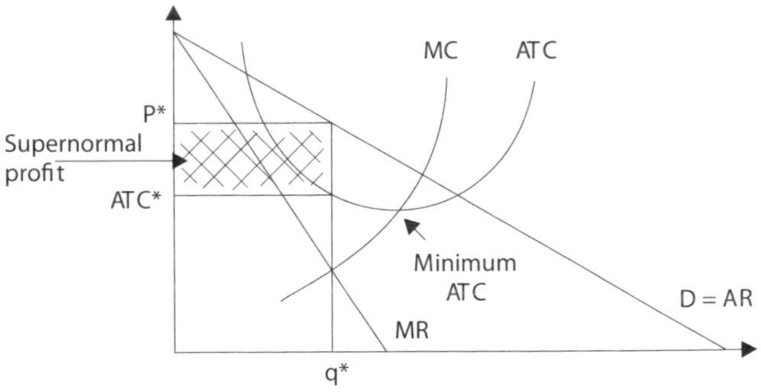

Monopolistic markets

Characteristics:

- A market with many competing companies, each making a product differentiated from that of other companies owing to branding and/or geographical fragmentation.
- Each company has a market for its version of the product and hence faces a downward sloping demand curve.
- In the short run companies can make supernormal profits. However, as there are no significant barriers to entry, new companies will be attracted into the industry in the long run. New entrants supply similar goods and take some of the customers of existing companies. Hence, their demand schedules shift to the left.

Monopoly

- A market that has a single producer of a good with no close substitutes.
- Usually due to barriers preventing other companies from entering the market.
- In the UK for legal purposes a monopoly is said to exist if a single company controls more than 25% of the market.

Monopoly and perfect competition compared

Monopoly	Perfect competition
Companies produce at cost higher than minimum ATC, therefore technically inefficient	Companies produce in long run at minimum ATC, therefore efficient
Supernormal profits persist in long run owing to barriers to entry	Only normal profits are made in long run (no barriers to entry)
Less is supplied (QM) at higher price (PM) than under perfect competition, therefore consumer may lose out – therefore allocatively inefficient	Consumer obtains lowest possible price with higher industry output
Consumer appears to lose out in monopoly, but benefits may exist	Hence, perfect competition appears best for consumer

Monopoly market structure

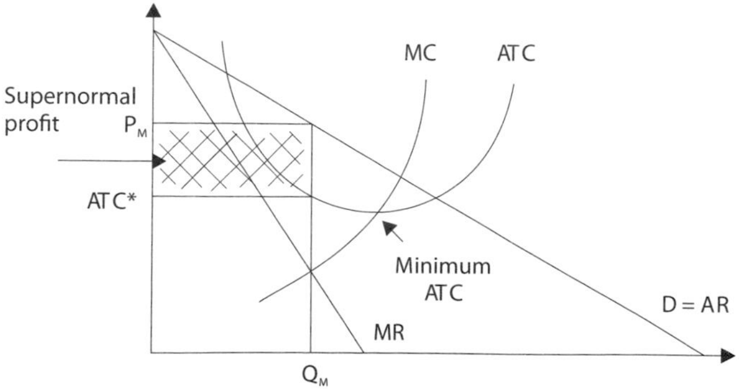

- A monopolist faces an industry demand curve, i.e. downward sloping, and sets output quantity at QM where MC = MR to maximise profits.
- A monopolist charges price PM determined by demand curve at quantity QM. As AR exceeds ATC the monopolist makes supernormal profits (shaded area) in the short and long run.

Mortgage

A loan to finance the purchase of property, usually with specified payment periods and interest rates. Characteristics of mortgages:

Returns	Interest
Risks	Lender usually expects security in the form of the asset (e.g. house) being bought. A fall in house prices would reduce the value of security offered (e.g. in the 1990s this gave rise to 'negative equity')
Timescales	Long term e.g. between 10 and 35 years
Liquidity	The mortgage cannot be resold by the lender to recover their funds but the borrower can repay the loan early, albeit with possible penalties

Multi-lateral trade agreements

Similar to bi-lateral agreements except more than two countries are involved, e.g. the North American Free Trade Agreement (NAFTA) between Canada, the United States and Mexico.

Multiple bar chart

Drawn where two or more related items are to be compared. The bars are placed next to each other and each represents a different item.

Multiplication law: dependent events

Two or more events are said to be dependent when the probability of the second event occurring is conditional upon the first event having taken place:
P(A and B) = P(A) × P(B given that A has occurred)
The probability that event B occurs given that A occurs is denoted by the symbol $P(B|A)$. The '$|$' is read as 'given' or 'if'.

* EXAMPLE *

A bag contains 3 black, 4 red and 13 blue marbles. The probability that if three are selected without replacement then they will be red, blue, black in that order is calculated as follows:
P(first red) = 4/20
P(second blue given first red) = 13/19
P(third black, given that the first two were red and blue) = 3/18

$$P(\text{red, blue, black}) = \frac{4}{20} \times \frac{13}{19} \times \frac{3}{18} =$$

156/6,840 = 13/570 (or 0.023)

Multiplication law: independent events

Two or more events are said to be independent if the occurrence or non-occurrence of one event does not affect the occurrence or non-occurrence of the other:
P(A and B) = P(A) × P(B)

* EXAMPLE *

The probability of drawing an ace from a pack of cards and throwing a 6 with an unbiased die is calculated as follows:
P(ace) = 4/52 P(6) = 1/6
∴ P(ace and 6) = P(ace) × P(6)
=1/13 × 1/6
= 1/78 (or 0.013)
The two events are independent because which card is drawn from the pack will have no influence on which number will be rolled by the die and vice versa.

Multiplier effect

The multiplier measures by how much more national income will increase relative to an initial increase in aggregate demand:

Increase in national income = 1/mps + mpt + mpm × increase in any type of expenditure

where mps = marginal propensity to save
(1 – mpc)
mpm = marginal propensity to import
mpt = marginal propensity to tax.

Note: 1/mps + mpt + mpm is known as the multiplier.

* EXAMPLE *

If an economy has an mpc of 0.8 and the government injects £500 million, the final increase in national income is:

Increase in national income = 1/ (1 - mpc) × increase in government investment
Increase in national income = 1 / (1 - 0.8) × £500 million = £2,500 million

Mutual organisations

Voluntary not-for-profit associations formed for the purpose of raising funds by subscriptions of members, out of which common services can be provided to those members. They include some building societies, trade unions and some working-men's clubs.

Name of company

The name in the Memorandum of Association is the company's legal name in which it will contract, sue and be sued. A company shall not be registered under the CA85 by a name:

- which includes otherwise than at the end of the name any of the following words and expressions limited, unlimited, or public limited company or their Welsh equivalents or abbreviations of any of those words or expressions
- which is the same as, or too like, a name appearing in the index of names which the Registrar is required to keep
- the use of which by the company would in the opinion of the Secretary of State constitute a criminal offence
- which in the opinion of the Secretary of State is offensive.

The company can change its name by passing a special resolution to that effect and presenting a signed copy of the resolution to the Registrar (with a fee).

Natural rate of unemployment

Monetarists recognise a concept called the natural rate of unemployment. Even if an economy is at capacity, significant unemployment can still exist due to imperfections in the labour market. These imperfections include:

- workers having the wrong skills relative to those demanded by the economy
- workers being located in the wrong place relative to economic activity
- workers having inadequate information about job opportunities
- occupational immobility due to trade unions and other restrictive working practices.

The natural rate of unemployment essentially has a structural cause. Boosting aggregate demand will do nothing to remove this problem. Inappropriate boosting of demand when the economy cannot respond for structural reasons will lead to inflation and will not decrease unemployment, i.e. stagflation.

Negative exponents

A number expressed to a negative exponent is equal to one over that number to a positive exponent. In general terms:

$$a^{-n} = \frac{1}{a^n}$$

* EXAMPLE *
$10^{-2} = 1/10^2$

Negative numbers

When a negative number is added to another number, the net effect is to subtract the negative number from the other number.

$$10 + (-4) = 10 - 4 = 6$$

When a negative number is subtracted from another number, the net effect is to add the negative number to the other number.

$$15 - (-10) = 15 + 10 = 25$$

When two negative numbers are multiplied or divided, the result is a positive number:

$$(-2) \times (-3) = +6$$
$$(-12) \div (-4) = +3$$

If there is only one negative number in a multiplication or division, the result is negative:

$$(-2) \times (-3) = -6$$
$$15 \div (-3) = -5$$

So, for multiplication or division: two negatives make a positive; one negative makes a negative.

Negligence

The tort of negligence has three essential elements:

- the existence of a duty of case
- breach of that duty
- loss arising as a result of that breach.

Negligent statements

In Hedley Byrne v Heller, the House of Lords first recognised liability for negligent statements causing economic loss made in circumstances where there exists a special relationship between the parties.

Net book value (NBV)

The difference between the gross cost (or valuation) of an asset and the depreciation charged to date. The remaining balance is the book value which appears in the balance sheet.

Net dividend yield

For equities a net dividend yield is calculated as follows:
Net dividend yield = (Annual dividend/Market value) × 100%
This figures looks only at the current dividend so does not incorporate future growth expectations.

Net National Product (NNP)

Neither GDP nor GNP take into account depreciation on capital assets. NNP is calculated by subtracting capital consumption (depreciation) from GNP:

GDP at factor cost
+
Net property income from abroad
=
GNP at factor cost
–
Capital consumption (depreciation)
=
NNP

Net present value (NPV) (C04)

A technique used to evaluate investment projects:
Step 1: Assess the relevant incremental cash flows for the decision.
Step 2: Discount the cash flows using an appropriate discount rate.
Step 3: Sum/net-off the different present values to give a net present value or NPV.
Step 4: If the NPV is >0, then the project should be accepted.

* EXAMPLE *

RST plc is considering the following investment. Machinery will be purchased for £100,000, used for three years and then disposed of for £20,000. Other incremental sales and costs have been estimated as follows:

(£000)	Year 1	Year 2	Year 3
Incremental sales	50	70	30
Incremental costs	(20)	(25)	(10)

RST plc has a cost of capital of 12%. To calculate the NPV of the project:

	Now	Year 1	Year 2	Year 3
Sales		50	70	30
Costs		(20)	(25)	(10)
Machine	(100)			20
	------	------	------	------
Net cash flow	(100)	30	45	40
Discount factor @ 12%	1	0.893	0.797	0.712
	------	------	------	------
Present values	(100)	26.8	35.9	28.5
	------	------	------	------
NPV	(8.8)			

The NPV is negative, indicating that the project returns do not cover the cost of capital and thus the project should be rejected. Accepting this project would see the value of the company (and hence shareholder wealth) decrease by £8,800.

Net profit percentage/Net profit margin

A measure of performance, expressed as (Net profit / Sales) × 100. This ratio extends the information given in the gross profit percentage to indicate the effect of other operating costs and revenues.

Net property income from abroad

The difference between income earned by UK residents on assets abroad and income earned by foreign residents on assets in the UK.

Net realisable value (NRV)

The amount for which any asset could be disposed, less any direct selling costs. Each individual item or each group of similar items of inventory should be stated in financial statements at the lower of cost and net realisable value. At the balance sheet date it is necessary to make a reasonable estimate of NRV.

Nominal ledger

The record that contains all of the accounts that are part of the double entry bookkeeping system.

Nominal value of shares (par value)

Each share usually has a stated nominal (or par) value. This has little practical significance except as a base line price below which further shares may not generally be issued.

Non-current assets

Acquired for retention by an entity for the purpose of providing a service to the business, and not held for resale in the normal course of trading. They may be tangible or intangible.

Non-profit objectives

These could include the following, for instance:

- maximisation of sales (while earning a 'reasonable' level of profit)
- growth (in sales, asset value, number of employees, etc)
- survival
- research and development leadership
- quality of service
- contented workforce
- respect for the environment.

Normal losses

Losses that are expected. They may be caused by many factors which are normal features of the process, e.g. evaporation, material wastage, sediment, quality control. Losses may have no value, a scrap value or a disposal cost. Since normal losses are unavoidable, their value is incorporated in the valuation of the output units.

Normal profit

The accounting profit which is just sufficient to cover the opportunity costs, i.e. the minimum profit required for the entrepreneur to stay in business.

Not-for-profit organisations (NFPs or NPOs)

Organisations whose primary objectives are unlikely to be financial. Instead they seek to satisfy the particular needs of their members, or the sections of society which they have been set up to benefit.

* EXAMPLE *

- Government departments and agencies (e.g. HM Revenue and Customs)
- Trade unions
- Schools
- Charities (e.g. Oxfam, Red Cross, Red Crescent, Caritas)
- Mutual associations (e.g. some building societies)

Notice

Can be by either party giving notice for the specified period.

Notice periods (The Law of Employment)

Continuous employment	*Minimum notice period*
1 month – 2 years	1 week
2 – 12 years	1 week per year
12 years +	12 weeks

Notice periods (Company administration and finance)

AGM	21 days	Less if every member entitled to attend and vote agrees.
EGM	14 days	Less if members holding at least 95% of shares agree. (Can be reduced to 90% in private companies.)
Special notice	28 days	Required for: • removal of director/auditor • appointment of over-age director (plc).

O

Obiter dicta

Obiter dicta (literally: other things that were said) are other statements of law that did not form the basis of the decision.

Objects clause

Sets out the business of the company. It is intended to provide a measure of protection for investors in that they are aware of what type of business they are investing in.

Objective classification of cost

Grouping cost according to the reason they are incurred, e.g. as direct or indirect costs.

Objectives

Statements of what the company wishes to achieve.

Objectivity

Accounting choices are often influenced by a desire to be as objective as possible. For instance, historical costs are often preferred over other valuations because historical costs are known with certainty and there is no scope for subjective judgement in their ascertainment.

Objectivity convention

Financial statements should be as objective as possible. Transactions are to be recorded objectively as historical events; this is the main basis of historical cost accounting. Certain aspects of historical cost accounting do, however, represent departures from the objectivity convention. For instance, although the depreciation charge is often based on the original cost of an asset (objective), it depends also on the estimated useful life and estimated scrap value at the end of that useful life (subjective).

Offer (in law)

A definite and unequivocal statement of willingness to be bound by contract. The offer must be open (i.e. still in force) when the offeree accepts it; when an offer has been terminated it can no longer be accepted. An offer is terminated by:

- revocation
- rejection
- lapse.

Off-the-shelf company

When a person has decided to incorporate his activities, he can either form a new company or buy one 'off-the-shelf', i.e. buy an existing company.

Office of Fair Trading

Monitors the UK economy looking for monopolies and anti-competitive practices. It has the power to refer companies to the Competition Commission, which took over from the Monopolies and Mergers Commission in 1998.

Offsetting

Assets and liabilities should not be offset except when required or permitted by an accounting standard. Items of income and expense should only be directly offset and reported as a net amount if a standard requires or permits it, or if they arise from similar transactions or events and are not material.

Oligopolies

Characteristics:

- The market is dominated by a few very large companies, surrounded by barriers to entry.
- Companies are interdependent, which creates a high degree of uncertainty.
- Price stability and non-price competition is common.
- One company may act as a price leader, setting the market price to which others then adhere.
- Companies often make a wide range of products for different markets.
- Companies may form a cartel and agree to fix prices and share markets. In effect, they act like a monopoly.

Open items

Unpaid invoices in either the sales ledger or the payables ledger.

Open market operations

By buying and selling its own bonds the government is able to exert some control over the money supply. For instance, by buying back its own bonds it will release more cash into circulation. Conversely, when it sells bonds it receives cash in return, reducing the amount of money in circulation and thus restricting the ability of banks to lend.

Opening work-in-process (AVCO)

If there is opening work-in-process opening inventory values are added to the current costs to provide an overall average cost per equivalent unit.

* EXAMPLE *

The input to Process A was 3,700 litres of material. There were opening stocks of 300 litres valued at $2,300 (this is made up of material of $1,000, labour of $500 and overhead of $800). Output was 3,800 litres and at the end of the period 200 litres were still in progress. There is no loss in process. Costs are $15,000 for direct materials, $7,420 for direct labour and $11,080 for absorbed production overhead. An estimate has been made of the degree of completion of the closing inventory.

Estimate of degree of completion:

Materials	100%	Complete
Labour	80%	Complete
Overhead	80%	Complete

To calculate the cost per equivalent unit and to write up the process account for the period, start by calculating the equivalent units of production. This is simply the expected units of output, allowing for the unfinished closing stock. The fact that there is now opening inventory does not affect this calculation as equivalent units are concerned with output.

	Total units	*Equivalent units*	
		Materials	*Labour and overhead*
Finished output	3,800	3,800	3,800
Closing work in progress	200	200	160
	4,000	4,000	3,960

* EXAMPLE *

A cost per equivalent unit can now be calculated and used to work out the value of finished output and closing work-in-process. The value of opening inventory is added to the cost incurred in the period.

	Materials	*Labour and overhead*
Cost – opening inventory	$1,000	$1,300
– added in the period	$15,000	$18,500
Total cost	$16,000	$19,800
Equivalent units	4,000	3,960
Cost per equivalent unit	$4	$5

		Materials		*Labour and overhead*	*Total*
		$		$	$
Finished output	(3,800 × $4)	15,200	(3,800 × $5)	19,000	34,200
Closing WIP	(200 × $4)	800	(160 × $5)	800	1,600
		16,000		19,800	35,800

The process account would be drawn up as follows:

Process account

	Units	$		*Units*	$
Opening inventory	300	2,300			
Direct material	3,700	15,000	Output	3,800	34,200
Direct labour		7,420	Closing WIP	200	1,600
Process overhead		11,080			
	4,000	35,800		4,000	35,800

Operating plans

Short-term tactics of the organisation.

Operating ratios

Measure profitability, such as gross profit percentage and return on capital employed.

Operations order (BEDMAS)

Remember the order of operations via the acronym BEDMAS. It is particularly important to know how to multiply out brackets.

Order of operations: BEDMAS	
1	**B**rackets
2	**E**xponents
3	**D**ivision and **M**ultiplication (left to right)
4	**A**ddition and **S**ubtraction (left to right)

Operators and symbols

+	Plus
–	Minus
±	Plus or minus (e.g. 'the answer is 18 ± 2' is a shorthand way of saying 'the answer is between 16 and 20')
x	Multiply
*	Multiply (e.g. used in spreadsheet formulae)
÷	Divide
/	Divide (also used in spreadsheet formulae)
Σ	Sum of
=	Equals
≡	Exactly equals
≠	Does not equal
≈	Approximately equals
<	Less than (e.g. 2<3; to remember which way round these go, think that < looks like the L in 'Less than')
>	Greater than (e.g. 3>2)
≤	Less than or equal to
≥	Equal to or greater than
x^y	x to the power of y
x^y	x to the power of y (e.g. in a spreadsheet formula)
√	Square root
∛	Cube root

Opportunity cost

The benefit forgone from the next best alternative.

* EXAMPLE *

A business might have the following income statement:

	£
Sales	100,000
Cost of sales	(60,000)
Profit	40,000

The accounting profit for the company is £40,000. The entrepreneur could earn £30,000 elsewhere, receive £6,000 interest on the capital invested in the business and requires a risk premium for investing in the business of £4,000.

The opportunity cost is £40,000 in total.

An economist would report the profit for the business as follows:

	£
Sales	100,000
Cost of sales	(60,000)
Profit	40,000
	0

Ordinary shares/ Equity shares

The normal shares issued by a company. Ordinary shareholders usually have the right to vote at company meetings and to receive dividends from profits. They are the real owners of the business because they bear the risks and enjoy the rewards associated with the business' success or failure.

Ordinary shares ('equity')

Shares have a nominal or par value which is usually different from the market value if quoted. Characteristics of ordinary shares:

Returns	Potentially very high returns Dividends (decided by the directors) Increasing share value
Risks	High risk Danger of zero or low dividends Fall in share value Last in line in the event of the company being liquidated
Time-scales	Company usually has no intention of buying back the shares
Liquidity	For unquoted companies it is very difficult to sell the shares For quoted companies the shares are highly liquid

Organisation controls

The provision of clear lines of reporting and responsibility so that the system can be properly supervised.

Organisations

Social arrangements for the controlled performance of collective goals.

Output tax

VAT collected on sales.

Outstanding deposits

Listed when the bank reconciliation statement is prepared. These are lodgements that have been recorded in the cash book but that have not had a chance to go through the bank's record-keeping system in time to appear on the bank statement. Any long-delayed outstanding lodgements would be investigated as suspicious.

Overhead absorption

The attribution of total production cost centre overhead to the cost unit.

Overhead absorption rate (OAR)

An absorption rate is calculated based upon budgeted costs and activity levels:

$$OAR = \frac{\text{Budgeted cost}}{\text{Budgeted activity level}}$$

A number of activity measures may be used, the most common being labour hours or machine hours depending on the extent to which the departmental activity is automated.

Overhead allocation

Overhead allocation occurs when whole costs can be related to a cost centre, e.g. the machine shop supervisor's cost can be wholly related to the machine shop.

Overhead apportionment

Apportionment is the sharing of common costs amongst the cost centres benefiting from the resource on an equitable basis. Each cost should be shared relative to the benefit obtained by each cost centre.

* EXAMPLE *

There are three departments in a factory:

Dept A occupies	2,000	square feet
Dept B occupies	2,500	square feet
Dept C occupies	500	square feet
	5,000	

The annual factory rent is £40,000. This is shared between the departments:

$$A \quad \$40{,}000 \times \frac{2{,}000}{5{,}000} = \$16{,}000$$

$$B \quad \$40{,}000 \times \frac{2{,}500}{5{,}000} = \$20{,}000$$

$$C \quad \$40{,}000 \times \frac{500}{5{,}000} = \$4{,}000$$

Overtime premium

The additional amount paid over and above the normal hourly rate for overtime hours.

* EXAMPLE *

If a worker is paid $10 per hour and overtime is paid at time and a half the overtime premium is £5.

P

Paid up share capital

The amount of nominal value of the issued share capital that is paid at the current date. The personal liability of the shareholders for the company's debts is limited to any unpaid amount of the issued share capital.

Paradox of thrift

Describes how, in an economy where people planned to save more, the economy would finish up saving less. This is because to save more out of a given income involves spending less. This would reduce money incomes via the multiplier process and therefore result in a lower level of savings in total.

Pareto charts

Used to highlight key areas for management.

* EXAMPLE *

Delays from a warehousing department:

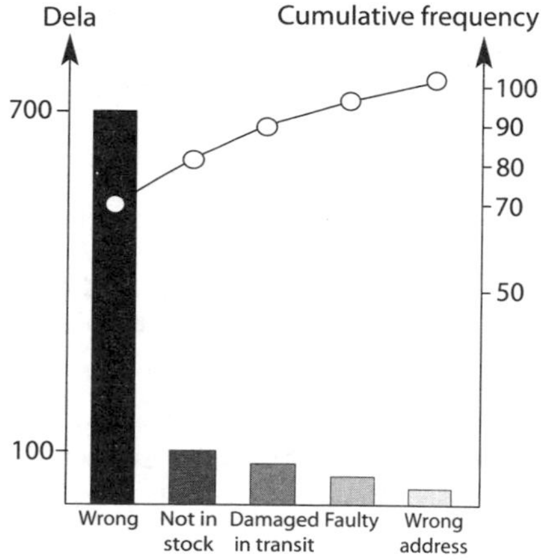

The cumulate frequency shows that 80% of delays are due to just two causes. Focusing on these first will ensure maximum management efficiency.

Pareto distribution and the '80:20' rule

Named after Vilfredo Pareto who, in the late 18th century, studied the distribution of wealth in Europe and found that 80% of the wealth was held by 20% of the population. The 80:20 aspect of this has been encapsulated into the '80:20' rule which has many variations, including:

- 80% of a company's business comes from 20% of its customers
- 80% of process defects arise from 20% of the process issues.

Parliament

Parliament consists of the House of Lords and the House of Commons.

Partnership

The relationship which subsists between persons carrying on a business in common with a view of profit. A partnership is not a separate person and so it is the partners personally who:

- own property
- are party to contracts
- are liable if sued.

Part-payment

Payment of a lesser sum in satisfaction of a greater sum cannot be satisfaction for the whole sum.

* EXAMPLE *

A creditor who agrees to accept £50 from a debtor in payment and satisfaction of a debt for £100, does not receive any benefit for his promise not to claim the balance; consequently the creditor's promise is unenforceable at common law.

Past consideration (in law)

If one party makes a promise in return for an act or promise which has already been performed unilaterally, the two promises are not a response to one another and do not support a contract. Past consideration is insufficient.

Payables ledger

Independent of the double entry bookkeeping system, it contains an account for each and every supplier. It is kept up to date using the detailed entries on the various day books dealing with credit purchases, returns to suppliers and cash payments. The balances according to the payables ledger should be totalled regularly and these should agree to the balance on the payables ledger control account.

Payables ledger control account

In the general ledger and part of the double entry bookkeeping system. It is kept up to date using the totals from the various day books dealing with credit purchases, returns to suppliers and cash payments. This gives the total due to suppliers and should be agreed to the total of the balances according to the payables ledger.

PAYE/NI control account

UK businesses must collect tax (PAYE and NI) from their employees. They pay the net sum left to the employees and the tax collected to HM Revenue & Customs (HMRC). The PAYE/NI control account is used to keep track of the amounts collected and due to be paid to HMRC.

Pension fund

An entity which administers a business' pension scheme. The fund takes cash from the company, invests it and uses the proceeds to pay pensions to retired employees.

Percentages

'Percent' means 'out of 100'. The rule is:

- to convert a fraction into a percentage, multiply the fraction by 100
- to convert a percentage into a fraction, divide by 100, e.g.:

$$40\% = \frac{40}{100}$$

$$2\tfrac{1}{2}\% = \frac{2\tfrac{1}{2}}{100}$$

*** EXAMPLE ***

Equipment is sold for £240 and makes a profit of 20% on cost. What is the cost price? What is the profit? Whatever the percentage is 'on' or 'of' is 100%. In this case we are told that profit is 20% on cost.

If cost price = 100%

and profit = <u>20%</u> (as it is 20% of cost)

Selling price = <u>120%</u> of cost

120% of cost = £240

$\therefore$ 100% of cost $= \frac{£240}{120} \times 100$

Cost price = £200

$\therefore$ Profit = £240 – £200

= £40

The figure of 20% on cost is usually referred to as a 'mark-up'.

Percentage component bar chart

A component bar chart in which the component values are expressed and drawn as percentages of the bar total. Each bar will have the same total height, representing 100%.

Perfect competition

Key assumptions:

- Infinitely large number of buyers and sellers, none of whom alone can influence the market price.
- Homogeneous/identical product.
- Free entry to/exit from the market place in the long run.
- No economic friction, i.e. factors affect only some individuals.
- Free access to perfect information on all market conditions.
- In addition, companies seek to maximise profits.

Perfect competition in the long run

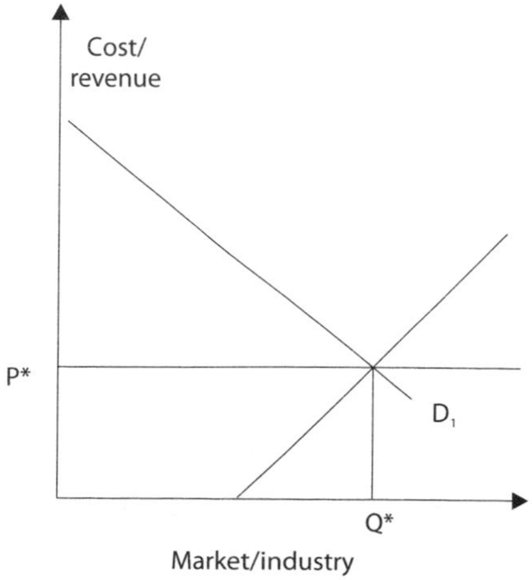

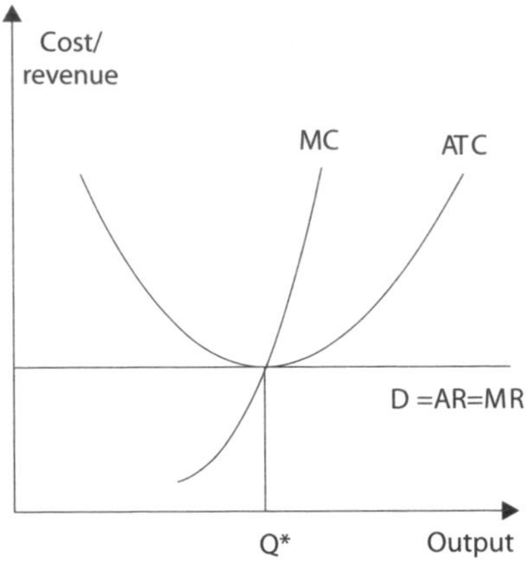

Firm

- Market price P* is determined by interaction of industry supply and demand.
- Companies perceive a perfectly elastic demand at price P* and produce output quantity Q* where MC = MR to maximise profits.
- Companies make only normal profits as ATC = AR. Therefore, there is no incentive for companies to enter or leave the industry in the long run.
- Companies produce efficiently, i.e. where ATC is minimised.

Perfect competition in the short run

Whilst normal profits represent the long-term position for perfect competition, it is possible for supernormal profits to be earned in the short term. This is shown in the diagram below:

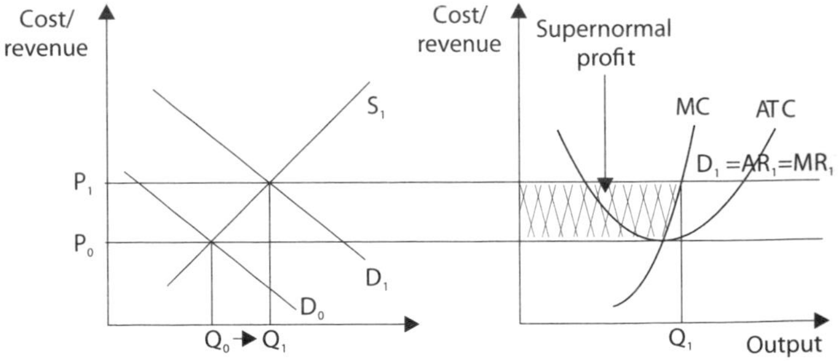

Market/industry

Firm

Performance (in law)

The general rule is that a contract is discharged by performance only when both parties have complied fully and exactly with the terms of the contract. A party who has substantially performed his contractual duties in the manner stipulated may recover the agreed price, less a deduction by way of a claim for damages in respect of duties not properly executed. This is an equitable exception to the rule of full performance.

Permissible capital payment

A private company limited by shares or limited by guarantee and having a share capital, if authorised to do so by its Articles, may redeem or purchase its own shares out of capital through a permissible capital payment, but only to the extent that its distributable profits (and proceeds of a new issue, if any) are insufficient.

Perpetuity

An annuity that continues forever. Such cash flows are rare in reality but a perpetuity is often used as an approximation for a very long annuity. A perpetuity discount factor is given by the simple formula:

Perpetuity factor = 1 / r

* EXAMPLE *

£500 received per annum in perpetuity with a discount rate of 10% has a present value of:

Present value = 500 × 1/0.10 = 500 × 10
= £5,000

Perpetual inventory

The recording **as they occur** of receipts, issues, and the resulting balances of individual items of inventory in either quantity or quantity and value.

Perpetuities

A periodic payment continuing for a limitless period. Referring back to the formula for the annuity discount factor:

$$\frac{1}{r} - \frac{1}{r(1+r)^t}$$

If t gets very large (tends to infinity) the second term gets very small, and will be zero at t = infinity.
Thus the perpetuity discount factor is 1/r.

Personnel controls

The selection and training of staff so that their abilities match up to their responsibilities.

Petty cash system

The system used to record cash payments. Not to be confused with the 'cash system' which is often associated with receipts and payments involving the bank.

Phillips Curve

Research by Phillips indicated that there is an inverse relationship between inflation and unemployment, i.e. during periods of low inflation unemployment is high and vice versa. This was subsequently discredited due to the stagflation which occurred in the 1970s.

The Phillips Curve

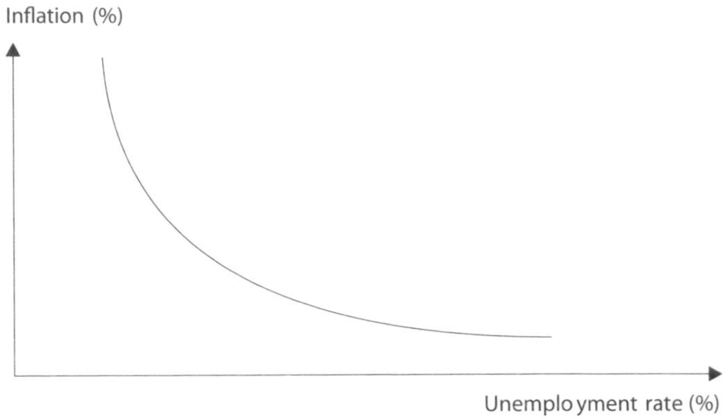

Physical (or operating) capital maintenance

The concept that profit is earned only if the physical productive capacity (or operating capability) of the enterprise at the end of the period exceeds the physical productive capacity at the beginning of the period, after excluding any distributions to, and contributions from, owners during the period. In other words, the profit of a manufacturing company would be calculated by taking into account the physical quantity of inventory at the beginning and end of the year and also the condition of non-current assets at the beginning and end of the year. More wear and tear will lead to a smaller profit.

Physical controls

The restriction of access to records and assets to prevent theft and forgery by those who are not authorised for access.

Pictograms

Pictures (or symbols) that can readily be associated with the data under consideration. One picture or symbol is used to represent a unit of the variable.

* EXAMPLE *

The following pictogram represents the car sales for British Mayland for the three consecutive years 20X1 to 20X3:

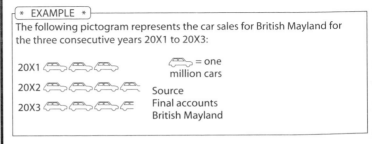

Pie charts

Usually drawn when the proportion of each class to the whole is important, rather than the absolute value of each class. A circle is drawn, and divided into sectors such that the area of each sector is proportionate to the size of the figure represented.

* EXAMPLE *

The following pie chart represents the proportion of each type of grain produced in Disney Land in the year 20X5:

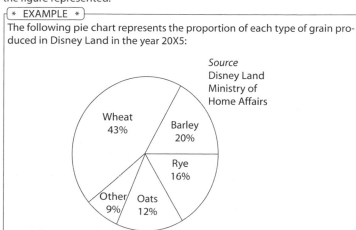

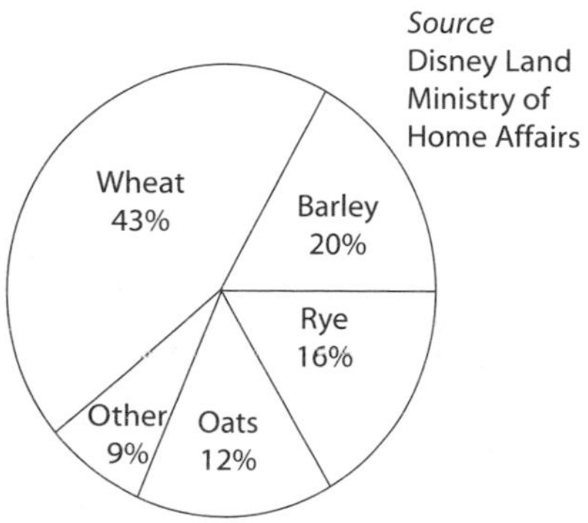

Piecework

Piecework schemes pay workers for each item of good output produced. There may be a guaranteed minimum wage.

Pillars of Islam

Sharia law regulates all human actions and puts them into five categories. The ultimate worth of an action is based on the individual's intention and sincerity.

- Obligatory actions must be performed and, when performed with good intentions, are rewarded.
- Forbidden actions are the opposite of obligatory actions.
- Recommended actions (or meritorious actions) are those that should be done.
- Disliked actions (or reprehensible actions) are the opposite of recommended actions.
- Permitted actions are those that are neither encouraged nor discouraged. Most human actions fall into this last category.

Planning process

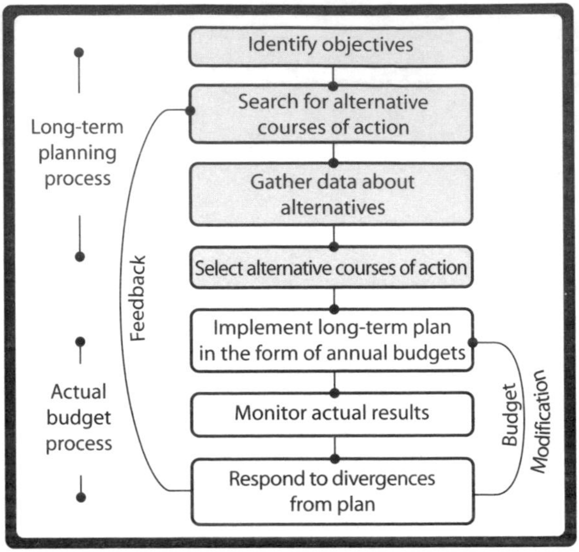

Postal rule (in law)

The communication of acceptance will be complete and effective when the letter is posted. Only applies when acceptance by post is either the chosen, obvious or reasonable method of acceptance. The letter must be properly stamped addressed and posted. Handing a letter to a postman who is authorised to deliver is not equivalent in law to posting a letter.

Power of a power

When a power is raised to a power the powers are multiplied. In general terms:

$(a^m)^n = a^{m \times n}$

* EXAMPLE *

$(10^2)^3 = 10^{(2 \times 3)}$

Power of a product

A product is the result of two numbers multiplied together. When taking a power of a product the exponent should be applied to each factor of the product. In general terms:

$(3ab)^m = 3^m a^m b^m$

* EXAMPLE *

$(10 \times 2)^2 = 10^2 \times 2^2$

Power of a quotient

A quotient is the result of one number divided by another. When taking a power of a quotient the exponent should be applied to both the numerator and the denominator.

* EXAMPLE *

$(10 \div 2)^2 = 10^2 \div 2^2$

Power of one

Any number expressed to the power of one is equal to that number.

* EXAMPLE *

$10^1 = 10$

Powers – division

When dividing a power of a number by another power of the same number the exponents are subtracted. In general terms:
$a^m \div a^n = a^{(m-n)}$

* EXAMPLE *

$(10^5 \div 10^2) = 10^{5-2}$

Powers – multiply

When two or more powers of the same number are multiplied the individual exponents can be added. In general terms:
$a^{m} \times a^n = a^{(m+n)}$

* EXAMPLE *

$(10^2 \times 10^3) = 10^{(2+3)}$

Powers and roots

When equal numbers are multiplied together the result is known as a power and is denoted by a superscript to the right of such a number.

* EXAMPLE *

$10^2 = 10 \times 10 = 100$ (100 is the 'second power of' 10, or 10 to the power of 2)

A number raised to the power of 2 is said to be squared, and if raised to the power of 3 is said to be cubed. A power (or root) is also called an 'exponent'.

Pre-emption rights

To safeguard the position of existing shareholders, no company can allot equity securities without first offering them pro rata to existing equity shareholders on the same or more favourable terms than it is proposing to offer them to other people. The shareholders must be given 21 days in which to decide whether to accept or reject the offer.

Preference

A company gives a preference if it does anything to put a creditor in a better position in the event of the company's insolvent liquidation than he would otherwise be. The liquidator (or administrator) may apply to the court to set aside the preference. The court will only set it aside if the company is insolvent and the preference was made within the relevant period which is within:

- two years of the onset of insolvency if the preference is given to a connected person
- six months of the onset of insolvency if the preference was given to other persons.

The preference will not be set aside unless, at the time it was made, the company was unable to pay its debts or became unable to pay its debts as a result.

Preference shares (preferred shares)

Shares carrying a fixed rate of dividend, the holders of which have a prior claim to any company profits available for distribution.

Pre-incorporation contract

Made by a person on behalf of or purporting to be the company at a date prior to that on the company's certificate of incorporation. A company cannot be bound by a contract that was made on its behalf by any person (including a promoter) before the company itself had been formed. A company cannot, after its formation, ratify a contract to which it could not have been a party when the contract was made.

Prepaid expenses

An item of expense that has been paid during the current accounting period, but relates to the next accounting period. The cost shown in the income statement should comprise only costs incurred in respect of the present period. Prepaid expenses should be removed from operating expenses and carried forward in the balance sheet as current assets.

Present value (PV)

The main implication of the time value of money is that cash flows at different times cannot be compared directly. Instead they need to be converted to their equivalent value at the same time:
Present value = Future cash flow x Discount factor

* EXAMPLE *

The present value of £110 received in one year's time at an interest rate of 10% is: $110 \times 0.909 = 100$

So present value is the cash equivalent now of a sum receivable or payable at a future date. The general formula for the present value (PV) of an amount A receivable/payable in n years' time at a discount rate of r% (as a decimal) is:

$$PV = \frac{A}{(1+r)^n}$$

The PV of an amount A receivable in n years' time is thus defined as that amount that must be invested now at r% pa to accumulate to A at the expiry of n years.

* EXAMPLE *

Calculate the present value of £2,000 at 10% pa for 1 year, 2 years, or 3 years.

1 year:	PV	= 2000/(1+0.1)	= 2000/1.1
			= £1,818.18
2 years:	PV	= $2000/(1+0.1)^2$	= $2000/1.1^2$
			= £1,652.89
3 years:	PV	= $2000/(1+0.1)^3$	= $2000/1.1^3$
			= £1,502.63

This means that £1,818.18 must be invested now to yield £2,000 in one year's time, £1,652.89 must be invested now to yield £2,000 in two years' time, etc.

Present value tables

Because discounting is so widely used in business problems, PV tables are available to shortcut the computations. They provide a value (the 'discount factor') for a range of years and discount rates. Thus, the discount factor is the factor by which the future sum (A) is multiplied to get its present value:

$1/(1+r)^n$

where r is the discount rate
n is the number of years

Note the timescale:

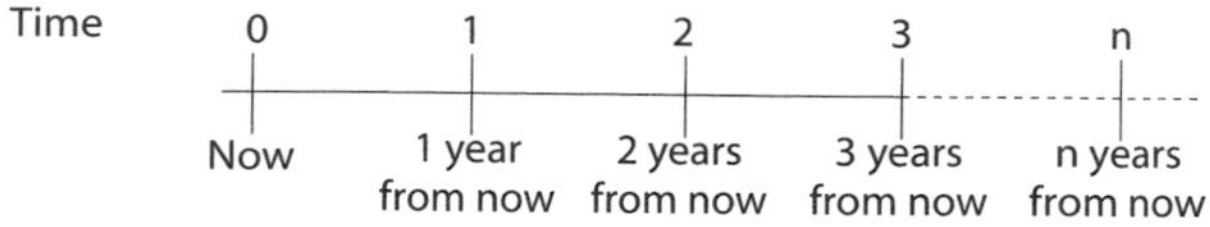

*** EXAMPLE ***

Calculate the present value of the given cash flows using a 15% discount rate.

Time	Cash flow £	Discount factor	PV £
0	(60,000)	1.000	(60,000)
1	(10,000)	0.870	(8,700)
2	15,000	0.756	11,340
3	20,000	0.658	13,160
4	20,000	0.572	11,440
5	20,000	0.497	9,940
6	20,000	0.432	8,640

Price Elasticity of Demand (PED)

Measures how responsive demand is to change in price. It is calculated as follows:

PED = %ΔDemand / %ΔPrice

It is convention to ignore the sign of PED as it is almost always negative.

PED is determined by a number of factors, including:

- Availability and closeness of substitutes, i.e. if readily available or close substitutes exist, then demand will tend to be much more elastic.
- Proportion of income accounted for by the good. This will also be related to the level of income. If a good accounts for a large proportion of income, demand will tend to be elastic; if it accounts for only a small proportion, demand will be much less elastic.
- Time: generally in the short run demand tends to be much less elastic, while in the long run it tends to be much more elastic.
- Nature of product: in the case of durable products demand tends to be more elastic, with perishable products less elastic.

Relationship between elasticity and total revenue when price changes

Elastic demand PED>1	Price increase	Revenue falls
Elastic demand PED>1	Price decrease	Revenue rises
Inelastic demand PED<1	Price increase	Revenue rises
Inelastic demand PED<1	Price decrease	Revenue falls

Price Elasticity of Supply (PES)

Measures how sensitive supply is to change in price.

$PES = \%\Delta Supply / \%\Delta Price$

Determinants of the price elasticity of supply

The primary determinant of elasticity of supply is the cost of making one more unit (the marginal cost). Factors related to this include:

1. Availability/production of stocks.
2. Availability of excess/spare capacity.
3. Time period:short run – generally inelastic
   long run – generally elastic (compare with costs).
4. Nature of production process:
   - factors readily available: more elastic
   - factors not readily available: less elastic.

   Availability influenced by:
   - degrees of specialisation
   - degree of substitutions between factors (NB: joint supply).

Primary markets

Securities are issued in primary markets.

Prime cost

The total of all of the direct costs (direct materials, labour and expenses) of production.

Principal-agent problem

Shareholders delegate control to professional managers, i.e. the board of directors, to run the company on their behalf. Thus shareholders normally play a passive role in the day-to-day management of the company. The resulting separation of ownership and control leads to a potential conflict of interests between directors and shareholders. This conflict is an example of the principal-agent problem. The principals (the shareholders) have to find ways of ensuring that their agents (the managers) act in their interests.

Principal budget factor/limiting factor

The factor that places a limit on the activities of the organisation.

Priority of charges

In the event of winding up, the priority of charges is as follows:

- Equal charges – first created has priority.
- Fixed charge – priority over floating charge.
- An unregistered registrable charge has no priority over a registered charge.
- A chargee can prohibit the creation of later a charge with priority, but the prohibition is only effective if the subsequent chargee has notice of the prohibition as well as the charge.

Private company

Any company that is not a public company.

Private law

Governs the relationship of individuals between themselves. Examples of private law are company law, the law of tort and the law of contract.

Private sector

The part of a nation's economy that is not controlled by the government. It includes businesses, charities and clubs. Within these will be both profit-seeking and not-for-profit organisations.

Privity of contract

A contract creates a personal obligation and only the original contracting parties can acquire enforceable rights or be subject to legal liabilities under it: Dunlop Pneumatic Tyre Co v Selfridge. date? However, the Contract (Rights of Third Parties) Act 1999 states that a person who is not a party to the contract (a third party) may in his own right enforce a term of the contract if the contract contains an express term which states that he can and the term confers a benefit on him.

Probability

Measured on a scale from 0 to 1, where 0 represents impossibility and 1 represents certainty. The probability of event 'A' occurring is represented by the symbol P(A).

* EXAMPLE *

An ordinary pack of playing cards consists of 52 cards. If the pack is well shuffled and one card is selected at random, the following probabilities can be calculated:

(a) the card is the ace of clubs
(b) the card is a king.

When a card is selected at random, there are 52 equally likely outcomes.

(a) P(ace of clubs) = 1/52 because there is only one ace of clubs in the pack.
(b) P(king) = 4/52 (or (1/13) because there are four kings in a pack.

Probability trees

Another useful way to break down complex problems is to use a probability tree – a diagram that sets out all the possibilities.

* EXAMPLE *

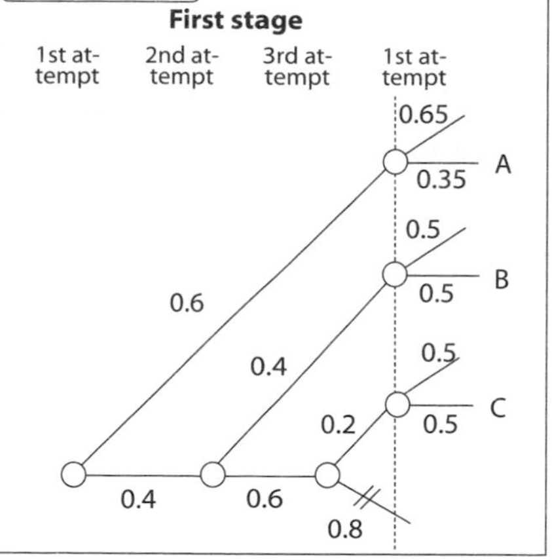

Process costing

Process costing has the following features:

- It is used where identical units of product are produced from a continuous process.
- Output from one process may be input into the next process.
- Losses may be inherent in the process, due to wastage, evaporation, scrap, etc.
- Partially completed units are valued using the concept of equivalent units.

Output is valued by averaging net cost over the expected output of the process (input less normal loss).

$$\text{Cost per output unit} = \frac{\text{Total process costs incurred - Scrap value of normal loss}}{\text{Expected output units}}$$

Production budget

Derived from the sales budget as follows:

		Product X	*Product Y*
Sales		1,000	200
Add:	closing inventory finished goods	200	40
Less:	opening inventory finished goods	(150)	(60)
		———	———
Production		1,050	180
		———	———

Production overhead control account

The costs of production overheads incurred are debited to the production overheads account, e.g. indirect materials, indirect production labour and indirect production expenses. The total cost of overheads incurred is therefore built up on the debit side of the account.

Absorbed overheads are charged to production. This is recorded by crediting the production overhead account and debiting work in progress.

Any difference between overheads incurred (debit) and overheads absorbed (credit) are recorded as the balancing item in the account. This balancing item is the amount of overhead under-absorbed or over-absorbed.

* EXAMPLE *

In June a manufacturing company incurred indirect production materials costs of $5,800 and indirect labour costs of $6,400. Indirect expenses were $17,500. Overheads are absorbed on a direct labour hour basis at $20 per hour. During the period, 1,550 direct labour hours were worked.

* EXAMPLE *

The production overhead account for June would look like this:

Production overhead			
	$		$
Raw materials inventory	5,800	Work in progress (1,550 × $20)	31,000
Wages and salaries	6,400		
Cost ledger control	17,500		
Income statement	1,300		
	31,000		31,000

Here, overheads incurred are $29,700 and overheads absorbed are $31,000, so there is over-absorbed overhead of $1,300.

Profit and cash

Profit and cash flows can be very different. For instance, a business could have a substantial profit and still suffer a large cash outflow because of cash transactions that are not reflected in the profit calculation (such as the acquisition of non-current assets, the repayment of loans, and so on).

Profit centre

The manager is responsible for revenue and costs. Performance is measured by comparing profit earned against budgeted profit.

Profit maximisation

Maximum profit occurs at the output level where MC = MR (marginal cost = marginal revenue). This does not always coincide with the point of lowest average total cost.

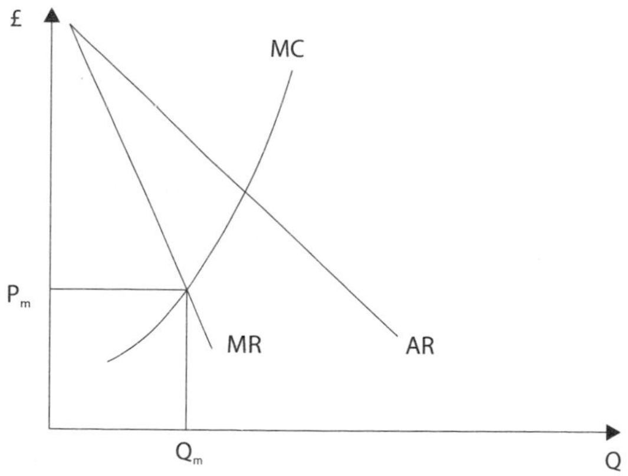

Graph showing profit maximisation
Q_m is the profit-maximising output; P_m is the profit-maximising price

Profit-seeking organisations

Organisations, such as companies and partnerships, that see their main objective as maximising the wealth of their owners. The objective of wealth maximisation is usually expanded into three primary objectives:

- to continue in existence (survival)
- to maintain growth and development
- to make a profit.

Profits available for distribution

Accumulated, realised profits so far as not previously utilised (whether by distribution or capitalisation) less accumulated, realised losses, so far as not previously written off.

Profit/Volume chart

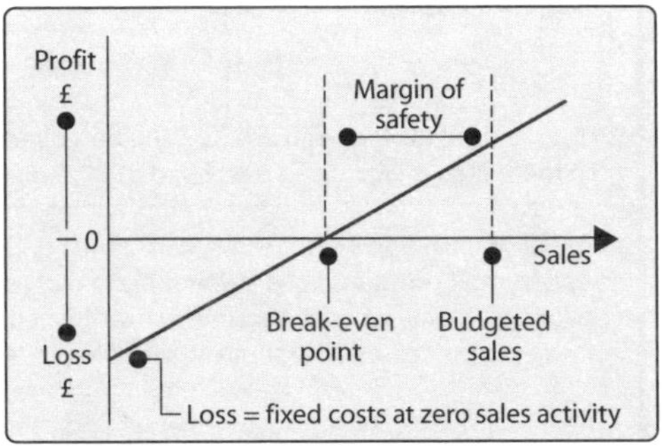

Progressive taxes

These are taxes where the proportion of tax paid increases with wealth or income.

Promissory estoppel

The equitable concept of estoppel, referred to as promissory estoppel, may operate to prevent a person going back on his promise to accept a lesser amount, at least for a period of time. It must be clear that one party has made an unequivocal representation whether by words or conduct, which he intends the other party to rely upon.

Promoter

A person who undertakes to form a company with reference to a given project and to set it going, and who takes the necessary steps to accomplish that purpose: Twycross v Grant (1877).

Proportional taxes

These are taxes where the proportion of tax paid stays the same regardless of wealth or income.

Proportions

Describe the relationship of some part of a whole to the whole itself and are usually given as a fraction.

* EXAMPLE *

In a class there are 20 girls and 10 boys. The ratio of girls to boys is 2:1. The proportion of girls in the class is 20 out of 30 or 2/3.

Protectionism

Many countries do not engage in free trade but seek, through a variety of mechanisms, to restrict the flow of imports into the domestic economy. National governments provide a number of 'justifications' for this behaviour:

- protection of infant industries that have yet to gain scale economies
- protection of declining industries to buy time for structural readjustment
- protection of domestic markets from heavily subsidised overseas production
- prevention of over-specialisation for strategic reasons (e.g. most countries would feel uneasy if totally dependent on imports for food as they could be cut off in the event of war)
- prevention of a huge balance of payments deficit.

Protectionist policies (e.g. quotas, tariffs, embargoes, exchange and administrative controls) often backfire on governments as the countries whose imports are involved will often retaliate with similar restrictions. The costs involved in operating a protectionist trade policy can also be high.

Proxy

Used both to denote a person authorised to vote on behalf of a member and the paper or proxy card that gives them that authority.

Prudence

Refers to caution when making estimates under conditions of uncertainty, so that income and assets are not overstated and expenses and liabilities are not understated.

Public company

A company limited by shares (or limited by guarantee and having a share capital), being a company:

- the Memorandum of which states that the company is to be a public company
- in relation to which the provisions of the Companies Act as to the registration or re-registration of a company as a public company have been complied with – in particular the requirement relating to a minimum authorised share capital of £50,000.

A newly incorporated public company needs to obtain a trading certificate.

Public goods

- Have the property of non-excludability, i.e. a person can benefit from the good without having to pay for it (the free rider concept).
- Provision of the good for one member of society automatically allows the rest of society to benefit also.
- Consumption of the good by one person does not reduce the amount available for consumption by others.
- Consequently, a market for this type of goods does not exist and would not be produced without government intervention, e.g. street lighting.

Public law

Governs the relationship between the individual and the state. Examples of public law are international law, constitutional and administrative law and the criminal law.

Public sector

The part of a nation's economy concerned with providing basic government services and thus controlled by government organisations. In most countries the public sector includes such services as the police, military, public roads, public transit, primary education and healthcare for the poor.

Public Sector Net Cash Requirement (PSNCR)

Government borrowing required to fund a budget deficit.

Purchase return

Goods returned to a supplier. Purchase returns are usually offset against purchases in calculating cost of sales in the income statement.

Purchases day book

Used to record credit purchases. Each transaction is shown at its net, VAT and gross total. The individual purchases are entered gross in the relevant accounts of the payables ledger. The total for gross purchases is credited to the payables ledger control account. Net purchases are debited to purchases and VAT is debited to the VAT account.

Purchases returns day books

Used to record returns to suppliers. Each transaction is shown at its net, VAT and gross total. The individual returns are entered gross in the relevant accounts of the payables ledger. The total for gross returns is debited to the payables ledger control account. Net purchases are credited to purchases and VAT is credited to the VAT account.

Purchases system

The system used to authorise and record the purchase of inventory, balances due to suppliers and final payment of amounts due.

Purchasing power parity

An exchange rate set by considering the amount of each currency needed to buy a standard basket of goods in each country.

* EXAMPLE *

If the price of corn were £100/tonne in one country and $200 in another, and this is the only good traded, it would seem reasonable to conclude that the exchange rate must be £1 = $2 (i.e. based on the relative prices of the traded commodities).

Q

Quadratic equations

A quadratic expression that is set to be equal to zero, e.g. $x^2 + 3x = -2$ can be re-arranged as a quadratic equation: $x^2 + 3x + 2 = 0$
In an equation like this there may be two values of x that satisfy the equation. These are called the roots of the equation.

Quadratic equations – solving by factorisation

If a quadratic expression can be seen to factorise, then this gives a quick and neat way of solving the equation.

Quadratic equations – solving by formulae

Consider the general quadratic equation:
$ax^2 + bx + c = 0$
There is a formula for solving this (given in the exam) as follows:

$$x = \frac{-b \pm \sqrt{b^2 - 4ac}}{2a}$$

The most important part of this formula is
$b^2 - 4ac$. There are three possibilities:

(a) If $b^2 - 4ac$ is zero there is only one solution to the quadratic equation.
(b) If $b^2 - 4ac$ is positive there are two distinct solutions to the quadratic equation.
(c) If $b^2 - 4ac$ is negative there are no real solutions to the quadratic equation since it is not possible to take the square root of a negative number.

* EXAMPLE *

$(x + 3)^2 = 25$
$(x + 3)^2 = 25$ but $(x + 3)(x + 3) = x^2 + 6x + 9$
$\therefore x^2 + 6x + 9 = 25$
$x^2 + 6x + 9 - 25 = 0$
$x^2 + 6x - 16 = 0$ so, $a = 1, b = 6, c = -16$

then $x = \dfrac{-6 \pm \sqrt{6^2 - 4 \times 1 \times (-16)}}{2 \times 1}$

$= \dfrac{-6 + \sqrt{100}}{2}$

$= \dfrac{-6 + 100}{2}$

$= \dfrac{4}{2}$, i.e. 2 or $-\dfrac{16}{2}$, i.e. -8

Quadratic function graphs

* EXAMPLE *

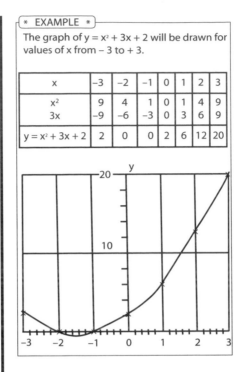

The graph of $y = x^2 + 3x + 2$ will be drawn for values of x from – 3 to + 3.

x	–3	–2	–1	0	1	2	3
x^2 3x	9 –9	4 –6	1 –3	0 0	1 3	4 6	9 9
$y = x^2 + 3x + 2$	2	0	0	2	6	12	20

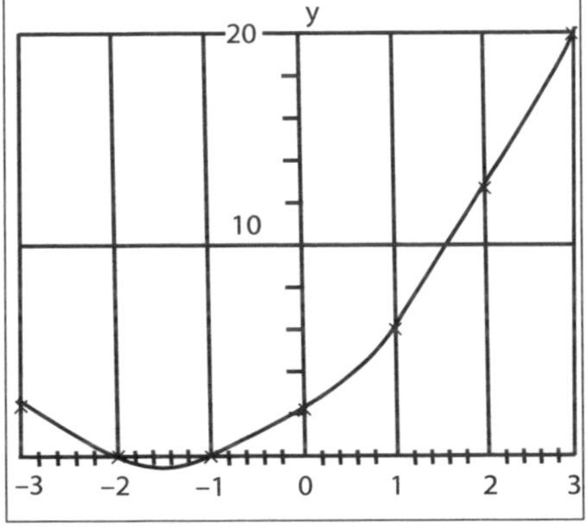

Quantity Theory of Money

MV = PT

M = money supply
V = velocity of circulation (frequency with which money is spent)
P = average price of a transaction
T = volume of transactions

In a given period monetarists believe that V is constant. T is also constant as it is limited by the supply of goods and services in the economy. Therefore, if the money supply increases quickly, for the equation to remain in balance P has to increase, i.e. inflation occurs.

QuickBooks®

A proprietary piece of accounting software, primarily intended for relatively small enterprises.

Quorum

The minimum number of persons whose presence is required in order that a meeting may validly conduct business.

Quotas

Imposition of a maximum number of units that can be imported, e.g. quotas on the number of cars manufactured outside of Europe that can be imported into the EU.

R

Range

By far the simplest measure of dispersion, being the difference between the extreme values of the distribution.

Range = Highest value – Lowest value

Ratio analysis

It is normally easier to derive useful information from a set of financial statements if ratios are calculated to show the relationships between the figures, e.g. profit means very little unless it can be compared with capital employed for instance.

Ratio decidendi

Ratio decidendi (literally: the reason for the decision) is the statement of law on which the judges based their decision.

Ratios

Show how something should be divided up or shared. The relative shares are usually (but not necessarily) expressed as whole numbers (integers) and they are separated by a colon, e.g. 2:5:7.

Dividing in a given ratio
To divide a number into separate parts in a given ratio, the ratios must be converted into fractions.

* EXAMPLE *

To divide 275 into three parts in the ratio 2:4:5 proceed as follows:

- Add the three ratio numbers: 2 + 4 + 5 = 11.
- Express each as a fraction of the total:

  $\frac{2}{11}, \frac{4}{11}, \frac{5}{11}$

- Multiply the number you want to share out by each fraction in turn:

$$\frac{2}{11} \times 275 = 50$$

$$\frac{4}{11} \times 275 = 100$$

$$\frac{5}{11} \times 275 = 125$$

Thus 50, 100 and 125 are in the ratio 2:4:5 and add up to 275.

Raw material control account

The purpose of the raw material account is to:

- record purchases of material at actual price (debit entry)
- analyse the cost of material issued according to whether it is a direct or indirect cost and by function (credit entry). Material may be issued using FIFO, LIFO, weighted average or standard cost.

The balance at the end of the period represents the closing inventory value of raw materials.

* EXAMPLE *

Raw material control

	$		$
Opening inventory	2,550	WIP	5,400
Creditor	8,500	Production overhead	1,200
		Administration overhead	550
		Sales and distribution overhead	780
		Closing inventory	3,120
	11,050		11,050

Realisation concept

Gains or profits, such as those made on sales, should be recognised and accounted for at the time that the transaction is made if the receipt of cash from that transaction is reasonably certain. Therefore, there is no need to wait until the cash from a credit sale is received before the sale is recognised.

Real wage unemployment

This type of unemployment can occur in industries that are highly unionised. By keeping wages artificially high through the threat of strike action and closed shops, the number of people employed in the industry is reduced.

* EXAMPLE *

In the graph below, in the absence of a union the equilibrium wage is W0, which would lead to Q_0 workers being employed. However, if the union can keep wages artificially high at W_1, the number of workers employed falls from Q_0 to Q_1.

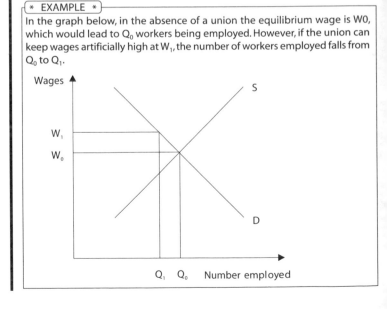

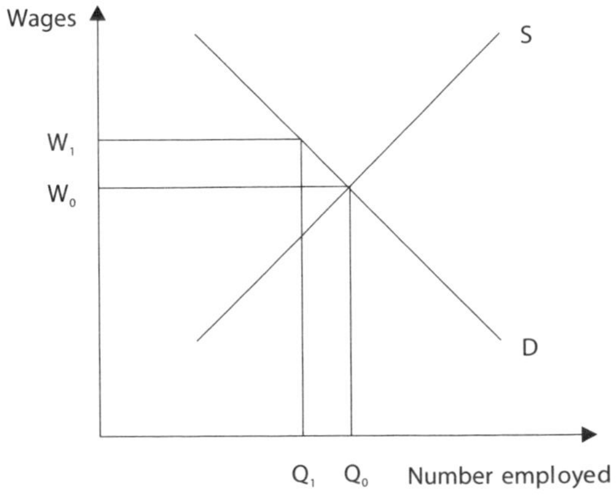

Rebasing an index

From time to time it may be desirable to rebase an index to a more recent year. An index number for any year can be rebased using the following formula:

$$\frac{\text{Old value for year in question}}{\text{Old value in new base year}} \times \text{New base index (usually 100)}$$

* EXAMPLE *

The following table shows the index of prices (2000 = 100) for a certain commodity over the period 2000–2005.

2000	*2001*	*2002*	*2003*	*2004*	*2005*
100	105	115	127	140	152

It has been decided to rebase the index so that 2003 = 100. To construct the new index, rounding to whole numbers:

$$\frac{\text{Old value for year in question}}{\text{Old value in new base year (here 127)}} \times \text{New base index (here 100)}$$

For example for the year 2001 the new figure is 105/127 × 100 = 83 (rounded).

2000	*2001*	*2002*	*2003*	*2004*	*2005*
79	83	91	100	110	120

Receipts and payments account

An alternative to an income and expenditure account for a club. It is not based on the accruals principle, so it is restricted to cash receipts and payments.

Receivables collection period/ Receivables turnover

A ratio used to measure how well a business is managing its relationship with credit customers. To give the average number of days it takes to collect cash from a customer, it is expressed as:

$$\frac{\text{Trade receivables}}{\text{Sales}} \text{x } 365$$

Too long a period suggests that the company is tying up excessive capital in trade receivables. Too short a period suggests that it is hounding its customers for payment and may be losing business.

Receivables written off

Amounts due from credit customers that have been written off because their recovery has been deemed unlilkely.

Reciprocal exponents

The 'reciprocal' of a number is 1 divided by that number. For instance, the reciprocal of 2 is ½. In general terms:
$a^{1/n} = \sqrt[n]{a}$

* EXAMPLE *

$10^{1/2} = \sqrt{10}$

Reconciliation (operating) statement

The purpose of calculating variances is to identify the different effects of each item of cost/income on profit compared to the expected profit. A reconciliation statement lists all variances to show the reasons for the difference between budgeted and actual profit or contribution.

* EXAMPLE *

			$
Budgeted contribution			15,000
Total sales price variance			300
Less: Cost variances:	*Adv.*	*Fav.*	
	$	$	
Material price		40	
Wages rate	80		
Material usage	180		
Labour efficiency		120	
	260	160	
			100
Actual contribution			15,200

Redeemable shares

Those shares which, under their contractual terms of issue, must be bought back by the company at a certain time. In general, redemption may only take place by using the proceeds of a fresh issue, and/or distributable profits. Any premium payable on redemption must also be paid out of the company's distributable profits. On redemption out of the profits of the company, the company is required to establish a capital redemption reserve equivalent to the amount by which the company's issued share capital is thereby reduced.

Reducing balance method

A method of depreciation. A percentage of the asset's book value is written off during each year of its estimated useful life so that its book value is reduced to its estimated residual value by the end of that time. This method leads to heavier depreciation charges when the asset is relatively new, but these decline year by year when the asset gets older.

Reduction of capital

If a company wishes to reduce its issued share capital it must pass a special resolution to that effect and obtain the approval of the court.

Redundancy

A person will be redundant if his dismissal was attributable wholly or mainly to the fact that:

- the employer has ceased (or intends to cease) to carry on the business for the purposes of which or in the place where the employee was employed
- the requirements of that business for employees to carry out work of a particular kind, or in a place where they were so employed, have ceased or diminished or are expected to cease or diminish.

Re-engaement

Re-employment under a new contract of employment.

Registration documents

The following documents must be sent to the Registrar in order to form a company:

- Memorandum signed by two subscribers.
- Articles (or a statement that Table A is adopted).
- Form 10 – names and addresses of directors and secretary (plus consent to act); and address of registered office.
- Form 12 – Declaration of compliance sworn by a director, secretary, or solicitor stating that the requirements of the Companies Act have been complied with.
- Registration fee.

Regressive taxes

These are taxes where the proportion of tax paid declines as income or wealth increases.

Regulatory system

The regulatory framework of accounting is made up of a number of legislative and quasi-legislative influences: company legislation (e.g. the UK Companies Act 1985), accounting standards (e.g. the IASB's International Financial Reporting Standards) and stock exchanges.

Reinstatement

Resumption of work as though there had been no break and nullifies totally the effect of the dismissal.

Relevance of information

Information should be relevant to the needs of users, in order to help them evaluate the financial performance of the business and draw conclusions from it.

Reliability of information

Information should be of a standard that can be relied upon by external users, so that it is free from error and can be depended upon by users in their decisions.

Remedies for breach of contract

Remedies include the following:

- Action for the price: Where the breach of contract is non-payment of the price, the seller sues for the price. This is an action for a specified sum – no question of remoteness or quantum arising. There is also no duty to mitigate.
- Injunction: An order of the court that either requires a person to do something (mandatory injunction) or prohibits a person from doing something (prohibitory injunction).
- Quantum meruit: A claim for the value of work done or services rendered, rather than for the contract price. The words literally mean 'as much as is merited'.
- Rescission: An equitable remedy that restores the parties to their exact pre-contractual position.
- Specific performance: An equitable remedy whereby the court orders a person to complete their obligations under a contract. It is usually only available in contracts for the transfer of land or goods (not work or services).

Remoteness of damage (in law)

There are two types of loss for which damages may be recovered:

- that which arises naturally in the usual course of things – general damages sometimes known as normal loss
- that which does not occur naturally in the usual course of things but which both parties could foresee, when the contract was made, as the likely result of breach – special damages sometimes known as 'abnormal loss.

Repeated distribution method

A technique for re-apportioning service centre overheads to production cost centres when service cost centres work for each other.

Overhead costs allocated and apportioned to service cost centres are apportioned to production and service cost centres using an iterative process according to the benefit received until all overhead costs have been re-apportioned to the production cost centres.

Replacement cost

The cost of replacing an asset, as closely as possible, with an asset that is identical in terms of technical capacity, age and condition.

Reserves

Equity comprises share capital and reserves. Reserves arise mainly from the retention of profits and the revaluation of non-current assets.

Responsibility centres

- Cost centre
  The manager is only responsible for costs incurred. A suitable measure of the performance of a cost centre may be performance against budget or variance analysis.

- Revenue centre
  The manager is only responsible for revenue earned. A suitable measure of performance may be performance against budgeted sales targets or performance indicators such as sales per store, sales per salesperson or sales per location.

- Profit centre
  The manager is responsible for revenue and costs. Performance is measured by comparing profit earned against budgeted profit.

- Investment centre
  The manager is responsible for costs, revenues and assets. Performance is measured by ROCE or other measures.

Retention monies

An agreed proportion of the contract price held by the client for a period specified in the contract as security against rectification costs.

Return on capital employed (ROCE) (C02)

The primary measure of profitability. The higher the ROCE the better. It can be expressed as:

$$\frac{\text{Net profit before interest and tax}}{\text{Equity and long term liabilities}}$$

or

$$\frac{\text{Net profit before tax}}{\text{Equity}}$$

or

$$\frac{\text{Earnings before interest and tax}}{\text{Capital employed}} \times 100\%$$

Revaluation reserve Arises when an increase in the value of a non-current asset is recognised. It is the excess of the new value over the previous book value.

Revenue centre The manager is only responsible for revenue earned. A suitable measure of performance may be performance against budgeted sales targets or performance indicators such as sales per store, sales per salesperson or sales per location.

Revenue curves Total revenue (TR)
Total sales revenue made in the period = Sales volume x Average sales price.

Average revenue (AR)
Average price paid per unit.

Marginal revenue (MR)
Change in total revenue as a result of selling one more unit. Assuming a normal demand curve, revenue is maximised when MR = 0.

Graph showing total, average and marginal revenue

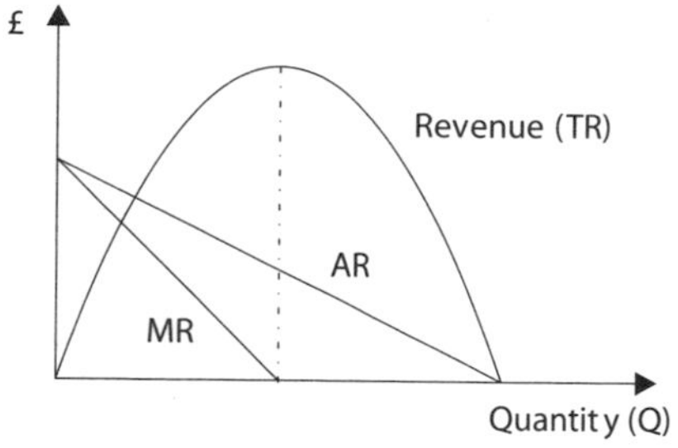

Revenue receipts One that would be regarded as revenue in the income statement.:

Revenue reserve Essentially retained profits that are available for distribution as dividends.

Revocation of an offer (in law) An offer can be revoked by the offeror or a person authorised to act on his behalf at any time before it has been accepted by the offeree. The revocation may be by express words or it may be implied from the offeror's conduct. The revocation will not take effect until it has been received and clearly understood by the offeree. Until then, the offer remains open, and can be accepted. An offer can be revoked at any time before acceptance, even if the offeror has stated that they will keep the offer open for a stated time.

Rights issue

Represents the offer of shares to existing shareholders in proportion to their existing holding at a stated price. Unlike the bonus issue, the shareholders do not have to take up their offer and have the alternative of selling their rights on the stock market.

Risk

Refers to the possibility that actual results, events or outcomes in the future will be different from what is expected. Downside risk, or pure risk, is a risk involving the possibility of loss, with no chance of gain, e.g. the risk of losses from theft or fraud, and risks to the health and safety of employees at work. Two-way risk is sometimes called speculative risk, e.g. a new product launch might be more or less successful than planned.

Rounding

The usual rules of rounding:

- If the number you want to sacrifice is between 0 and 4 leave the number to the left as it is.
- If the number you want to sacrifice is between 5 and 9, round up (add 1 to) the number to the left.

You should only look at one extra number when rounding.

* EXAMPLE *

To round the number 1.3748 to two decimal places, the answer is 1.37. You do not round to three decimal places (1.375) and then round this result to two decimal places (1.38).

S

Sage®

A proprietary piece of accounting software, primarily intended for relatively small enterprises.

Salaries book

Used to calculate and record the amounts due to individual employees for their salaries. The totals are entered in the various accounts relating to net pay and deductions, e.g. PAYE/NI.

Sale by sample

Occurs when the buyer is given the opportunity of examining a small part only of the goods to be bought, but such as to be typical of the bulk of the goods. The Sale of Goods Act 1979 implies a condition that the goods supplied will correspond with the sample.

Sale of Goods Act (SOGA) 1979

Governs contracts for the sale of goods in return for a sum of money. It implies the following terms into such contracts in order to protect buyers from unscrupulous sellers. These terms cannot be excluded from the contract; any attempt to do so is void.

- Title – s12: Implied condition that the seller has the right to sell the goods. Breach means buyer can return goods and sue for full contract price. S12 applies to all sales (whether the seller is in business or not).
- Description – s13: Implied condition that, where goods are sold by reference to a description upon which the buyer relies, the goods will correspond with that description (quality, quantity, etc). Breach means buyer can reject goods and recover full sale price, or sue for damages. Remedies apply even if buyer inspected goods, unless it was obvious the goods did not match their description. S13 applies to all sales (whether the seller is in business or not).
- Satisfactory quality – s14: When sales are made in the course of a business, implied condition of satisfactory quality and fitness for purpose. Fitness for purpose means fit for their normal purpose and for any purpose the buyer specifies even if it is unusual. Breach means buyer can reject the goods and recover the full price, or sue for damages, unless:
  - the buyer did not rely on the seller's judgement
  - it was unreasonable for the buyer to rely on the seller's judgement.

Sales budget

Forecast sales units × sales price.

Sales cycle

Long-term plans made by senior managers.

Sales day book

Used to record credit sales. Each transaction is shown at its net, VAT and gross total. The individual sales are entered gross in the relevant accounts of the sales ledger. The total for gross sales is debited to the sales ledger control account. Net sales are credited to sales and VAT is debited to the VAT account.

Sales ledger

Independent of the double entry bookkeeping system, it contains an account for each and every credit customer. The sales ledger is kept up to date using the detailed entries on the various day books dealing with credit sales, returns from customers suppliers and cash receipts. The balances according to the sales ledger should be totalled regularly and should agree to the balance on the sales ledger control account.

Sales ledger control account

In the general ledger and part of the double entry bookkeeping system. It is kept up to date using the totals from the various day books dealing with credit sales, returns from customers and cash receipts. This gives the total due from trade payables which should be agreed to the total of the balances according to the sales ledger.

Sales returns

Goods returned from a customer. Usually offset against sales in calculating gross profit in the income statement.

Sales system

Strategy is the course of action, including the specification of resources required, that the company will adopt to achieve its specific objective.

Sales variances

Sales price variance
Actual sales units should have earned:
(units of actual sales × standard price per unit)
But did earn:
(actual revenue)
The difference is the sales price variance
If the actual sales revenue is greater than expected, then the variance is favourable.

Sales volume profit or contribution variance
The sales volume variance is calculated differently depending on whether a marginal or absorption costing system is being used.

Absorption costing	Marginal costing
Budgeted volume Less actual volume Valued at standard profit per unit	Budgeted volume Less actual volume Valued at standard contribution per unit

* EXAMPLE *

D Limited manufactures and sells a single product for which the following standard data are available:

	$ per unit	$ per unit
Selling price		86
Variable cost	21	
Fixed cost	15	36
Profit		50

Budgeted sales volume for the latest period was 480 units.

* EXAMPLE *

Actual sales volume was 420 units, earning a sales revenue of $37,380.
The sales price variance is calculated as follows:

420 units should have earned × $86	36,120
But did earn	37,380
Sales price variance	1,260 F
The **sales volume variance** is calculated, **using absorption costing**:	
Standard profit	$50 per unit
Budgeted volume	480 units
Actual volume	420 units 60 A
Value at standard profit × $50	$3,000 A
The **sales volume variance** is calculated, **using marginal costing**:	
Standard contribution	$65 per unit
Budgeted volume	480 units
Actual volume	420 units 60 A
Value at standard contribution × $65	$3,900 A

Sampling

Auditors draw conclusions about populations of items from the accounting systems by extracting samples, testing them and extrapolating the results to draw inferences about the population as a whole. Sampling schemes can be judgemental and rely on common sense or they can be based on statistical analysis.

Sarbanes-Oxley Act 2002 (SOX)

Introduced requirements relating to corporate governance into the federal law in the USA. It extended protection to internal and external whistleblowers in publicly traded companies for the first time. The provisions:

- make it illegal to 'discharge, demote, suspend, threaten, harass or in any manner discriminate against' whistleblowers
- establish criminal penalties of up to 20 years for document shredding and obstruction of justice
- set up the Public Company Accounting Oversight Board to enforce auditing standards
- require the Chief Executive Officers and chief finance directors of companies listed in the US to sign 'oaths of honesty' certifications about the integrity of their company accounts
- restrict the types of audit work that can be carried out by the audit firm for a client company.

Satisfactory quality (in law)

Goods that meet the standard that a reasonable person would regard as satisfactory, taking account of any description of the goods, the price (if relevant) and all other relevant circumstances.

Scarce resource

A good or service which is in short supply and which, because of this shortage, limits the ability of an organisation to provide greater numbers of products or service facilities.

Scatter diagrams

Information about two variables that are considered to be related in some way can be plotted on a scatter diagram, each axis representing one variable. The independent variable is usually marked along the horizontal (x) axis and the dependent variable along the vertical (y) axis. It is convenient to think in terms of the x-axis being the cause, and the y-axis the effect.

Scattergraph (scatter chart)

A graph on which data values are plotted.

Scatter chart showing the relationship between total inspection costs and output

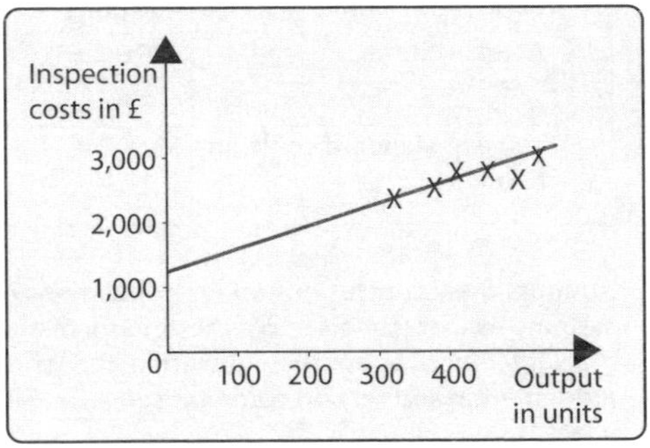

Seasonal unemployment

Demand for some goods and services is highly seasonal, e.g. demand for fruit pickers, which creates a highly seasonal demand for workers. This can lead to regional economic problems in areas where a significant proportion of the workforce is employed in these seasonal industries.

Seasonally adjusted figures

A popular way of presenting a time series is to give the seasonally adjusted or deseasonalised figures. Deseasonalisation is the process of removing the effect of seasonal variation from a time series.

For the additive model:

Seasonally adjusted data =
Original data - Seasonal variation = A – S

For the multiplicative model:

Seasonally adjusted data =
Original data / Seasonal indices = A / S

Secondary markets

Secondary markets trade existing securities.

Segregation of duties

Every transaction requires three steps: authorisation, handling assets and recording. Each step should be in the hands of a separate person or section so that fraud requires collaboration between them, e.g. the buying department should authorise the purchase of inventory and the stores department should take receipt of the resulting goods. That means it would require two people to work together in order to buy goods for personal use.

Semi-variable costs

Include an element of both fixed and variable cost, e.g. telephone bills, machine maintenance.

Graph showing relationship between machine maintenance costs and output

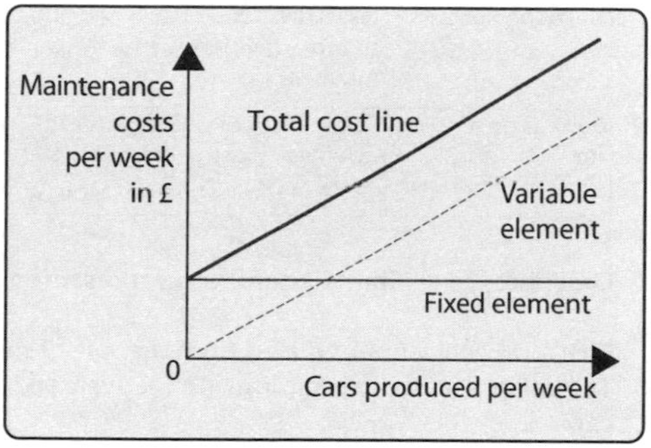

Separation from management

In all but the smallest of companies, the shareholders rarely have any direct influence over the management of the business. that is delegated to the directors.

Sequence and series

A sequence is a succession of numbers, of which each number is formed according to a definite law which is the same throughout the sequence. When each term in the sequence is summed the result is called a series.

Sequential codes

Allocated to items in strict numerical order. This means that there is no obvious connection between a code and what it stands for.

Service contracts of directors

A company cannot include a term in a director's service contract that it should continue for more than five years during which time it cannot be terminated by the company by notice or can only be terminated in specified circumstances, without first obtaining the approval of the shareholders in general meeting by an ordinary resolution.

Service costing

Services have the following features:

- intangible, i.e. have no physical substance
- heterogeneous, i.e. different for each customer
- simultaneously produced and consumed
- perishable.

* EXAMPLE *

A train journey cannot be clearly defined and it may be different each time. As it is produced it is consumed and once the journey is over a new journey begins. The implications are that services cannot be held in stock and are difficult to monitor and control.

Shadow director

A person in accordance with whose directions or instructions the directors of the company are accustomed to act. However, a person is not a shadow director by reason only that the directors act on advice given by them in a professional capacity.

Share

The interest of the shareholder in the company measured by a sum of money, for the purpose of liability in the first place and of interest in the second, but also consisting of a series of mutual covenants.

	Preference shares	**Ordinary shares (equity)**
Voting rights	None, or restricted	Full
Dividend rights	Fixed dividend paid in priority to other dividends, usually cumulative	Paid after preference dividend. Not fixed
Surplus on winding up	Prior return of capital, but cannot participate in any surplus	Entitled to share surplus assets after repayment of preference shares

Share capital

Describes the capital of a company represented by shares.

Share premium

The additional amount raised from the sale of shares over their nominal value. The balance on share premium is effectively an additional component of share capital.

Shareholder wealth

Can be measured in terms of:

- income value, e.g. dividend payments, and
- capital value, e.g. increase in share prices. Share prices will reflect short-term returns and long-term prospects.

Shareholders' liability

The personal liability of the shareholders for the company's debts is limited to any unpaid amount of the issued share capital.

Sharia law

Refers to an Islamic religious code for living that governs all elements of life. Considered to be divine, it is adopted by most Muslims to a certain extent as a matter of personal conscience, but it has also been formally instituted as law by certain countries and enforced by the courts. The primary sources of Sharia law are:

- the Qur'an – the Muslim holy book
- the Hadis – the sayings and conduct of the prophet Mohammed.

Short run

The time period during which there is at least one fixed factor of production (there may be more than one).

Significant digit codes

Significant digit codes incorporate digits that are part of the description of the item, e.g. 503028 = Jeans – 30" waist, 28" leg.

Significant figures

In a mathematical context the word 'significant' means 'precise'. The number of significant figures is not an indication of how large or small the number is.

Rules of significant figures

Rule	Examples	Significant figures
All non-zero figures are significant.	127	3
	2.5	2
All zeros between non-zeros are significant.	10204	5
	10.03	4
Leading zeros in a decimal are not significant.	0.12	2
	0.034	2
Trailing zeros are not significant unless followed by, or to the right of, a decimal point.	1540	3
	320	2
	320.	3
	320.00	5

Do not confuse rounding to a certain number of significant figures with rounding to a certain number of decimal places:

- 102.0304 to four decimal places is 102.0304.
- 102.0304 to four significant figures is 102.0.

Simple bar chart

* EXAMPLE *

The following bar chart represents the production of wheat in the UK for the years 20X1 to 20X3:

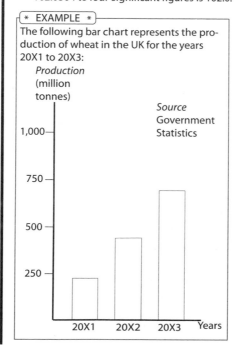

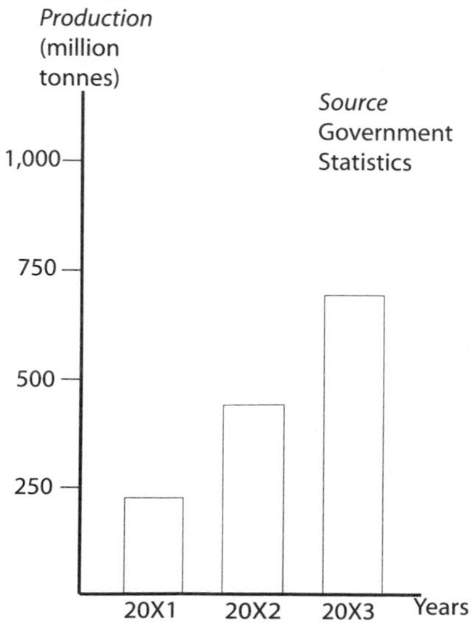

Simple contract

Any contract that is not a specialty contract is a simple contract.

Simple indices

Percentage relatives

Based on a single item. There are two types:

- Price relatives – a number expressing a current year money value of a series as a percentage of a base year money value of the same series.
- Quantity relatives – the same, except not expressed in money.

The base year is the year with which all changes in the series are compared, in other words the reference point of the series. The formulae for calculating these index numbers are:

$$\text{Simple price or price relative index} = \frac{P_1}{P_0} \times 100$$

$$\text{Simple quantity or quantity relative index} = \frac{Q_1}{Q_0} \times 100$$

Where P_0 is the price at time 0
P_1 is the price at time 1
Q_0 is the quantity at time 0
Q_1 is the quantity at time 1

* EXAMPLE *

If a commodity costs £2.60 in 20X4 and £3.68 in 20X5, the simple price index for 20X5, using 20X4 as base year (i.e. time 0) can be calculated:

$$\text{Simple price index} = \frac{P_1}{P_0} \times 100 = \frac{3.68}{2.60} \times 100 = 141.5$$

This means that the price has increased by 41.5% of its base year value, i.e. its 20X4 value.

Multi-item indices

By using appropriate weights, price relatives can be combined to give a multi-item price index.

* EXAMPLE *

The Retail Price Index (RPI) is such an index and consists of a list of items as diverse as the price of bread, the cost of watch repairs, car repairs and cinema tickets.

Simple interest

When money is invested it earns interest; similarly when money is borrowed interest is payable. The sum of money invested or borrowed is known as the principal. The usual notation is:

$$I = Xrt$$

where X = initial sum invested/borrowed (principal)
r = interest rate % pa (expressed as a decimal; 15% = 0.15)
t = time in years
I = interest in £

* EXAMPLE *

A man invests £160 on 1 January each year. On 31 December simple interest is credited at 12% but this interest is put in a separate account and does not itself earn any interest. Find the total amount standing to his credit on 31 December following his fifth payment of £160.

Year (1 January)	Investment (£)	Interest (31 December)
1	160	12/100×160 = £19.20
2	160+160=320	12/100×320 = £38.40
3	160+320=480	12/100×480 = £57.60
4	160+480=640	12/100×640 = £76.80
5	160+640=800	12/100×800 = £96.00
Total		£288.00

Simultaneous equations

Can be solved algebraically by eliminating one of the variables. This is achieved by adding or subtracting the equations.

Simultaneous equations with two unknowns

1 By multiplying one or both of the equations, make the coefficients of either x or y equal.
2 Eliminate one of the unknowns by addition or subtraction.
3 Obtain a value for y.
4 This value of y is now substituted back in one of the equations.

The result can be checked by substituting the values of x and y in the other equation. It is not always possible to eliminate one of the unknowns by simply adding or subtracting the equations. In such a case it will be necessary to multiply one or both of the equations to make the coefficients of x or y equal. One of the unknowns may then be eliminated by addition or subtraction of the amended equation(s).

* EXAMPLE *

$2x + 3y = 42$ (1)
$5x - y = 20$ (2)

1 By multiplying equation (2) by 3, the coefficients of y become equal:

(1): $2x + 3y = 42$
$3 \times$ (2): $15x - 3y = 60$ .... Equation (3)

2 Equation (2) when multiplied is called equation (3). You can add equation (1) to equation (3) to eliminate y:

(1) $2x + 3y = 42$
(3) $\underline{15x} - 3y = \underline{60}$
$\underline{17x}$ $\underline{102}$

3 Obtain a value for x by rearranging the equation:

$17x = 102$

$$x = \frac{102}{17}$$

$$x = 6$$

* EXAMPLE *

4 Substitution into any of (1), (2) or (3) is possible but in this case (2) is most convenient giving:

$(5 \times 6) - y$	=	20
$30 - y$	=	20
$30 - 20$	=	y
y	=	$30 - 20$
	=	10

So the solution is $x = 6, y = 10$.

Check by substituting in (1):

$2 \times 6 + 3 \times 10$	=	42
$12 + 30$	=	42
42	=	42

As this is a true statement, the solution is correct.

Simultaneous equations – solving graphically

By finding the point of intersection of the two lines:

* EXAMPLE *

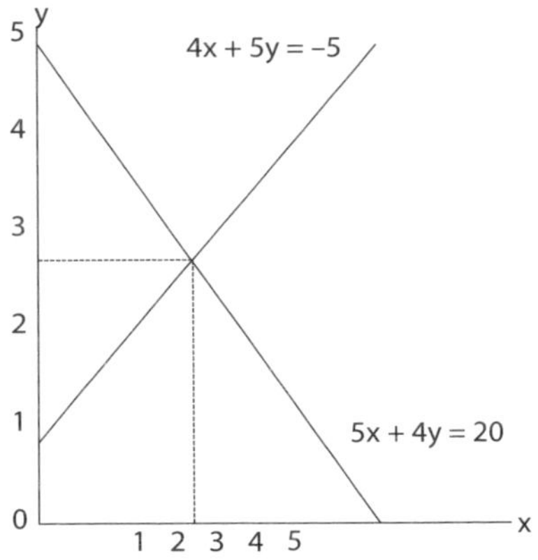

From the graph, the point of intersection of the lines is:

$x \approx 2$

$y \approx 2\frac{1}{2}$

Single currency zones

One way of avoiding exchange rate risk is for each country to use the same currency. The best known example of such an arrangement is the Economic and Monetary Union (EMU), which seeks to establish a single currency and monetary authority within the European Union. Two major components of this integration are:

- a single European currency – the Euro
- the European Central bank.

Single markets (economic communities)

A single market is a customs union with common policies on product regulation, and freedom of movement of all the four factors of production (i.e. goods, services, capital and labour), e.g. the Economic Community of West African States (ECOWAS).

Sinking fund

Money put aside periodically to settle a liability or replace an asset. The money is invested to produce a required sum at an appropriate time.

* EXAMPLE *

£2,000 is invested at the end of each year for five years at 8% compound interest. What is the accumulated amount at the end of five years? The first contribution to the fund will earn interest for four years, the second contribution for three years and so on.

Summarising in a table:

Instalment	Amount (£)	Duration (yrs)	Accumulated amount (£)
1	2,000	4	$2,000\ (1 + 0.08)^4$
2	2,000	3	$2,000\ (1 + 0.08)^3$
3	2,000	2	$2,000\ (1 + 0.08)^2$
4	2,000	1	$2,000\ (1 + 0.08)^1$
5	2,000	0	2,000

The total amount in the fund at the end of the period is the sum of the values in the final column. Thus, taking these from the bottom upwards:

Total = $2,000 + 2,000(1 + 0.08) + 2,000(1 + 0.08)^2 + 2,000(1 + 0.08)^3 + 2,000\ (1 + 0.08)^4$

This is a geometrical progression with A = 2,000, R = 1.08, n = 5.

Hence the total is $\dfrac{A\ (R^n - 1)}{R - 1}$

(R is the common ratio of the GP)

$$= \frac{2,000 \times (1.08^5 - 1)}{1.08 - 1}$$

= £11,733

If the instalments are paid into the fund at the start of each year instead of the end, the first term will become $2,000\ (1.08)^5$ and the last, 2,000(1.08). Each term is therefore increased by a factor 1.08, so that the total would then be £11,73 × 1.08 = £12,672.

Skewness

The tendency in a distribution to deviate from symmetry. Can be positive or negative.

Normal distribution

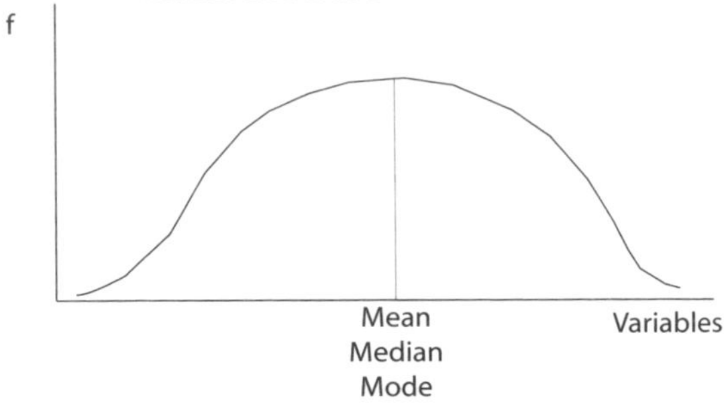

A positively skewed distribution

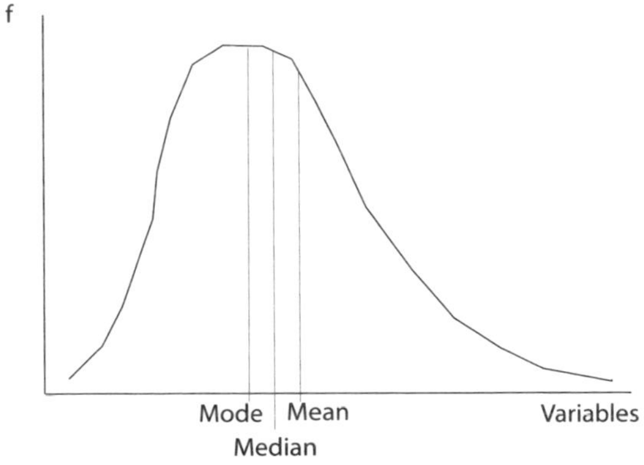

A negatively skewed distribution

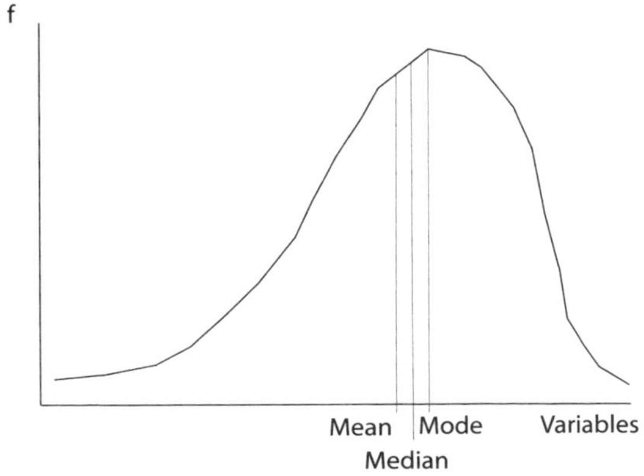

Skewness and averages

(a) In a symmetrical distribution, the mean, median and mode all have the same value, and are located at the same point on the frequency curve.
(b) In a skewed distribution, the mean will be drawn away from the mode, which is always found at the peak of the curve. The median lies between the mean and the mode. (Remember the order mean, median, mode – alphabetical order.)

Smith Report (2003)

Conclusions:

- The role of the audit committee is to ensure that the interests of shareholders are properly protected in relation to financial reporting and internal control.
- The role, responsibilities and activities of the audit committee should be noted in the annual report.
- The committee should contain a majority of non-executives.

Social club

A non-profit making entity that exists for social or religious purposes. It may produce very simple, cash-based financial statements for its members.

Social responsibility

Refers to how the company behaves towards the community in which it operates.

Special notice

Special notice, when required, is given to the company by a member at least 28 days before the meeting. It is notice that the member intends to move a resolution at the meeting.

Specialty contract

A contract made by deed is called a specialty contract.

* EXAMPLE *

- A conveyance of land.
- A lease for three years or more.

Specific allowance for doubtful receivables

An allowance for receivables that is calculated by identifying particular balances that are in greater danger of default (e.g. older balances).

Specific order costing

The cost accounting method applicable where work consists of separately identifiable contracts, jobs or batches.

Spreadsheets

Spreadsheets can be used for anything with a rows and columns format and normally have the following elements:

- Worksheet (or spreadsheet): the basis of all the work you do. It could be considered to be the electronic equivalent of an accountant's ledger.
- Workbook: a collection of worksheets. Simply a folder that binds together your worksheets. When you open a new workbook, it automatically contains 16 worksheets.
- Cells: the worksheet is divided into columns and rows. The intersection of a column and a row is known as a 'cell'. To refer to a particular cell, use its column and row location. This is called a 'cell address', for example A1, B22, etc.
- Columns: each is referenced by one or two letters in the column heading. The whole worksheet consists of 256 columns, labelled A through IV.
- Rows: each is referenced by the row number shown in the row heading to the left of a row. There are 65,536 rows in Excel®.

- Data: each cell can contain numbers, text or a formula. Formulae are not visible when you are entering data but reside in the background. A formula normally involves a mathematical calculation on the content of other cells, the result being inserted in the cell containing the formula. This allows the spreadsheet to automatically update itself when data is altered.

Spreadsheet applications: budgeting and forecasting

Preparing budgets and forecasts are classic applications of spreadsheets, as they allow estimates to be changed without having to recalculate everything manually.

* EXAMPLE *

An extract from a cash flow forecast:

Apart from the formatting to make the forecast easy to read, the key formulae are as follows:

Total payments: e.g. B14: =SUM(B7:B13)

Net cash flow: e.g. B16: =+B4-B14

Bal. c/f: e.g. B19: =+B18+B16

	A	B	C	D	E
1	**Revised cashflow forecast for 05/06**				
2	**£000**	**Jul-05**	**Aug-05**	**Sep-05**	**Oct-05**
3					
4	**Sales receipts**	**1867**	**1828**	**1893**	**1939**
5					
6	**Payments**				
7	Purchases	1691	1644	1701	1798
8	Overheads	57	57	57	57
9	Capex	50	50	50	25
10	Bank loans	12	12	12	12
11	VAT	160			171
12	CT				
13	Bank o/d intererst	2	2	2	1
14		**1972**	**1765**	**1822**	**2064**
15					
16	Net cash in/out flow	**-105**	**63**	**71**	**-125**
17					
18	Bal b/f*	-134	-239	-176	-105
19	Bal c/f	-239	-176	-105	-230

Apart from the formatting to make the forecast easy to read, the key formulae are as follows:

Total payments: e.g. B14: =SUM(B7:B13)

Net cash flow: e.g. B16: =+B4-B14

Bal. c/f: e.g. B19: =+B18+B16

Spreadsheet applications: discounted cash flow calculations

An NPV calculation can be set up using formulae with any layout you choose.

* EXAMPLE *

	A	B	C	D	E	F	G
1	**NPV Calculation**						
2	Discount rate		10.00%				
3							
4	Time	Narrative		CF	DF	PV	
5	0	Invest		-10,000	1	-10,000	
6	1	Returns		4,000	0.909091	3,636	
7	2	Returns		5,000	0.826446	4,132	
8	3	Returns		3,000	0.751315	2,254	
9	4	Returns		2,000	0.683013	1,366	
10		NPV				1,389	

Examples of formulae used:

Discount factors: E6: = (1+C2)^(-1*A6)

Present values: F6: = D6*E6

NPV: F10: = SUM(F5:F9)

Excel has the capability to calculate NPVs and IRRs if the spreadsheet is set out in an appropriate way.

The function is NPV(rate,value1,value2, ...), where

- rate = discount rate
- value1 = cash flow at end of the first year
- value2 = cash flow at the end of the second year, etc.

The NPV could thus be calculated by the formula:

=NPV(C2,D6:D9)+D5

Likewise the IRR can be calculated using IRR(values,guess), where:

- values are the cash flows in order (including now time zero if required), and
- guess is your first guess at the IRR.

The IRR for this example could thus be calculated as 17.07%, using:

=IRR(D5:D9,C2)

Spreadsheet applications: reporting performance

Performance appraisal usually involves calculating ratios, possibly involving comparatives between companies and from one year to the next. A neat way of doing this is to input the raw data, such as financial statements, on one sheet and calculate the ratios on another..

* EXAMPLE *

An extract from the five years results for a company called Parkland, input on a sheet titled 'historic data':

	A	B	C	D	E
1					
2					**Rutwater**
3	£000		2005	2004	2003
4					
5	Revenue		319,361	316,197	309,119
6	Cost of sales		-81,428	-84,627	-83,039
7	Gross prodfit		237,933	231,570	226,080

* EXAMPLE *

Here are some ratios set up on a separate sheet (titled 'current and historic ratios') in the same workbook:

	A	B	C	D	E
1					
2	**Historic ratio analysis**		**Rutwater**		
3					
4					
5	RoC		11.70%	12.50%	12.50%
6	margin		27.80%	27.80%	26.80%
7	Asset turnover		£0.42	£0.45	£0
8	Gross margin		74.50%	73.20%	73.10%
9	EBITDA margin		49.20%	48.10%	47.20%
10					

* EXAMPLE *

Taking just one as an example, gross margin is calculated as gross profit divided by revenue. The answer has been formatted to show as a percentage to one decimal place and the formula for cell C8 is as follows:

='Historic data'!C7/'Historic data'!C5

The 'historic data'! part indicates which worksheet the information came from. While this looks complex, setting up the formula was simply a matter of clicking on the correct cells in the first place:

- On the sheet 'current and historic ratios' click on cell C8 and press '='
- Switch to sheet 'historic data' and click on cell C7
- Type '/'
- Click on cell C5 while still on sheet 'historic data'
- Press enter and you will automatically return to the 'current and historic ratios' sheet.

Spreadsheet applications: variance analysis

Involves management comparing actual results with budget and then investigating the differences. A relatively simple statement could be along these lines:

	A	B	C	D	E	F	G
1				**Variance Report**			
2	Project Name:						
3	Employee Name:						
4							
5	**ID#**	**Task name**		**Planned effort** (Baseline)	**Actual Effort** (or Estimated Completion)	**Variance / Slippage**	**Comments**
6						0.0	
7						0.0	
8						0.0	
9						0.0	
10						0.0	
11						0.0	
12							

Spreadsheet formulae

Spreadsheet packages can incorporate most formulae. All start by inputting '=' into the cell but some formulae have to be entered in a particular way to work:

- Addition can be performed within a formula, e.g. typing '=4+10' into a cell formula would display '14' in the cell. The addition function is more useful when used to sum the values in different cells, e.g. suppose we want to sum the figures in a column from cell C2 down to C11. This can be done simply as '=SUM(C2:C11)'.
- Multiplication: spreadsheet multiplication uses the symbol * instead of ×.
- Division: spreadsheet division uses the symbol / instead of ÷.
- Powers: to raise to a power the easiest approach is use the ^ symbol.

Formulae can be copied across cells.

Spreadsheet software compared to manual analysis

Advantages
- Speed
- Accuracy
- Legibility
- Management reporting

Disadvantages
- Security

Spreadsheet software compared to other software applications

Spreadsheets

Advantages
- Relatively easy to use
- Require little training to get started
- Most data managers are familiar with them

Disadvantages
- Have to re-copy data over and over again to maintain it in separate data files
- Inability to efficiently identify data errors
- Lack detailed sorting and querying abilities
- Can be sharing violations among users wishing to view or change data at the same time
- Restricted to a finite number of records, and can require a large amount of hard-drive space for data storage

Databases

To store large amounts of raw data, it is best to use a database.

Advantages
- Ease of reporting and sharing data
- Require little or no duplication of data between information tables
- Changes made to the data do not corrupt the programming (like at the cell level of a spreadsheet where calculations are running)
- Better security to restrict users from accessing privileged information, and from changing coded information in the programming

Disadvantages
- Require the user to learn a new system
- Require a greater investment in training and software
- Initial time and cost of migrating all of the data into a new database system

Spurious correlation

Spurious or accidental correlation may result between two variables when there is no direct casual relationship. A hidden third variable could be present.

Stagflation

Inflation and unemployment occurring together.

Stakeholders

Interested parties in an organisation, each with different objectives and degrees of influence.

* EXAMPLE *

Stakeholders	Objectives
Internal stakeholders • Managers • Employees	Career development, pay, security, enjoyable jobs
External stakeholders • Government • Pressure groups	Compliance with the law, tax revenue Protecting the environment
Connected stakeholders • Shareholders • Customers • Suppliers • Financiers	Profit, growth in share price Low prices, quality High prices, assured demand Interest payments, security

Standard cost

A predetermined cost for a single unit of a product based on a prescribed set of working conditions. Standard costs represent the long-run average cost per unit and are most relevant in businesses where large numbers of similar products are being produced.

Standard cost card

Standard costs are made up of two estimates which are multiplied to produce the standard cost of the output unit. These two estimates are:

- a physical measure of the resources required for each unit of output
- the price expected to be paid for each unit of the resource.

These are recorded on a standard cost card:

Standard cost card – cost per unit of product X

		$
Raw materials:	5 kgs P @ $2/kg	10.00
	3 kgs Q @ $1.5/kg	4.50
Labour	4 hrs grade A @ $4/hr	16.00
	1 hr grade B @ $5.50/hr	5.50
Variable overheads	5 hrs @ $1.50/hr	7.50
		43.50 (MC)
Fixed overheads	5 hrs @ $1.30/hr	6.50
		50.00 (TAC)

Standard costing

A control technique which compares standard costs and revenues with actual results to obtain variances that are used to stimulate improved performance.

Standard deviation

The most valuable and widely used measure of dispersion, but the most complex to calculate and understand. A measure of the amount by which the values in a set of numbers differ from the arithmetic mean. It is defined as the square root of the mean square deviations of the values from the mean. The defining formula is therefore:

$$\text{Standard deviation} = \sqrt{\frac{\Sigma(x - \bar{x})^2}{n}}$$

where n is the number of x values. The standard deviation is usually denoted by σ (the Greek lower case sigma) or by the abbreviation SD.

* EXAMPLE *

Calculate the standard deviation of 3, 5, 8, 11, 13.

$\bar{x}$ is $\Sigma x/n$ 40/5 = 8

x	$\bar{x}$	$(x - \bar{x})$	$(x - \bar{x})^2$
3	8	−5	25
5	8	−3	9
8	8	0	0
11	8	3	9
13	8	5	25
40			Σ 68

$$\sqrt{\frac{\Sigma(x - \bar{x})^2}{n}} = \sqrt{\frac{68}{5}} = \sqrt{13.6} = 3.69$$

Standard deviation for a frequency distribution

The defining formula is:

$$\sigma = \sqrt{\frac{\Sigma fx^2}{\Sigma f} - \left(\frac{\Sigma fx}{\Sigma f}\right)^2} \quad \text{or} \quad \sqrt{\frac{\Sigma fx^2}{\Sigma f} - \bar{x}^2}$$

* EXAMPLE *

Weight (stones)	*Mid-value x*	*Frequency f*	*fx*	*fx²*
8 – 9	8.5	4	34	289.0
9 – 10	9.5	10	95	902.5
10 – 11	10.5	14	147	1,543.5
11 – 12	11.5	22	253	2,909.5
12 – 13	12.5	16	200	2,500.0
13 – 14	13.5	12	162	2,187.0
14 – 15	14.5	2	29	420.5
Totals		80	920	10,750.0

Substituting in the computational formula:

$$\sigma = \sqrt{\frac{10{,}752}{80} - \left(\frac{920}{80}\right)^2}$$

$$= \sqrt{134.4 - (11.5)^2}$$

$$= \sqrt{2.15}$$

$$= 1.47 \text{ stones}$$

Standard form contract — A person faced with a standard form cannot usually bargain. He must take it or leave it, e.g. conditions of rail travel.

Standard hour — The amount of work achievable, at standard efficiency levels, in an hour. (CIMA *Official Terminology*)

Standard-rated supplies — Transactions that are subject to the standard rate of Value Added Tax.

Standing data — Data that is retained and referred to in the course of routine processing, e.g. suppliers' bank details might be input once, kept up to date and used every month whenever processing payments.

Statement of changes in equity — Used to indicate how each of the equity balances has changed in the course of the period. e.g. retained profits will increase because of the retained profit for the year and decrease because of dividends.

Statutes — Acts of Parliament, or statutes, are legislation made by Parliament itself.

Stepped costs (semi-fixed costs) — Costs may be fixed over a certain range of activity (e.g. production volume) but rise in steps over higher ranges. In the short term stepped costs may be largely fixed costs as it would be difficult to employ more resources. In the long term stepped costs may behave more like variable costs as organisations can adjust resources to match production volume.

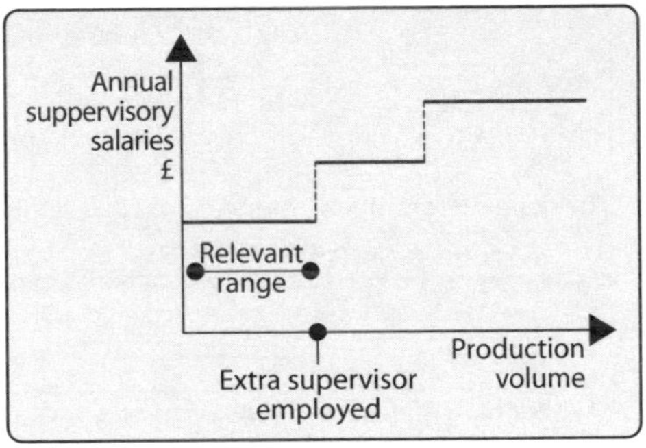

Stewardship — The safeguarding and good management of a principal's wealth by an agent, e.g. the directors are expected to protect a company's assets and put them to good use on behalf of their shareholders.

Straight line method — A method of calculating depreciation. The same amount is written off each year throughout the asset's estimated useful life so that the book value is reduced to its estimated residual value by the end of that time.

Strategic plans — Long-term plans made by senior managers.

Strategy — Strategy is the course of action, including the specification of resources required, that the company will adopt to achieve its specific objective.

Structural and technological unemployment — Caused by structural change in the economy, often leading to both a change in the skills required and the location where economic activity takes place.

Subjective classification

Classification by the type of cost, e.g. by cost element.

Subjective probability

Estimates made by individuals of the relative likelihood of events occurring.

> * EXAMPLE *
>
> An individual may estimate that the likelihood of the Conservative Party winning the next British election is 0.4.

This is a personal view, though it may be based on the individual's own predictive model of the political future. It cannot be confirmed by either a priori reasoning or experimentation, i.e. it is 'subjective probability'. Some statisticians would say that this type of probability is invalid, but many business problems are of this nature, and it is difficult to find any other method of quantifying the relative likelihood of forecasts. Subjective probabilities are assumed to follow the same laws as objective probabilities.

Substance over form

The legal form of an agreement can be very different from its economic substance. For instance, if a third party has an option to ask the company for money but has not yet exercised that option then, legally, there is no liability. If, however, the third party is almost certain to exercise the option, then the economic substance is that a liability does exist.

Substance over form convention

Financial statements should reflect the economic substance of a transaction, rather than its legal form, where these are different. For instance, sometimes a business will take out a long-term lease on an asset for the whole of its useful life. It would be necessary to account for this as the acquisition of a non-current asset and the creation of a long-term liability to the lessor, even though the legal form of the agreement states that ownership of the asset does not pass to the company and that there is no major lump sum due to the lessor.

Substantial property transactions

A transaction exceeding the lower of £100,000 or 10% of the company's assets (but with a minimum value of £2,000). A company cannot enter into such a transaction with a director without first obtaining approval by ordinary resolution in general meeting. If the resolution is not obtained, the transaction is voidable unless restitution is no longer possible.

Substantive tests

Tests of transactions and balances that seek to provide audit evidence as to the completeness, accuracy and validity of the information contained in the accounting records or in the financial statements.

Substitutes

When two or more goods are interchangeable in terms of giving consumers utility, e.g. if the price of margarine were to rise, it is likely that demand for butter would increase as individuals switch to the cheaper product.

Summary dismissal

Termination without notice by the employer is summary dismissal of the employee.

Summing an infinite geometrical progression

Where the series is infinite it may still have a finite sum. This will only occur if R is between –1 and +1. Substituting into the formula gives:

$$S_\infty = \frac{A\,(1 - R^\infty)}{1 - R} \text{ where } \infty \text{ means infinity}$$

But, if -1 < R < +1, as n gets larger R^n gets smaller, hence R^∞ becomes zero,

$$\therefore \quad S_\infty = \frac{A}{1-R}$$

* EXAMPLE *

5, - 1, 1/5, ...

A = 5, R = –1/5

$$S_\infty = \frac{5}{1-(-1/5)}$$

$$= \frac{5}{(6/5)} = \frac{5}{1} \times \frac{5}{6}$$

$$= \frac{25}{6} = 4.167$$

Sunk costs

Amounts already spent.

Supernormal profit

Profit earned in excess of normal profit.

Supervision controls

Responsible officials should supervise on a day-to-day basis the carrying out and recording of transactions.

Supply curve

Shows quantities that suppliers are willing and able to supply at each price, assuming that all other variables are constant. It is normally upward sloping and an increase in price causes a movement along the supply curve.

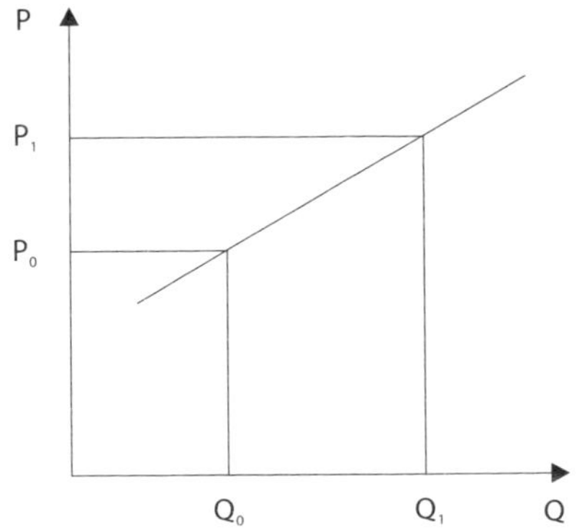

Factors that cause the whole supply curve to shift include:
- technology
- factor cost
- weather
- price of alternative products
- price of joint products
- expectations of price movements.

Anything that increases the cost of production is likely to cause a decrease in supply, i.e. an upward and leftward movement of the supply curve. In the example below, improved technology has increased the efficiency of production and thus lowered costs. As a result the supply curve has shifted downwards and to the right, increasing the quantity supplied at any particular price.

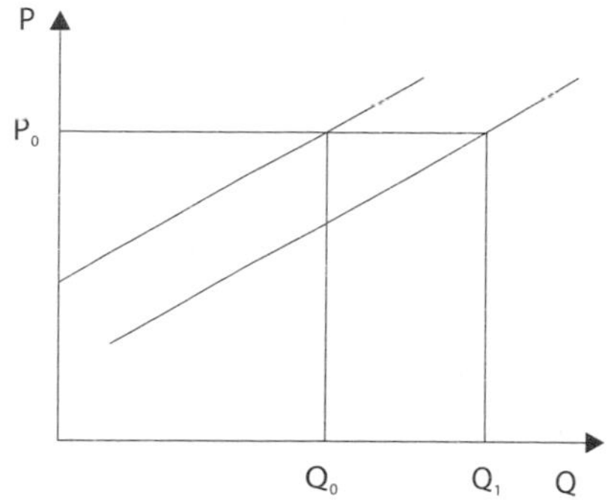

Supply of Goods and Services Act 1982

Concerns contracts for the supply of services:
- S13 implies a term that the supplier will carry out the service with reasonable care and skill.
- S14 implies a term that the supplier will carry out the service within a reasonable time.
- S15 implies a term that the party contracting with the supplier will pay a reasonable charge.

Supply-side (monetarist) policies

These policies seek to improve the supply of factors of production in the economy and are more likely to be effective remedies for structural unemployment than increasing aggregate demand. Measures could include:
- government-funded retraining schemes
- tax breaks for redevelopment of old industrial sites
- grant aid to encourage relocation of industry
- business start-up advice and soft loans
- help with worker relocation costs
- improved information on available employment opportunities.

Suspense accounts

Used to make a temporary entry in the bookkeeping records. For instance, if a sum is received for an unknown reason, it could be recorded as a debit to bank and a credit to suspense. When the transaction has been investigated the entry can be corrected by debiting suspense and crediting the correct account.

T

Tabulation of data

When tabulating data to make it easier to comprehend, the following principles need to be borne in mind.

- Simplicity: the material must be classified and detail kept to a minimum.
- Title: the table must have a comprehensive and self-explanatory title.
- Source: the source of the material used in drawing up the table should always be stated.
- Units: the units of measurement that have been used must be stated.
- Headings: all column and row headings should be concise and unambiguous.
- Totals.
- Percentages and ratios should be shown if meaningful.

Tariffs

Imposition of an import tax on goods being imported into the country to make them uncompetitive on price.

Taxation

- The effect of imposing a tax is to both increase the cost of the product and reduce the amount demanded and supplied.
- If negative externalities exist, the tax forces the market to work efficiently.

The diagram below assumes that a flat rate tax has been imposed on the good. If this is the case, the supply curve will shift upwards by the exact amount of the tax, and the old and new supply curves will be parallel.

If an ad valorem indirect tax is imposed, the old and the new supply curves will not be parallel, as the absolute amount of tax per unit will increase as the selling price increases, e.g. VAT.

Equilibrium prior to taxation

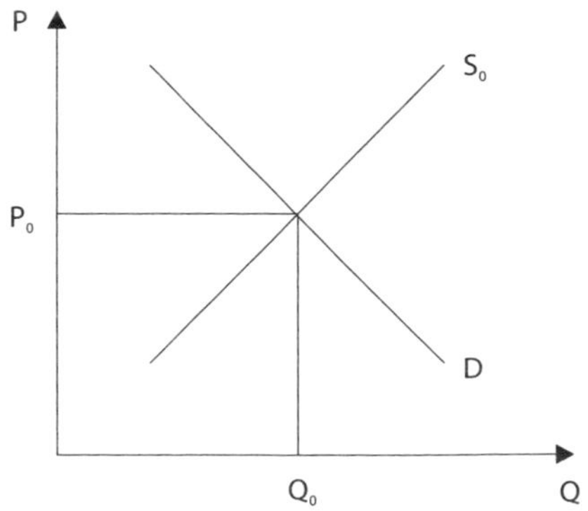

Equilibrium after taxation

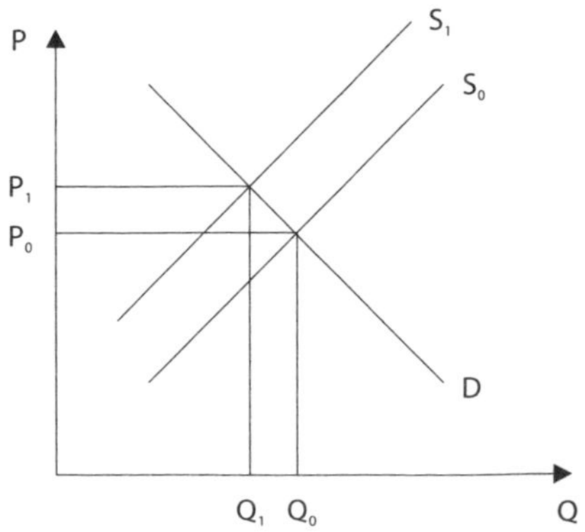

Taxation principles

Adam Smith in his book, *Wealth of Nations*, defined four principles of taxation:

- *Equity* – Taxes should be fair and based on ability to pay.
- *Certainty* – Taxpayers should know how much they are expected to pay and when they are expected to pay it.
- *Convenience* – Taxes should be easy to pay and should not involve the taxpayer in unnecessary inconvenience or expense.
- *Economy* – The cost of tax collection should be minimised.

Teeming and lading

A technique for concealing fraud where accounts are falsified to conceal the misappropriation of a remittance from a customer. Cash subsequently received from another customer is credited to the misappropriated customer's account, a remittance from a third customer is credited to the second customer's account and so on.

Term structure of interest rates (yield curves)

The longer the term of a security, the higher its gross redemption yield will be, i.e. the return to the investor.

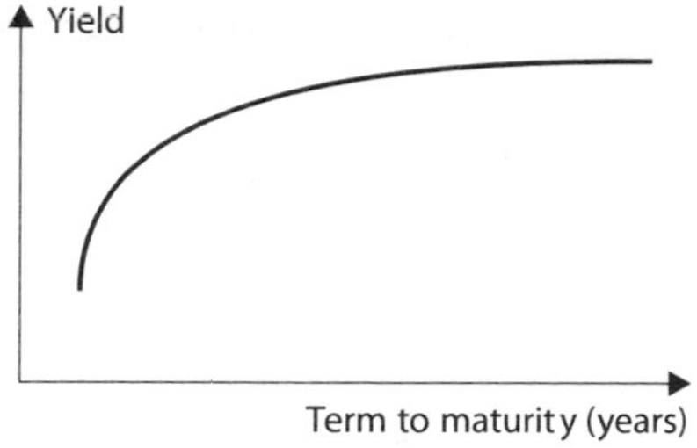

This is owing to:

- *Expectations theory:* the normal upward sloping yield curve reflects the expectation that inflation levels, and therefore interest rates, will increase in the future.
- *Liquidity preference theory:* investors have a natural preference for more liquid (shorter maturity) investments. They will need to be compensated if they are deprived of cash for a longer period.
- *Market segmentation theory* suggests that there are different players in the short-term end of the market and the long-term end of the market. Investors are assumed to be risk averse and to invest in segments of the market that match their liability commitments, e.g. banks tend to be active in the short-term end of the market and pension funds would tend to invest in long-term maturities to match the long-term nature of their liabilities.

The supply and demand forces in various segments of the market in part influence the shape of the yield curve. If there is an increased supply in the long-term end of the market because the government needs to borrow more, this may cause the price to fall and the yield to rise and may result in an upward sloping yield curve.

Time series

A time series is the name given to a set of observations taken at equal intervals of time, e.g. daily, weekly, monthly, etc. The observations can be plotted against time to give an overall picture of what is happening. The horizontal axis is always the time axis.

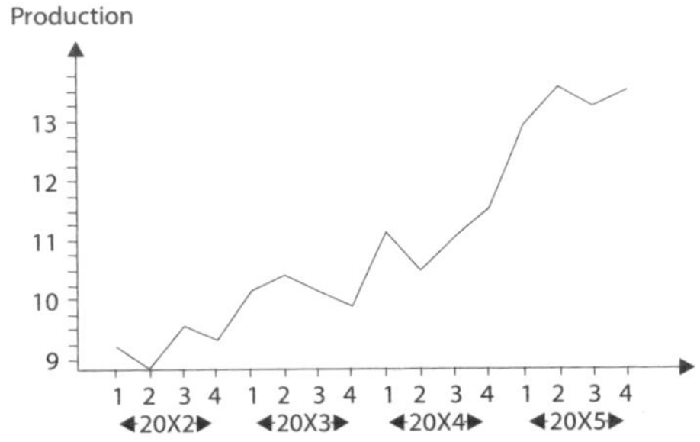

Time series – additive models

Additive time series is a model of a time series where the overall series is obtained by adding the separate trend, seasonal, cyclical and random components. Used when fluctuations about the trend are constant.

A = actual value for the period
T = trend component
C = cyclical component
S = seasonal component
R = residual component

Then $A = T + C + S + R$
This is called an additive model.

Time series – multiplicative models

Multiplicative time series is a model of a time series where the overall series is obtained by multiplying the separate trend, seasonal, cyclical and random components. Used when fluctuations about the trend increase as the trend increases.

$A = T \times C \times S \times R$
This is called a multiplicative model.

Time series – variations in observations

A time series is influenced by a number of factors, the most important of these being:

(a) Long-term trends
The way in which the graph of a time series appears to be moving over a long interval of time when the short-term fluctuations have been smoothed out. The rise or fall is due to factors which only change slowly.

(b) Cyclical variations
The wave-like appearance of a time series graph when taken over a number of years. The distance in time from one peak to the next is often approximately five to seven years.

(c) Seasonal variations
A regular rise and fall over specified intervals of time. The interval of time can be any length – hours, days, weeks, etc, and the variations are of a periodic type with a fairly definite period.

(d) Residual or random variations
Any other variation happening entirely at random due to unpredictable causes.

Time value of money

Cash received in the future is less valuable than the same sum received now.

> * EXAMPLE *
>
> A £1 million receipt anticipated in five years' time is not equal in value to £1 million received now because:
>
> - Inflation erodes the purchasing power of the money. The £1 million in five years' time will not buy as much as £1 million today.
> - Risk – £1 million today is more certain than the estimated £1 million in five years' time.
> - Interest – £1 million received today could be invested to earn interest. In five years' it will have grown to more than £1 million.
> - Alternatively, the £1 million received today could be used to repay a loan or reduce an overdraft, thus saving interest.

Tort

A breach of a legal duty or infringement of a legal right, arising independently of contract, which gives rise to a claim for unspecified damages.

Total gearing

A measure of gearing calculated using the formula:

$$\frac{\text{Debt (including preference shares}}{\text{Debt + Equity}}$$

Trade cycle

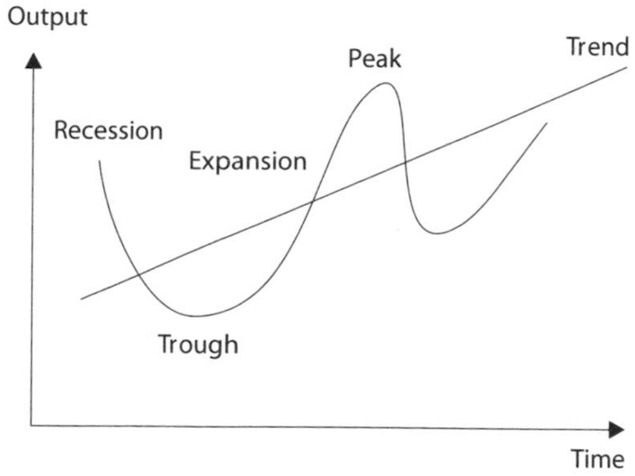

Although there a number of other explanations for this cyclical economic behaviour, attempts have been made to combine the accelerator and multiplier effects to explain the cycle:

- Investment initially rises due to expectations of recovery.
- Triggers multiplier, leading to rising incomes.
- Rising incomes increase consumption and therefore demand.
- Triggers accelerator as companies invest further to meet demand.
- Triggers multiplier, leading to rising incomes and so on.

This process cannot continue indefinitely as the economy will eventually reach full capacity, i.e. all factors are employed. As this point is reached investment tails off and incomes start to fall, thus triggering a reverse multiplier. As incomes fall, so does consumption and demand. This is in turn reduces investment and so on.

Trading certificate

A public company cannot do business or exercise any borrowing powers unless it has obtained from the Registrar a 'certificate of entitlement to do business' (more commonly called the trading certificate .To obtain the certificate, the public company must deliver to the Registrar a statutory declaration in the prescribed form signed by a director or secretary stating:

- the nominal value of the company's allotted share capital is at least £50,000
- each allotted share is paid up to at least one-quarter on the nominal value and the whole of any premium.

If a public company which does not have a trading certificate:

- does business or exercises borrowing powers, the company and any officer in default commits a crime punishable by a fine
- enters into a transaction with a third party, the directors are jointly and severally liable with the company to the third party on the transaction
- has been in existence for more than one year (whether or not it has done business or borrowed money), it may be wound up under s122 Insolvency Act 1986.

Transactions at an undervalue

A company enters into a transaction at an undervalue if it makes a gift or otherwise enters into a transaction on terms such that it receives either no consideration or insufficient consideration. The liquidator (or administrator) may apply to the court to set aside the transaction. The court will only set it aside if the company is insolvent and the transaction was made within the relevant period which is within:

- two years of the onset of insolvency if the transaction were entered into with a connected person
- six months of the onset of insolvency if the transaction were entered into with other persons.

The transaction will not be set aside unless, at the time it was made, the company was unable to pay its debts or became unable to pay its debts as a result.

Transposition errors

An error where two digits of a number are reversed, e.g. a transaction worth $18 is entered as $81. Interestingly, the resulting error is always divisible by 9, e.g. 81 - 18 = 63; 63/9 = 7.

Trend

Can be estimated by using a graph, by using linear regression or by smoothing out the fluctuations using moving averages.

* EXAMPLE *

The following are the sales figures for Bloggs Brothers Engineering Ltd:

Year	Sales (£000)
20X1	491
20X2	519
20X3	407
20X4	452
20X5	607
20X6	681

*** EXAMPLE ***

Using a five-point moving average:

Sales	5-year moving total
491	
519	
407	495
452	533
607	
651	

The five-year moving total is the sum of five successive years of sales. These are then plotted to obtain the trend. The number of points to use will be specified in a question.

*** EXAMPLE ***

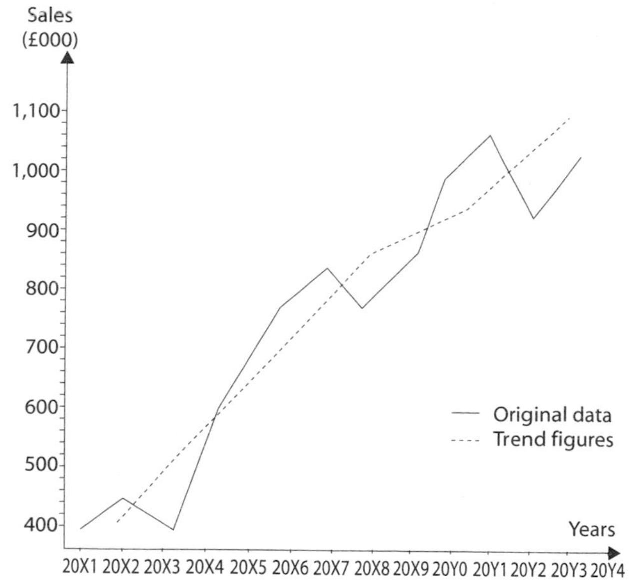

Trend – cyclical variation

The long-term variation about the trend.

Trend – seasonal variation

For data covering only a few years, the cyclical component can be ignored and the seasonal component can be identified. The seasonal component is the short-term variation about the trend.

*** EXAMPLE ***

The following table gives the takings (£000) of a shopkeeper in each quarter of four successive years.

Qtrs	1	2	3	4
20X1	13	22	58	23
20X2	16	28	61	25
20X3	17	29	61	26
20X4	18	30	65	29

To calculate the trend figures and quarterly variations, and draw a graph to show the overall trend and the original data, using the additive model:
A = T + S + R,
it is necessary to draw up a table as follows:

	1 Year and quarter	2 Takings (£000) A	3 4-quarterly moving average	4 Centred value T	5 Quarterly + Residual variation S + R (= A – T)
	1	13	-	-	-
	2	22		-	-
20X1			29		
	3	58		30	28
			30		
	4	23		31	-8
			31		
	1	16		32	-16
			32		
	2	28		33	-5
20X2			33		
	3	61		33	28
			33		
	4	25		33	-8
			33		
	1	17		33	-16
			33		
	2	29		33	-4
20X3			33		
	3	61		34	27
			34		
	4	26		34	-8
			34		
	1	18		35	-17
			35		
	2	30		36	-6
20X4			36		
	3	65		-	-
	4	29	-	-	-

Notes on the calculation

Column 3
To smooth out quarterly fluctuations, it is necessary to calculate a 4-point moving average, since there are four quarters (or seasons) in a year:
(13 + 22 + 58 + 23)/4 = 116/4 = 29
then, advancing by one quarter.

Column 4
In order to subsequently find A – T, it is essential that A and T both relate to the same point in time. The four-quarterly moving averages do not correspond with any of the A values, the first coming between the second and third A values and so on down. To overcome this, the moving averages are 'centred', i.e averaged in twos. The first centred average will coincide with the third A value and so on.

In order to establish the quarterly variation another table must be drawn up to remove the residual variation R.

	Quarter 1	Quarter 2	Quarter 3	Quarter 4
	– –16 –16 –17	– –5 –4 –6	28 28 27 –	–8 –8 –8 –
Totals	–49	–15	83	–24
Seasonal variation	–16	–5	28	–8

The quarterly variations should total to zero again, but –16 + (–5) + 28 + (–8) = –1. However, the adjustment would only be –1 ÷ 4, i.e. –0.25 which means using a spurious accuracy of two decimal places. To avoid this, one value only need be adjusted, choosing the greatest value as this will give the lowest relative adjustment error.

1st	Quarter =			–16
2nd	Quarter =			–5
3rd	Quarter =	28 + 1	=	29
4th	Quarter =			–8
				0

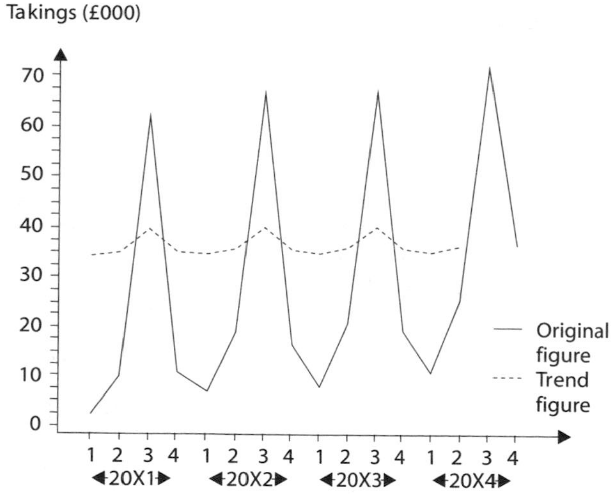

As can be seen from the calculations and the graph, the takings show a slight upward trend and the seasonal (quarterly) variations are considerable.

Trend extrapolation

The trend is the smoothed-out line through the data when plotted against a timescale. The timescale is taken as the x variable, and the trend is the line of best fit.

* EXAMPLE *

Year	Sales (£000)
20X3	12.0
20X4	11.5
20X5	15.8
20X6	15.0
20X7	18.5

To forecast sales for 20X8, the sales in £000 units are taken as the y values. Year 20X3 is taken as x = 1, 20X4 as x = 2, 20X5 as x = 3, etc, in which case the forecast for year 20X8 will be the value of y when x = 6.

The least squares regression line of y on x (the line of best fit) for this data is:

$$y = 9.61 + 1.65x$$

Hence, the forecast of sales for year 20X8 is obtained by putting x = 6 in this equation, giving:

$$y = 9.61 + 1.65 \times 6$$
$$= 19.51\ (£000)$$
$$= £19,510$$

Trial balance

A list of general ledger account balances, analysed to show debit and credit balances. If double entry has been maintained, then the trial balance totals will agree or 'square'.

True and fair view

UK company law requires that the financial statements published by companies must give a true and fair view. Truth and fairness is not adequately defined in any formal way and there is a great deal of debate as to how the quality of 'truth and fairness' might be measured. At the very least, financial statements must comply with the detailed requirements of the law and of accounting standards, although that might not be sufficient in dealing with issues that are not covered by the rules or in those exceptional cases where the rules themselves are not suited to a specific company's circumstances.

Turnbull Report (1999)

To give listed companies additional guidance on how to implement the provisions of the Combined Code with regard to internal control. It concluded that directors should:

- evaluate the likely risks facing a company ensure that effective safeguards and internal controls are put in place to prevent or minimise risk.

U

Ultra vires

Describes transactions entered into by a company that are not within the capacity of the company, as set out expressly or impliedly by its objects clause. At common law an ultra vires transaction is void. However, s35 CA85 provides that an ultra vires transaction is not void simply for being ultra vires.

Under/over-absorption of overhead

Under-absorption or over-absorption of overheads arises because actual overhead cost and/or activity level is different to budget.
It is calculated as follows:

Overhead absorbed (recovered):	Actual production × predetermined OAR
Compared to	Actual overhead (Overhead incurred)

* EXAMPLE *

A company budgeted to produce 3,000 units of a single product in a period at a budgeted cost per unit as follows:

	$/unit
Direct costs	17
Fixed overhead	9
	26

In the period covered by the budget:

- Actual production was 3,200 units.
- Actual fixed overhead expenditure was 5% above that budgeted – all other costs were as budgeted.

The amount of over- or under-absorption of fixed overhead is as follows:
Over/(under)-absorption = Absorbed overhead - Incurred overhead
Budgeted fixed overhead = 3,000 units × $9 = $27,000.

	$
Fixed overhead absorbed (3,200 units × $9)	28,800
Fixed overhead incurred (£27,000 × 1.05)	(28,350)
Over-absorbed fixed overheads	450

Understandability of information

Information should be in a form that is understandable to user groups.

Undistributable reserves

Undistributable reserves are:

- share premium account
- capital redemption reserve
- unrealised profits (less unrealised losses unless previously written off)
- any other reserve that the company is prohibited from distributing by any statute or by its Memorandum or Articles of Association.

Unfair Contract Terms Act 1977

Restricts the extent to which a person can exclude or limit his liability:
- A person in business cannot exclude or restrict liability for death or personal injury resulting from negligence.
- A person in business cannot exclude or restrict liability for negligence causing loss other than death or personal injury unless it is reasonable.
- Any exclusion of the s12 SOGA 1979 implied term as to title is void.
- The SOGA 1979 implied terms as to description (s13), satisfactory quality (s14(2)), fitness for purpose (s14(3)), and sample (s15)
  - cannot be excluded or restricted by reference to a contract term, as against a person dealing as a con sumer
  - as against any other person, such liability can only be excluded or restricted in so far as the term satisfies the requirement of reasonableness.
- If a contract contains a term that would exclude or restrict liability for pre-contractual misrepresentations, that term shall have no effect except in so far as it satisfies the requirement of reasonableness.

Unfair dismissal

This is a statutory claim. The procedure is as follows:
- The employee must have been continuously employed for one year.
- The employee must prove he was dismissed.
- Claim to Employment Tribunal within three months of dismissal.
- Employer must prove reason for dismissal.
- If found unfair, entitled to reinstatement, re-engagement or compensation.

Unfair prejudice

Any member of the company who complains that the affairs of the company are being conducted in a manner unfairly prejudicial to the interests of some or all of the members (including themselves) may petition for an order under s459. of which act? If the court is satisfied that the petition is well-founded, it may make such order as it thinks fit.

* EXAMPLE *

The court may order the shares of the petitioner to be purchased by the other members or by the company itself.

Unfair Terms in Consumer Contracts Regulations 1999

The rules apply only to standard form contracts for the supply of goods or services. They specify that written terms should be in plain and intelligible language. An unfair term in a contract is covered by the regulations if it '... contrary to the requirement of good faith causes a significant imbalance in the parties' rights and obligations under the contract to the detriment of the consumer'. To decide whether a term satisfies the requirement of good faith, the regulations specify a number of factors:
- the strength of the bargaining position of the parties
- whether the consumer had any inducements to agree to the term
- whether the goods or services were supplied to the special order of the consumer
- the extent to which the seller had dealt fairly and equitably with the consumer.

If a clause is held to be unfair, the clause is not binding on the consumer.

Unilateral contract

A contract whereby one person makes promises and the other person is free to perform or not is a unilateral contract. Once the party chooses to perform, the party making the promise is bound. This is a reward-type situation, where one person promises to pay another if the other does something as in Carlill v Carbolic Smoke Ball Company (1893).

Unit cost

The actual cost of purchasing identifiable units of inventory. This method is only likely to be used in situations where inventory items are of high value and individually distinguishable. e.g. a motor dealership would be able to identify each car in its inventory by its registration number or chassis number and determine the value of each.

Unlimited company

In the case of an unlimited company, there is no limit on the liability of its members to contribute to its assets if it goes into liquidation. Unlimited companies are not required to file their accounts at the Companies Registry. An unlimited company must be private.

Unpresented cheques

Listed when the bank reconciliation statement is prepared, these are cheque payments that have been recorded in the cash book but that have not had a chance to go through the bank's record-keeping system in time to be on the bank statement. Any long-delayed unpresented cheque would be investigated as suspicious.

Useful information

Accounting information is intended to be useful and to inform important economic decisions. Characteristics of useful information are relevance, understandability, reliability and comparability.

Users of accounts

Financial statements serve a wide variety of user groups who have different interests and also different levels of financial sophistication. The IASB identifies the following as users: investors, employees, lenders, suppliers and other trade creditors, customers, governments and their agencies, the public.

V

Value added

Value added = Sales revenue – Cost of materials and bought-in services.

Value Added Tax (VAT)

A tax on consumer expenditure collected on business transactions and imports. VAT on inputs may be reclaimed or set against output VAT collected.

Variable costs

Change in direct proportion to output, e.g. raw materials.

Graph showing relationship between raw materials cost and output

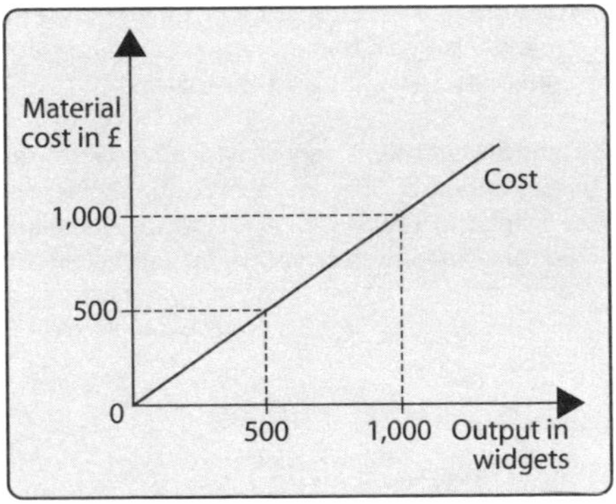

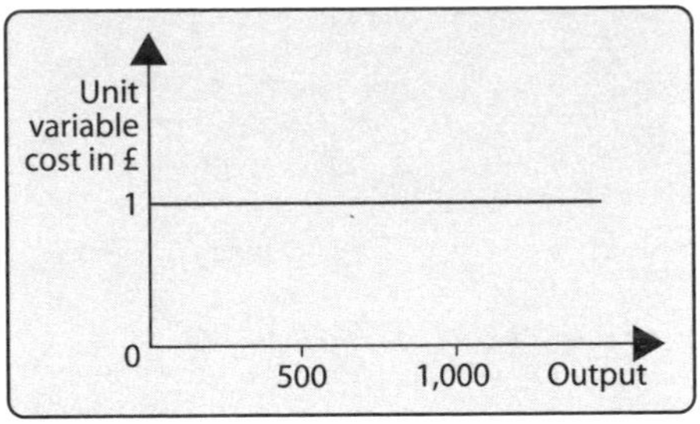

Variable overhead variances

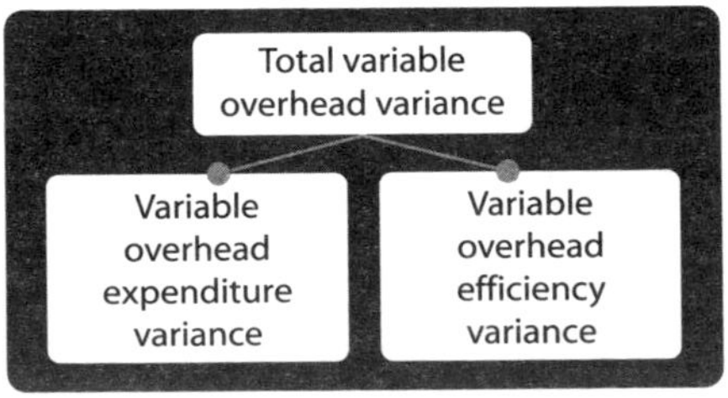

Total variable overhead cost variance

Assuming that variable overhead is absorbed to product on the basis of labour hours, standard variable overhead cost of actual output should have been:

(units of actual output × standard variable overhead absorption rate per unit)

But was:

(actual cost)

The difference is the total variable overhead cost variance

If the actual cost is greater than the standard cost, then the variance is adverse.

Variable overhead expenditure variance

Actual labour hours should have cost:

(actual hours × standard variable overhead absorption rate per hour)

But did cost:

(actual cost)

The difference is variable overhead expenditure variance

Variable overhead efficiency variance

Actual units produced should have used:

(actual units × standard hours per unit)

But did use:

(actual hours)

Difference is the variable overhead efficiency variance in hours

(Note: This is the same as the labour efficiency variance in hours.)

Value at standard variable overhead absorption rate per hour

* EXAMPLE *

K Limited has a budgeted variable overhead cost for August of $84,000. Budgeted production is 20,000 units of its finished product and direct labour hours are expected to be 40,000 hours. During August the actual production was 20,500 units. Actual hours worked were 41,600 hours and the variable overhead cost incurred amounted to $86,700.

The budgeted variable overhead cost per hour is calculated by:

$$\frac{\text{Budgeted cost}}{\text{Budgeted hours}} = \frac{\$84{,}000}{40{,}000} = \$2.10 \text{ per hour}$$

The budgeted variable overhead cost per unit is $84,000/20,000 = $4.20 per unit.

Or this could be calculated by identifying that each unit is budgeted to take 2 labour hours × $2.20 per hour = $4.20

	$
20,500 units should cost × $4.20	86,100
But did cost	86,700
Variable overhead total variance	600 A

* EXAMPLE * *(continued)*

The variance is adverse because the actual cost exceeded the standard cost and therefore profits would be lower than expected.

	$
41,600 hours should cost × $2.10	87,360
But did cost	86,700
Variable overhead expenditure variance	660 F

The variance is favourable because the actual rate of variable overhead expenditure is less than the rate expected.

20,500 units should use	41,000 hours
But did use	41,600 hours
Variance in hours	600 A
Value at the standard rate per hour × $2.10	
Variable overhead efficiency variance	$1,260 A

The variance is adverse because actual hours exceeded standard hours.

Variables

The characteristics that are being measured. Can be classified in two different and distinct ways:

(a) Variables can be either continuous or discrete. A continuous variable is one that can assume any value, e.g. height, temperature. A discrete variable is one that can only assume certain specific values, e.g. shoe sizes.

(b) Variables can alternatively be classified as independent or dependent. An independent variable is not affected by changes in another variable, whereas a dependent variable is affected by changes in another, e.g. changes in advertising expenditure in a year can be expected to affect sales, but a change in sales will not directly affect advertising expenditure. Hence, advertising is the independent variable and sales the dependent.

Variance

The square of the standard deviation.

$$\text{Variance} = \frac{\Sigma(x - \bar{x})^2}{n} \quad \text{for ungrouped data.}$$

$$\text{Variance} = \frac{\Sigma fx^2}{\Sigma f} - x^2 \quad \text{for a frequency distribution.}$$

Variance account

If standard costing is used there will be one or more variance accounts. The accounting entries will be to:

- debit all adverse variances
- credit all favourable variances.

The balance on the variance account is posted to the income statement. So, if adverse variances exceed favourable variances, the balancing entry will be to credit the variance account and debit the income statement account (as an expense).

Veil of incorporation

The legal consequence of the doctrine of incorporation, namely that a company is a separate legal entity from its members, is expressed by saying that there is a veil of incorporation drawn down between the company and its members. This legal separation and the concept of a company as an artificial entity means:

- perpetual succession
- the company itself owns its own property, not the members or directors
- members are not liable to creditors for the company's debts
- separation of ownership and management
- the company can sue and be sued in its own name.

Venn diagrams

A pictorial method used in mathematics and other fields to show the relationship between different sets, or groups, of objects. In probability theory these sets can be used to represent events and the resulting diagrams are a useful way of seeing key theories and solving some problems.

* EXAMPLE *

Suppose we are looking at the different possible outcomes of rolling a die.
Let A = rolling an even number = {2,4,6}
Let B = rolling a multiple of 3 = {3,6}
This can be shown in the following diagram:

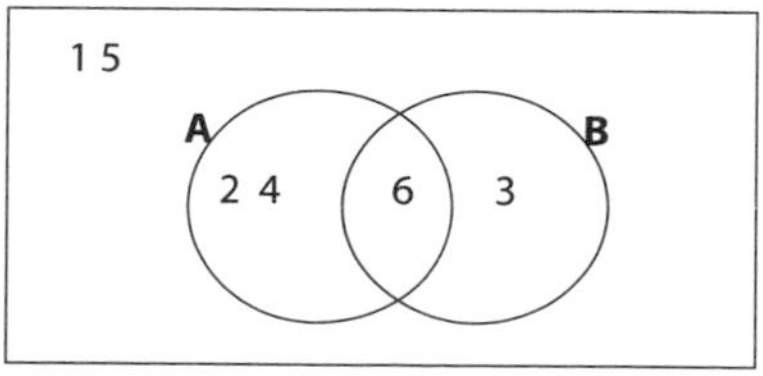

The diagram can be interpreted as follows:

- All possible outcomes are contained within the box – so, the outcomes '1' and '5' are within the box, even though they are not included within events 'A' or 'B'.
- 'A' and 'B' are shown as circles with each possible outcome contained within them.
- If asked to consider the probability of 'A or B' happening (in this case being the likelihood of the outcomes {2,3,4,6} occurring), then you need to look at the area shown by adding the two circles together.

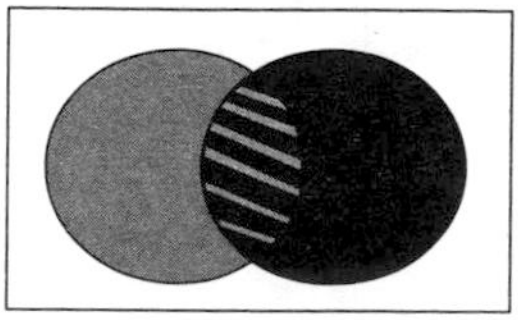

- If asked to consider the probability of 'A and B' occurring (i.e. in this example, just getting a six), then on the diagram this is represented by the overlap of A and

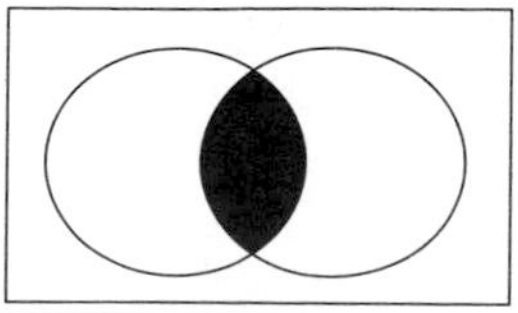

Vicarious liability

An employer will be vicariously liable for any tort committed by an employee if this act or omission occurred within the scope of the employment relationship.

Void contract

One that has no legal effect on either party – it is as if there is no contract. Any property which is transferred under a void contract must be handed back to the transferor, as he remains the owner of it.

Voidable contract

One that can be rescinded by one of the parties.

W

Wages book

A day book used to calculate and record the amounts due to individual employees for their wages. The totals are entered in the various accounts relating to net pay and deductions, e.g. PAYE/NI.

Weighted average

Each time there is a delivery a new weighted average price per unit is calculated and used to value issues until there is another delivery. The calculation is:

$$\frac{\text{Inventory value} + \text{Receipt value}}{\text{Quantity in inventory} + \text{Quantity received}}$$

* EXAMPLE *

1 November bought 300 kgs costing \$1 each
6 November bought 200 kgs costing \$1.20 each
8 November used 100 kgs

$$\frac{£300 + £240}{300 + 200} = £1.08 / \text{Kg}$$

The materials used on 8 November would be valued at \$1.08 per kg.

Weighted indices

Weighted average price relative =

$$\frac{\Sigma W \times P_1/P_0 \times 100}{\Sigma W}$$

where W = weight, P_1 = prices at time 1, P_0 = prices at time 0.

Whole and parts

A percentage (such as 5%) treats the whole in an abstract sense as 100%. You may have no idea what the actual number of the whole is.
A ratio (such as 3:5:8) focuses on the shares that make up the whole.
A proportion (e.g. 320 out of 1,600) is usually given as a fraction.

Any number to the power of zero equals 1.

* EXAMPLE *

Adding up to the whole

If you are told that 22% of people prefer Brand X, then you can deduce that a total of (100 – 22) = 78% of people do not prefer Brand X. Likewise, if you are given a proportion in the form '320 out of 1,600 people surveyed prefer Brand X', this information also (silently) tells you that (1,600 – 320) = 1,280 people prefer other brands.

Decimal equivalents

Any of these measures can also be expressed in decimal form:

- 5% is 0.05.
- The ratio 3:5:8 could be rewritten as 0.1875:0.3125:0.5000.
- 320/1600 (or 1/5) is 0.2.

Working capital

The liquid assets that are available to fund day-to-day transactions. It is usually expressed as current assets minus current liabilities.

Work-in-progress

Inventory that is in a partially completed state. It should be valued by determining the costs incurred in bringing it to its present location and condition.

Work-in-progress (WIP) control account

The work-in-progress account is:

- debited with direct materials, direct labour and production overheads absorbed
- credited with finished output.

* EXAMPLE *

Work-in-progress account

	$		$
Opening inventory b/d	4,000	Finished goods	60,000
Raw materials inventory	15,000		
Wages and salaries	19,000		
Production overhead absorbed	25,000	Closing inventory c/d	3,000
	63,000		63,000

Working Time Regulations 1998

Limit the hours which a worker can be required to work to an average of 48 a week. It also gives the right to four weeks paid leave a year and one day off each week.

World Bank

The International Bank for Reconstruction and Development (IBRD), also known as the World Bank, was created at the Bretton Woods meeting in 1944. Its original purpose was to help finance the reconstruction of economies damaged by the war. However, it soon shifted the focus of its lending to countries of the developing world.

World Trade Organisation (WTO)

In 1995 the WTO based in Geneva replaced the General Agreement on Tariffs and Trade (GATT). It has a number of roles:

- to ensure compliance of member countries with previous GATT agreements
- to negotiate future trade liberalisation agreements
- to resolve trading disputes between nations.

Written particulars of employment

An employer must provide an employee with a written statement of certain particulars of their employment within two months of the commencement of employment.

Wrongful dismissal

Where an employment contract is terminated not in accordance with the terms of the contract, there is a breach of contract and the innocent party will have a claim for damages.

Wrongful trading

Under s214 Insolvency Act 1986 if in the winding up of an insolvent company a past or present director (or shadow director) knew or ought to have known, before the commencement of the winding up, that there was no reasonable prospect that the company could avoid insolvent liquidation, and failed to take every step to minimise the loss to the company's creditors, then the court may declare on the application of the liquidator that the person is liable to make such contribution as the court thinks fit.

Z

Zero exponent

Any number to the power of zero equals 1.

* EXAMPLE *

$10^0 = 1$

Zero-rated supplies

Traders in zero-rated supplies charge VAT at 0% on their sales. As they are making taxable supplies they can thus recover VAT suffered on their purchases.